Sex in the Middle East and North Africa

Sex in the Middle East and North Africa

Edited by
L. L. WYNN AND
ANGEL M. FOSTER

VANDERBILT UNIVERSITY PRESS
Nashville, Tennessee

Library of Congress Cataloging-in-Publication Data
Names: Wynn, L. L., 1971– editor. | Foster, A. M. (Angelina Marguerite),
editor.
Title: Sex in the Middle East and North Africa / edited by L. L. Wynn and
Angel M. Foster.
Description: Nashville, Tennessee : Vanderbilt University Press, 2022. |
Includes bibliographical references and index. | Summary: "Wide-ranging
essays on sex and sexuality in the modern Middle East and North
Africa" — Provided by publisher.
Identifiers: LCCN 2022002096 (print) | LCCN 2022002097 (ebook) | ISBN
9780826504326 (paperback) | ISBN 9780826504333 (hardcover) | ISBN
9780826504340 (epub) | ISBN 9780826504357 (pdf)
Subjects: LCSH: Sex customs—Middle East. | Sex customs—Africa, North. |
Sex—Social aspects—Middle East. | Sex—Social aspects—Africa, North.
Classification: LCC HQ18.M628 S49 2022 (print) | LCC HQ18.M628 (ebook) |
DDC 306.70956—dc23/eng/20220217
LC record available at https://lccn.loc.gov/2022002096
LC ebook record available at https://lccn.loc.gov/2022002097

To a world where laws and policies are grounded in
human rights, social justice, and science

Contents

Acknowledgments

The success of an edited volume hinges on the contributors. We are grateful to all of the chapter authors for their efforts—we have enjoyed working with this dynamic group. We also appreciate the reflections and insights generated by participants in a series of Thematic Conversations at the annual meetings of the Middle East Studies Association. Those discussions helped shape our thinking and the structure of the volume. We also want to acknowledge the organizations and funders that supported the editors during different phases of this project: American Center of Research (ACOR), the Australian Research Council, Cambridge Reproductive Health Consultants, the Canadian Partnership for Women and Children's Health, the Centre for Academic Leadership (and Françoise Moreau-Johnson and Jean Quirion) at the University of Ottawa (uOttawa), Macquarie University, the Society of Family Planning Research Fund, and uOttawa.

We are also grateful to the friends, colleagues, and mentors who have supported the editors throughout this project and the journey that brought us here. Joel Beinin, Danielle Bessett, Kelly Cleland, Raywat Deonandan, Greg Downey, Majd Hammad, Saffaa Hassanein, Matteo Legrenzi, Annika Malmberg, Steve McCarroll, Chris Patil, Gordon Peake, Payel Ray, Eugene Rogan, and Tracy Weitz—thank you! We also want to thank our wonderful research assistant Mira Persaud and the team at Vanderbilt University Press, and Zack Gresham in particular, for sticking with us.

Lisa wants to thank Jeff, Louise, Jared, Valerie, Cory, DonRaphael, Saiph, Rigel, Alex, and Elijah, and especially David. Angel wants to thank Nancy and Emad Mancy, Linda Lemmens, and Gary Simms for their unwavering support, and Eddy Niesten for everything.

Sex in the Middle East and North Africa

Complicated Legacies and the Politics of Representation

ANGEL M. FOSTER

L. L. WYNN

Setting the Context

In 1798, Abd al-Rahman Al-Jabarti, Egypt's "unrivaled chronicler of the eighteenth century" (Tignor 1993, 5), wrote a history of the Napoleonic occupation of Egypt. In it, Al-Jabarti described the "manners and customs" of the French invaders, including their sexual and grooming practices:

> Their women do not veil themselves and have no modesty; they do not care whether they uncover their private parts. Whenever a Frenchman has to perform an act of nature he does so wherever he happens to be, even in full view of people. . . . They have intercourse with any woman who pleases them and vice versa. Sometimes one of their women goes into a barber's shop, and invites him to shave her pubic hair. If he wishes he can take his fee in kind. (Al-Jabarti 1993, 28–29)

In 1849, the French author Gustave Flaubert (who later became famous for his novel *Madame Bovary*) traveled through Egypt, chronicling his sexual exploits with dancers, sex workers, and courtesans in personal notes and letters to friends and family back in England. He describes one of the first courtesans he encountered, "Firm flesh, bronze arse, shaven cunt, dry though fatty; the whole thing gave the effect of a plague victim or a leperhouse" (Flaubert 1996, 40).

Al-Jabarti died in 1825 or 1826 (Tignor 1993), during the period of Muhammad Ali's rule of Egypt that followed the French occupation and more than two decades before Flaubert's own Grand Tour. But the juxtaposition of these two writers' observations, with their shared fascination with the pudenda, depilatory practices, and promiscuousness of foreign women, occupiers, and occupied, speaks to a long history of Orientalism and Occidentalism. Descriptions of the bodies and sexual practices of exotic others are far more than a set of neutral observations about cultural difference. Accounts of otherness construct one's own civilizational identity (Said 1978; Kabbani 1986).

But these two observers are not equivalent. Al-Jabarti wrote from the perspective of an Egyptian scholar observing the military occupiers, and his speculative portrayal of French women's sexual transactions with barbers carries no hint of personal familiarity.[1] This is in striking contrast with Flaubert's travel diary and letters, which are replete with accounts of his sexual encounters with Egyptian, Ottoman, and Nubian women and boys. As a member of the wealthy European elite, Flaubert's access to sex workers was enabled and structured by the European political and economic presence in the region, which eventually culminated in Egypt's occupation by the British in 1882. European power went hand in hand with the availability of Egyptian courtesans and sex workers to the European gaze (and penises); indeed, in the same letter to his mother sent from Alexandria in November 1849, Flaubert described the local women's visual availability to Europeans—"all the women are veiled. . . . On the other hand, if you don't see their faces, you see their entire bosoms"—and, two sentences later, noted that, "One curious thing here is the respect, or rather the terror, that everyone displays in the presence of 'Franks,' as they call Europeans" (1996, 29).

The history of European writing about the Middle East and North Africa as a space of exotic barbarism, sensuousness, and sexuality is much older than Flaubert's Grand Tour or even Napoleon's occupation. As Hsu-Ming Teo (2012) has documented, European-authored romances set in the Islamic world date all the way back to the twelfth century and the

Crusades. They flourished in the seventeenth through nineteenth centuries when European romances set in the Middle East evidenced a fascination with the despotic harem master and the lives of women of the harem. And they continued throughout the twentieth century with erotic historical romance novels of lusty Arab sheiks' sexual encounters with, and eventual taming by, White women (Teo 2012).

Why bring up these historical descriptions and romantic imaginations of sexual otherness at the start of a contemporary edited collection of mostly anthropological accounts of sex in the Middle East and North Africa? Because every author writing about the topic in European languages—and every person reading about it—is heir to this long history of Western fascination with sex in the region.

"Othering" Sex and Sexuality in Western Academia

In 1978, Palestinian-American literary critic Edward Said published his groundbreaking book *Orientalism*, in which he argued that European (and American) accounts of the Eastern other were a mirror for the Western self, a "flexible positional superiority, which puts the Westerner in a whole series of possible relationships with the Orient without ever losing him the relative upper hand" (Said 1978, 7). Syrian-British historian Rana Kabbani took Said's insights and applied them specifically to accounts of the sexuality of the "Orient" (Kabbani 1986). She showed how Western portrayals of gender roles and sexuality in the Middle East have historically transformed according to the sexual mores of the time to present a shifting reflection of difference. When the European bourgeoisie placed high moral value on marital monogamy and restrained sexuality, accounts of the Middle East described polygamous harems of sexual licentiousness; when European sexual norms shifted to value sexual freedom, portrayals of the Middle East rendered a landscape of sexual repression (Kabbani 1986). As Meyda Yegenoglu has argued, "representations of cultural and sexual difference are constitutive of each other" (1998, 1).

Although Said and Kabbani were writing specifically about a Western field of study focusing on the Arab and Islamic world, descriptions of sexual otherness in the history of Western academia extend far beyond the Middle East and North Africa. Anthropologists have been writing about the sexuality of exotic others from the earliest years of the discipline. For example, in 1929, Polish-British anthropologist Bronislaw Malinowski published his ethnography of the Trobriand Islanders titled *The Sexual Life of Savages*. In it, he describes everything from the sexual appeal of small eyes and large noses to the way Trobriander lovers bite each other's eyelashes off during the throes of passion, thus demonstrating that sexual aesthetics are culturally constructed and even orgasm has its own cultural rituals. In 1928, Margaret Mead published her ethnography *Coming of Age in Samoa*, which described the developing sexuality of Samoan teenagers. She argued that Samoan society's tolerance for adolescent sexual experimentation and nonmonogamy engendered a society that lacked the sexual pathologies and anxieties that she believed characterized American adolescence.

Malinowski and Mead were key founders of the discipline and their legacies are enduring. Malinowski, trained in the British ethnological tradition under Charles Seligman, was an early advocate for the ethnographic research method, characterized by long-term embeddedness and participation in the everyday life of the people being described. This methodological ideal has now become core to the discipline (Stocking 1994). Mead, trained in America by Franz Boas (who is often described as the "father of anthropology," and certainly its founder in the Americas), became a leading American public intellectual, perhaps the most famous anthropologist in history. For decades her book was the most widely read anthropological text in the world (Lutkehaus 2008). *The Sexual Life of Savages* and *Coming of Age in Samoa* were amongst the first monographs of a nascent discipline and captured American and European imaginations with their descriptions of exotic sexuality. But they were also, particularly for Mead (who was bisexual), explicitly written to deconstruct what was understood as "natural" about the sex and gender systems of our own societies.

In contrast, there is no equivalent description of the sex lives of Middle Easterners from the early years of the discipline. Why? Undoubtedly, there were a number of factors. For decades, anthropology of the Middle East and North Africa primarily focused on studies of local politics, economies, and to a lesser extent kinship systems. Further, the first generation of Americans and Europeans conducting anthropological research in the region were almost all men and local cultural norms excluded women and sexual practices from the male, foreign gaze. Thus, the interaction of Western sexism of the era with the norms of gender segregation in the Middle East likely played a role. There were a handful of cases in the 1950s and 1960s where male anthropologists leaned on their wives to obtain a glimpse of that part of society they were denied access to and used those insights to describe kinship and the world of women. For example, take the case of Elizabeth Warnock Fernea, who accompanied her anthropologist husband, Robert Fernea, to a small Iraqi village in the 1950s. She eventually published her own ethnography of the community of women of the village, *Guests of the Sheikh* (1965), and became more famous than her husband in Middle East studies. But, in general, the local cultural norms dictated not only the gender segregation that prevented male anthropologists from gaining access to half of society but also moral codes that considered discussing sex with unrelated men to be disrespectful to female kin.

Consequently, it is largely colonial-era travel and romance writers who shaped European understandings of sexuality in the Middle East and North Africa. When Western travel writers in the region (like Flaubert) described the sexual practices of locals, they were describing a very particular class of society that made its living through interaction with foreign tourists and traders. Women from more powerful classes of society were unavailable to the Western observer and so writers and artists created mythical harems of mysterious, sensuous, and imprisoned women (Alloula 1986)—though some nineteenth-century Western women travelers who gained access to these "harems" described them in much more mundane terms (Goffman 2005; Lewis 2004).[2]

But even in the 1970s and beyond, as anthropology of the Middle East and North Africa turned away from its fixation on economic and political systems to start examining a wider range of topics, there is very little ethnographic writing about sex in the Middle East and North Africa (a lack that Inhorn actually quantifies in her conclusion to this volume). This is most likely the result of the critiques of scholars like Said and Kabbani. These critiques ushered in a new era of Middle East studies, one where Western academics were increasingly aware of the ways that knowledge was political, neutrality was a powerful fiction (Said 1978, 10), and all who wrote about the Middle East were implicated in a highly charged transnational political economy of representation.[3] Contemporary academics are aware that they must situate their own research and writing within this intellectual history and acknowledge that their representations of gender and sexuality in the region have real political impact, at scales both large and deadly (for example, when the status of Afghani women under the Taliban was used by Laura Bush to justify the Gulf War; see Gerstenzang and Getter 2001) and small and intimate (for example, as it plays out in the micropolitics of tourism; see Wynn 2018; Jacobs 2009).

While the history of Western fascination with the hidden sexual practices of Middle Eastern societies generates the audience for this book and incentives for academics to do research on sex in the region, it also, thanks to such critiques, generates a cautionary wariness among academics about writing on sex in the Middle East and North Africa. Every contributor to this volume is part of this long history of the production of a spectacle of sexuality of the Middle East and North Africa and every contributor knows how fraught the politics of representing sex are. Said's legacy in the scholarship of the Middle East is a pervasive awareness that everything we write is political, even (perhaps especially) when it appears to be neutrally descriptive. The topics we choose to study, the regions and groups of people we get access to, the gendered and embodied ways that we gain knowledge, and the audiences for our work are all part of the politics of knowledge and representation of the region.

An Agenda for Writing about Sex in the Middle East and North Africa

In 2017, Vanderbilt University Press published our edited volume *Abortion Pills, Test Tube Babies, and Sex Toys: Emerging Sexual and Reproductive Technologies in the Middle East and North Africa.* That project, years in the making, brought together anthropologists and public health researchers to explore the ways that "new" global technologies are locally appropriated, adopted, adapted, and rejected. We aimed to bring together areas of sexual and reproductive health that are typically siloed and separated, explore issues throughout the Arab world, as well as Iran, Israel, and Turkey, and give voice to the experiences of populations that are often not centered in academia. We divided the volume into three sections—preventing and terminating pregnancy, achieving pregnancy and parenthood, and engaging sex and sexuality—and each chapter focused on a specific technology in a specific country within the region.

Unquestionably, the section on engaging sex and sexuality elicited the most interest and comment. The chapters included an exploration of the human papilloma virus (HPV) vaccine in Lebanon, hymenoplasty in Iran, Viagra in Egypt, sex toys in Morocco, and gender transformation practices in Turkey. The response to these chapters—both when we were promoting the book and after it was published—inspired us to embark on a dedicated project that moved away from technologies and instead explored sex and sexuality.

In deciding to edit a volume on sex in the Middle East and North Africa, we asked ourselves, our colleagues, and our contributors—in a series of three consecutive years of thematic conversations and roundtable discussions at the annual meetings of the Middle East Studies Association—these key questions: What would a critically aware scholarship of sex in the Middle East and North Africa look like? In the context of this history of representations and their politicization, what should we be writing about, how should we write about it, and who should be writing?

First, we decided as editors that it was critically important to present voices from the region. This includes both the voices of research participants and the voices of academic researchers who write from positions of deep embeddedness in the social phenomena they describe, from Saramifar writing about childhood friends in the militia in Iran to Chalmiers writing from the perspective of health service professionals working with Syrian refugees in the United States. This is not about only authorizing those who have been identified as carrying an essential nativity; it is a matter of giving space for the voices of people who have conducted deep ethnographic research in the lives of those they describe.

Second, and following from the first, we asked our contributors to follow Abu-Lughod's (1991) call for anthropologists (and others) to "write against culture," that is, to focus on the specificity of individual lives (see also Abu-Lughod 1993). Thus contributors to this volume do not try to flatten out diverse experiences into a generalized terrain of "culture" and "this is what 'they' do in X country." Rather, this approach entails using case studies of individual lives to understand not only hegemonic social norms (see Salem) but also how individuals interpret, inhabit, and defy those hegemonic norms (see Wynn, and Gagné), and what are the consequences for those who inhabit the centers *and* the margins (Wynn 2018).

Third, it is imperative to not write about Middle Eastern and North African societies and political movements as if they are enacting scenes from some Western past. This does not mean ignoring Western social movements that might be relevant to understanding the Middle East, but examining them to show the specifics of how global ideologies circulate and how local individuals and groups interpret and engage with them, not for comparison or to tacitly establish a universal timeline of social/political movements (see Feather). It means writing about social and cultural phenomena as things in themselves, not as comparative foils for excavating one's own cultural history or developing an implicitly evolutionary model of sexual repression or freedom (see Hassanein and Wynn).

Fourth, contributors to this volume explicitly and implicitly explore the relationship between intimacy and the state. In her book *The Empire of Love: Toward a Theory of Intimacy, Genealogy, and Carnality* (2006), anthropologist Elizabeth A. Povinelli argues that the state, and colonizing ideologies in particular, structure the ways we govern, categorize, define, and understand sex and intimacy. Authors in this volume reflect on the complex relationship between the state and the politics and practices of the intimate (see Fererro, and MacFarlane).

And finally, it means being reflexively aware of the international political economy of representations of sexuality in the region, how our own representations feed particular narratives, and what the incentives are for generating such representations, from pruriently voyeuristic to political and military (Abu-Lughod 2013; Amar 2011; Amar and El Shakry 2013; cooke 2008;[4] Inhorn 2013; Wynn 2018).

One way that the editors and contributors to this volume have deliberately engaged with the history of representations of sex in the Middle East and North Africa is by writing about topics that veer away from the standard tropes of representing sex in the region. The core themes of this book are pleasure, remuneration, and love in the context of both normative and nonnormative sexual practices. Contributors discuss social attitudes toward ideal and proscribed sexual behaviors (see El-Mowafi and Foster); assumptions about and challenges to normative gender roles (see Hayes), including ideals of gender aesthetics and comportment (see Gagné); beliefs about families, cosmologies about the relationship between sexuality and an individual's relationship with God (see Ibrahim); and expectations about the role of government, security forces, religious experts, and medical authorities in individuals' sexual and reproductive lives (see Michalak). Thus, while contributors examine ways that sex is part of broader systems of social hierarchies and political systems, by focusing on topics such as love and pleasure, they move away from representations of sex in the region as mainly an arm of patriarchal power, an assumption that has characterized so much feminist writing about the Middle East (Abu-Lughod 2001).

Studying sex and sexualities focuses our attention on the microphysics of power negotiations in gender relations and the ways that new and emerging sexualities come from, and produce, new relations, social hierarchies, and imaginations of bodies, physiological processes, and morality. The study of sex thus offers a unique vantage point for studying not only cultural attitudes toward religion, the state, and the body but also the structures through which religion, science, and the state compete for authority over individuals' sexual and reproductive lives.

The contributors to this volume examine the complexities surrounding normative, nonnormative, and illicit sexual behaviors and relationships, including married sex, nonheterosexual relationships, individuals whose bodies and lives reject binary categories of gender and sexual desire, those who have premarital and extramarital relationships, and those who engage in remunerative or transactional sex. The chapters of this book demonstrate that bright lines do not divide normative and nonnormative behaviors. Indeed, the marking off of certain behaviors as "nonnormative" is a social tool for disciplining women, men, and nonbinary folks and that is one of the critical projects that this book tackles in its commitment to exploring the microphysics of power.

Single and Dating, Engaged and Married, and It's Complicated

We have organized the book into three sections: "Single and Dating," "Engaged and Married," and "It's Complicated." The allusion to categories of relationship statuses on social media is at once a nod to the compulsion to categorize, recognition of the many ways that categorization is rarely straightforward, and acknowledgment that so much of the intimate lives described by our contributors are mediated by online technologies.

In Part I, "Single and Dating," I. M. El-Mowafi and Angel M. Foster start us off by exploring casual sex and dating practices in Jordan. Drawing from long-term residence and ethnographic fieldwork, they reflect on the ways that unmarried women, often with the aid of social media and dating apps, are able to navigate familial and social pressures to fulfill their sexual curiosities, experiment with new sexual partners, satisfy their sexual desires, and obtain the sexual and reproductive health services they want and need. Matthew Gagné's chapter on gay sex apps in Lebanon picks up the theme of how new technologies can be used to both construct and subvert heteronormative gender identities. The author draws from extensive ethnographic fieldwork among queer men in Beirut to show how digital technologies do not produce or transgress Lebanese norms of masculinity but extend and remediate them. Katrina MacFarlane's chapter on the use of withdrawal in Turkey follows. In this chapter, she reflects on the reasons why many Turkish couples, including those that are in new or casual relationships, choose to use nonbiomedical methods of contraception and argues that sexual pleasure, cultural and social norms, and intimacy and trust are key factors in decision-making. Saffaa Hassanein and L. L. Wynn then present an autoethnographic memoir of the Gulf dating scene in the early 2000s. Through several vignettes of queer Gulf women dating and finding allies among gay and straight men in a queer-friendly club, the authors show how lesbian sociability sometimes mimics and sometimes rejects heterosexual "toxic masculinity" and reflect on how class privilege enables queer sex. Finally, rounding out Part I, Shannon Hayes describes how women seek help from magic practitioners to navigate hookups, relationships, and breakups in Fez, Morocco. She argues that this practice is tied to premarital sexual intercourse and serves as a way for the woman to secure the relationship and prevent a loss of reputation.

Part II, "Engaged and Married," begins with Younes Saramifar's chapter on Iranian revolutionary women's encounters with pornography. He argues that his interlocutors are engaging with something widely viewed as "un-Islamic" as a way of fashioning compliance with Islam and commitment to Shi'i political Islam. Gendered attitudes is an important theme in Rania Salem's chapter on customary ('urfi) marriage in Egypt. Based on in-depth interviews in Cairo and Minya, the author examines the meanings that young Egyptians ascribe to customary marriages as well as toward the relationship between sex and marriage. Morgen Chalmiers's chapter on the politics of intimacy among Syrian refugees in the United States follows. Through telling the story of one married couple, the author reflects on how disciplinary institutions often require refugees to "perform love" in ways that resonate with liberal ideals of autonomy and intimacy. This section concludes with Laura Ferrero's chapter on sperm smuggling in Palestine in the context of continued occupation. Drawing from interviews with women who marry political prisoners, the author reflects on how procreation without sexual intercourse—particularly in the case of marriage by proxy between a man and woman who never had sex—is justified.

Part III, "It's Complicated," begins with L. L. Wynn's chapter on defining—and problematizing—transactional sex in Egypt. Drawing from ethnographic research conducted over many years, the author reflects on how the commodification of intimate relationships is understood and experienced by those involved and argues that the exchange of money is irrelevant to local understandings of the legitimacy of sexual intimacy. The volume then turns to Laurence Michalak's chapter on legal and illegal sex work in Tunisia. Structured around three case studies, the author argues that the restrictions on legal sex work that emerged after the 2011 Tunisian revolution reflect changing social mores and have considerable public health consequences. Ginger Feather's chapter on normative and non-normative sexual relationships in Morocco follows. Using the Advocacy Coalition Framework, she analyzes the core tenets underpinning activists' positions on Moroccan laws and public policies governing love, sex, and sexuality, and the gendered consequences. Part III ends with a chapter from Egyptian anthropologist Mina Ibrahim, who uses excerpts from a woman's diary to reflect on unmarried sexual relationships in the Coptic community in Egypt. Ibrahim's account of the blurred lines around transactional sex makes a powerful argument about the relationship between women's transgressive sexuality and the compulsion of the largest minority group in the Middle East to present a morally unified self vis-à-vis the nation and the wider international community.

The volume concludes with some reflections by Marcia C. Inhorn. The author situates the volume within Middle East studies and draws ten insights from the chapters. She argues that the ethnographic research conducted throughout the region and reflected in the volume collectively makes a unique and important contribution to the growing body of research on sex, sexualities, and sexual health in the Middle East and North Africa.

NOTES

1. It is not quite clear in the text if Al-Jabarti is describing the Frenchwomen who traveled with Napoleon's expedition or women of other nationalities who were associated with the Frenchmen while they were in Egypt.
2. Indeed, the Arabic word that "harem" derives from, *hareem*, means "women" and refers to nothing more or less exotic than the woman's side of a large gender-segregated household. This use of language in and of itself tells a whole story about the production of Western fantasies about Arab sexuality.
3. They also reflected Arab intellectuals' own critical writing about this history of European representations, which had predated Said's critique. Ridwan al-Sayyid (2004, 95) has argued that Said's writings in English brought to Western attention the concept of *al-istishraq* (Orientalism) that was being elaborated among nationalists and Islamists in the Middle East long before Said's seminal work, and Ida Nitter (2017) has described two Egyptian intellectuals who anticipated Said's critique of Orientalism by over a hundred years.
4. miriam cooke prefers her name to be spelled without capitalization.

REFERENCES

Abu-Lughod, Lila. 1991. "Writing against Culture." In *Recapturing Anthropology: Working in the Present*, edited by Richard Fox, 137–62. Santa Fe, NM: School of American Research.

———. 1993. *Writing Women's Worlds: Bedouin Stories*. Berkeley: University of California Press.

———. 2001. "Review: 'Orientalism' and Middle East Feminist Studies." *Feminist Studies* 27, no. 1: 101–13.

———. 2013. *Do Muslim Women Need Saving?* Cambridge, MA: Harvard University Press.

Al-Jabarti, Abd al-Rahman. 1993. *Al-Jabarti's Chronicle of the French Occupation, 1798*. Translation by Shmuel Moreh. Princeton, NJ: Markus Wiener Publishing.

Al-Sayyid, Ridwan. 2004. "Commentary." In *Penser l'Orient: Traditions et actualité des orientalismes français et allemande*, edited by Youssef Courbage and Manfred Kropp, 95–102. Beirut: Presses de l'Ifpo.

Alloula, Malek. *The Colonial Harem*. 1986. Translated by Myrna Godzich and Wlad Godzich. Minneapolis: University of Minnesota Press, 1986.

Amar, Paul. 2011. "Turning the Gendered Politics of the Security State Inside Out?" *International Feminist Journal of Politics* 13, no. 3: 299–328.

Amar, Paul, and Omnia El Shakry. 2013. "Introduction: Curiosities of Middle East Studies in Queer Times." *International Journal of Middle East Studies* 45, no. 2: 331–35.

cooke, miriam. 2008. "Deploying the muslimwoman." *Journal of Feminist Studies in Religion* 24, no. 1: 91–99.

Fernea, Elizabeth Warnock. 2010. *Guests of the Sheikh*. New York: Random House [1965].

Flaubert, Gustave. 1996. *Flaubert in Egypt*. Translated and edited with an introduction by Francis Steegmuller. New York: Penguin.

Gerstenzang, James, and Lisa Getter. 2001. "Laura Bush Addresses State of Afghan Women." *Los Angeles Times*, November 18, 2001. https://www.latimes.com/archives/la-xpm-2001-nov-18-mn-5602-story.html.

Goffman, Carolyn. 2005. "Authenticity, Orientalism, and the Female Traveler: Writings from Inside the Harem." *Turkish Studies Association Journal* 29, no. 1/2: 91–104.

Inhorn, Marcia C. 2012. *The New Arab Man: Emergent Masculinities, Technologies, and Islam in the Middle East*. Princeton, NJ: Princeton University Press.

Jacobs, Jessica. 2009."Have Sex Will Travel: Romantic 'Sex Tourism' and Women Negotiating Modernity in the Sinai." *Gender, Place and Culture* 16, no. 1: 43–61.

Kabbani, Rana. 1986. *Europe's Myths of Orient: Devise and Rule*. London: Pandora.

Lewis, Reina. 2004. *Rethinking Orientalism: Women, Travel and the Ottoman Harem*. London: IB Tauris.

Lutkehaus, Nancy C. 2008. *Margaret Mead: The Making of an American Icon*. Princeton, NJ: Princeton University Press.

Nitter, Ida. 2017. "Fictional Writing as Western Resistance: How Two Writers Challenged Western Orientalist Depictions of the Arab 'Other.'" *Maydan: Politics and Society*, May 25, 2017. https://themaydan.com/2017/05/fictional-writing-western-resistance-two-writers-challenged-western-orientalist-depictions-arab.

Povinelli, Elizabeth A. 2006. *The Empire of Love: Toward a Theory of Intimacy, Genealogy, and Carnality*. Durham, NC: Duke University Press.

Said, Edward. 1978. *Orientalism*. New York: Vintage Books.

Stocking, George. 1994. *The Ethnographer's Magic and Other Essays in the History of Anthropology*. Madison: University of Wisconsin Press.

Teo, Hsu-Ming. 2012. *Desert Passions: Orientalism and Romance Novels*. Austin: University of Texas Press.

Tignor, Robert L. 1993. Introduction to *Al-Jabarti's Chronicle of the French Occupation, 1798*, by Abd al-Rahman Al-Jabarti. Translated by Shmuel Moreh. Princeton, NJ: Markus Wiener Publishing.

Wynn, L. L., and Angel M. Foster, eds. 2017. *Abortion Pills, Test Tube Babies, and Sex Toys: Emerging Sexual and Reproductive Technologies in the Middle East and North Africa*. Nashville, TN: Vanderbilt University Press.

Wynn, L. L. 2018. *Love, Sex, and Desire in Modern Egypt: Navigating the Margins of Respectability*. Austin: University of Texas Press.

Yegenoglu, Meyda. 1998. *Colonial Fantasies: Toward a Feminist Reading of Orientalism*. Cambridge, UK: Cambridge University Press.

PART I

SINGLE AND DATING

CHAPTER I

Anywhere but Home

Dating, Hooking Up, and Casual Sex in Jordan

I. M. EL-MOWAFI

ANGEL M. FOSTER

We are navigating competing priorities; we want to live our lives but are highly aware of the disappointment our parents would feel if they were to become aware of how we participate in these haram [prohibited] acts. Living double lives is both exhilarating and exhausting. More importantly, it is a necessity if we want to express ourselves freely in a country and culture that condemns these behaviors, both socially and politically, and especially for women. (Leila, 2020)

Marriage patterns have changed dramatically in Jordan over the last two decades according to the Jordan Population and Family Health Survey (JPFHS; Department of Statistics (DOS) and ICF 2002, 2013, 2018). The 2017–2018 JPFHS reports that the average age of first marriage among Jordanian women was twenty-six years; over a third of women between the ages of twenty-five and twenty-nine were unmarried (DOS and ICF 2018). Level of education, socio-economic status, employment status, and region of residence are associated with age of first marriage (Economic Research Forum 2016; DOS and ICF 2018; Salem 2012; UNWomen and REACH 2017; Foster and El-Mowafi, 2019). Overall, Jordanian women are spending longer and longer periods of their sexual and reproductive lives unmarried.

Consistent with dynamics documented in other parts of the Middle East and North Africa (MENA) region (see, for example, DeJong et al. 2005; Foster 2014; Hayes, this volume), dating and courtship are changing in Jordan. However, laws, policies, and services lag behind. Jordanian Personal Status Law governs issues surrounding marriage and sexual and reproductive health (SRH) for Muslim families in Jordan. According to Article 282 of the Penal Code, a man or a woman who commits *zina* (adultery or illicit sexual relations) can be subjected to one to three years in prison.[1] In practice, these crimes are difficult to prosecute and generally require a complaint by specific relatives, forensic medical evidence that documents the liaison, and/or a confession. However, Article 282 creates a chilling effect and sends a strong and clear message that sex before or outside of marriage is taboo and punishable.

Current programs through both the private and public sectors largely ignore the SRH needs of unmarried women (OECD Development Centre 2018; Gausman et al. 2019; Almasarweh 2003; Foster and El-Mowafi 2018). Research also indicates that youth are unsatisfied with existing SRH services (Gausman et al. 2019; Khalaf, Abu-Moghli, and Froelicher 2010) and experience judgment and intrusive questioning when seeking services (Khalaf, Abu-Moghli, and Froelicher 2010; Sieverding, Berri, and Abdulrahim 2018; Foster, Hammad, and El-Mowafi 2019). As a result, the uptake of SRH services through Ministry of Health (MOH) clinics among youth is extremely low.

What does this mean for unmarried women in Jordan? How do unmarried women engage in sexual relationships and navigate SRH services given the larger legal, policy, and socio-cultural context? Drawing from extensive fieldwork and observations during long periods of residence in Jordan by both authors, this chapter reflects on current dating, hooking up, and casual sex practices in Jordan. We argue that among unmarried young adult women who are educated, resourced, and living in Amman, the availability of Internet and smart phone technologies has changed the dating game. Dating and hook up apps, online ads for short term rentals, and SRH information provided through Facebook help young unmarried women navigate legal, policy, service delivery, and socio-cultural barriers to sexual experimentation. These new avenues for sexual expression differ from those available to unmarried Jordanian women of previous generations and introduce complicated dynamics for unmarried women to negotiate.

Our chapter draws from the reflections of both authors. El-Mowafi, a multi-national, multi-lingual graduate student, resided in West Amman over a three-and-a-half-year period from 2016 to 2020 and conducted both formal and informal interviews with unmarried, recently engaged, and newly married women. West Amman is a metropolitan area characterized by upper middle-income neighborhoods, open spaces, and higher quality infrastructure in comparison to East Amman. Located just ten minutes away, East Amman is characterized by significant poverty, overcrowding, and weak infrastructure. Foster, an American anthropologist and medical doctor, began conducting research on young and unmarried women's sexual behaviors and practices in the early 2000s as an ACOR-CAORC postdoctoral fellow and has continued this line of research ever since. Her early research focused on the perspectives and experiences of university students in both Amman and Irbid and later expanded to study the experiences of a broader array of unmarried women in both urban and semi-urban areas. In this chapter, we principally focus on the experiences and narratives of unmarried women collected between 2016 and 2020; we have assigned pseudonyms and removed or masked identifiable information.

This chapter focuses primarily on heterosexual women's experiences with dating and sexual practices outside of marriage. We explore the ways women identify partners, their experiences with "courting practices," and their access to SRH services. We begin by looking at unmarried women's experiences navigating familial and social pressures to fulfill their sexual curiosities, experiment with new sexual partners, and satisfy their sexual desires. We then turn to unmarried women's experiences with SRH services and identify ways that these services could better meet the changing needs of unmarried women. We use both illustrative quotes and narrative vignettes to give voice to unmarried women's lived experiences.

How Casual Partners and Couples Meet

────────────────────*Maha's Story*────────────────────

Maha is a twenty-two-year-old university student who lives in West Amman. She has not been actively dating or seeking a relationship but has strictly been interested in casual sexual encounters. Maha is an artist and her open Instagram page is filled with her photography and pictures of hikes with her friends. She often receives direct messages from fellow students and young men who claim to have seen her "around" and frequently comment on her physical appearance. Maha had been hesitant to respond and had not been engaging with men on this platform, until Ibrahim sent her a message one day inquiring about the type of lens she uses for her photography.

Maha was intrigued by the approach and the subsequent conversation with the fellow photographer who was very complimentary about her art. Maha and Ibrahim proceeded to talk on Instagram for a few days; they shared tips on their photography which led to flirtatious conversation. Ibrahim invited Maha for a drink. They met at a local bar and talked to the late hours. They eventually ended up at a restaurant; they had a sexual encounter in his car in the parking lot. Although Maha and Ibrahim never spoke again, Maha remembers the encounter fondly.

SLIDE INTO MY دم

Since the late 2000s, access to the Internet and smart phones has vastly increased throughout Jordan, changing the way that people, in general, and youth, in particular, interact with one another. Globally, adolescent (those between the ages of ten and nineteen) and youth (those between the ages fifteen and twenty-four) populations are the primary users of social media as a communication tool. They have been able to leverage the medium to navigate their lives outside the expectations and pressures of their families and society at large, as reflected in clandestine communication between members of the opposite sex.

Given that all public schools and most private schools are sex segregated in Jordan, university campuses are often the first opportunity for youth of the opposite sex to interact with one another at an intellectual and social level, outside of playtime as children in family environments (Salem 2012). However, gendered differences in the types of degrees men and women pursue persist. Men are more likely to pursue degrees in engineering, medicine, and computer science, whereas women are more likely to pursue degrees in teaching, nursing, and social science fields. In the early 2000s, unmarried university students often used text messaging on low-end mobile phones to arrange encounters on campus or in malls. Use of these technologies allowed young men and women who might not otherwise cross paths to orchestrate "accidental" meetings, generally involving a small group of friends, thereby creating a veneer of respectability.

However, our interviews with unmarried women suggest that technological advancements and social media have provided them with an additional layer of social protection in their interactions with male peers outside of class time. Nora, who was enrolled in the social work program at the University of Jordan, explained:

> You know, social media has changed the way we can talk to guys . . . when I was in my first year of university, we used this app called ASKfm. You could choose a private or public forum that allowed you to ask questions online and other people at the university would reply or submit their own questions. . . . This is how I met my first boyfriend of four years. I would write to his profile saying I had seen him around campus, and I thought he was cute, and he would call me out and say, "I know it's you." He asked for my number and this is how I started my first four-year relationship.

WhatsApp has been particularly transformative for our unmarried interlocutors. The messaging service has enabled unmarried women to be in constant contact with their male interests, whether casual or serious. Lama explained:

> WhatsApp allowed us to text with men from the confinement of our homes. We had to make intricate plans in advance to be able to meet up with our boyfriends. . . . To avoid being caught by my parents I would save my boyfriends' names under girl names and I would use selected emojis that would have meaning only to me. This made it possible for constant communication and allowed us to really get to know one another without having to be face-to-face with that person.

Lama's story echoed the experiences of many of our Jordanian interlocutors. Although young women are attending university and going to their day jobs, they often have familial obligations that limit their free time. In addition to those restrictions, they have male family members ensuring their "obedience." Anecdotal evidence suggests that unmarried women do not always have the level of freedom of mobility and socialization as their male family members, irrespective of age.

WhatsApp has not only enabled women in Amman to maintain contact with their immediate intimate and sexual interests, but it also facilitates exploration and identification of potential partners. Miriam recounted an experience from when she was twenty-three years old:

> My friend and I were bored, so we were prank calling these guys' numbers and we started speaking with these groups of guys. We were like "Oh my God, they actually seem pretty cool." They invited us to go clubbing with them and we were like, "Oh my God, no of course we could never go clubbing with them." Once we hung up, my friend and I decided that we wanted to go. You must understand that we have never been clubbing before and that the majority of our interactions and dates with men up to that point consisted mostly of cruising in their cars or parking in their car and looking out onto a view. We called them back and told them where to pick us up. We told our parents that we had a C shift at the hospital to cover up our time out with these guys. We got picked up in a Mustang and it was the first time we had anything like that. I stayed with one of the guys for two years. He never promised me marriage, but we had a lot of fun, and I learned a lot during that time.

Miriam's story exemplifies how social media platforms can facilitate women's ability to explore intimate contact with men, even at the risk of social consequences. The fact that Miriam and her friend were primary care providers provided them with mobility that they otherwise would not have had.

Conversations with women in Jordan provided an opportunity to understand how methods have changed in identifying potential sexual and intimate partners. The transition from men cruising the streets and initiating conversations with women from their car windows to using WhatsApp and dating applications such as Tinder and Bumble has provided women with greater power and autonomy in their interactions with men. However, most of the women we spoke with used Instagram and direct messages (DMs) to connect with men whom they were interested in sexually. Dunya, who had a similar story to Maha, explained:

> Have you ever heard of the term "*dakhal 'al khas*" (entered my private messages), "sliding into my DMs"? Anyone can look up your Instagram profile and send you a message. If you are set to private mode, they won't see that you saw their message unless you accept the message. . . . Anyone can reach out to you, but you have the choice whether to answer that person or not. I receive messages from guys saying *oooo, ya gamil* or *ya amar* (ooo,

beauty or you are the moon). But the guy I am hanging out with right now sent me a message with a goat meme. I was charmed, we chatted for a bit, met up for a drink, and then [had a sexual encounter.]

#NOTYOURHABIBTI: THE UNWANTED "DICK PIC"

————————————————*Alia's story*————————————————

Alia, a twenty-seven-year-old woman, works for a nongovernmental organization. After unfortunate dynamics arose from breakups with men who were integrated into her friend group, she decided that she wanted to branch out from her current social and work circles. Not knowing how to navigate the "outside" dating world, she brought up these concerns with a colleague from Italy. Her colleague advised her to set up Tinder and Bumble profiles.

In the beginning, Alia was hesitant; the concept of online dating seemed decidedly foreign. However, after some encouragement from her colleague, Alia set up her Bumble and Tinder profiles. Initially Alia became overwhelmed by the abundance of choice, but quickly started to enjoy the journey of swiping left and right. One day Alia and Abdullah both swiped right. At her lunch break they began to chat and exchanged good banter. Abdullah asked for her number so that they could switch their communication to WhatsApp, claiming that it would be easier. Not giving it much thought she gave him her number and soon they started chatting through that medium.

Abdullah asked Alia what it was she was looking for, to which she answered that she wasn't fully sure what to expect from the app but wanted to see how it goes. Abdullah responded to her answer by sending a picture of his penis and asked her "were you looking for this?" Alia, shocked, did not respond and proceeded to block Abdullah. Alia remains confused as to what she did or said to instigate such behavior.

The incorporation of social media, dating apps, and the Internet into the dating scene in Jordan has opened opportunities for young women to navigate social and familial pressures, engage in consensual casual sexual encounters, and establish relationships. However, the use of social-media outlets and dating apps for surreptitious flirtations has also ushered in a new phenomenon: the unwanted "dick pic." Many of our interlocutors shared stories of having initiated or responded to fun and consensual exchanges on dating and social media platforms only to eventually be greeted with an image of a penis and testicles. As Jasmine explained:

> It is disheartening; you start to build a connection with someone on the other screen and out of nowhere, and I really mean out of nowhere, they send you this weirdly angled picture and ask: "You like? You want? Let me see you habibti." You can't help but sit there and ask why . . . ? And more often than not I will not respond. . . . I have had men here realize they made the wrong move because of me not responding but will double down and call me names or claim that I am "not fun."

Sharing photos of male genitalia (either a picture of one's own member or an impressive stock image) has become a global phenomenon (Oswald et al. 2019). Indeed, the legislature in the US state of Texas recently made sending unsolicited penis pictures a misdemeanor (North 2019). Further, there are efforts underway to leverage artificial intelligence to create algorithms to delete such images from social media accounts in an attempt to protect women (Hu 2019). However, interlocutors in our study were unaware of this broader context and generally perceived this to be a uniquely Jordanian male behavior. Women we spoke with also correctly perceived this as being a recent phenomenon and noted that little sage advice for how to navigate the situation exists.

As demonstrated by Alia's story, receipt of an unsolicited phallus image instigated confusion surrounding the meaning of these images: if sent before sexual intimacy had occurred, women often found this off-putting and a signal that reciprocal images and sexual intercourse were expected. Indeed, an online study conducted by Oswald and colleagues among men in Canada found that the motivation behind men who send unsolicited pictures is to receive naked pictures and arouse the receiver (Oswald et al. 2019). Our interlocutors expressed that the receipt of such images not only created the opposite effect, but this expectation of reciprocity put women in socially vulnerable positions. This vulnerability stems from the potential social consequences that arise from the distribution of women's naked pictures. The #notyourhabibti hashtag was started in Palestine in 2018 to push back against revenge porn and online harassment. Although there is little empirical evidence surrounding the extent of "revenge porn" in Jordan, this is addressed in the Cyber Crimes Act, which, in theory, should provide women and men with the ability to report cyber sexual harassment, general harassment, and revenge porn (Nahhas 2018). However, both conversations with our interlocutors and a statement by the Sisterhood Is Global Institute suggest that women are not aware of being able to report this behavior (Cuthbert 2019).

Location, Location, Location

──────────────────────────────*Lina's story*──────────────────────────────

At twenty-nine years old, Lina has been in a committed relationship with Amer for one year and recently decided to get married. Their parents are under the impression that their courtship is part of a "traditional" marriage trajectory. Amer showed up to Lina's house with his parents to ask for her hand in marriage; her family assumed that they did not know each other and agreed to the match.

Lina and Amer wanted to spend some time alone together before their engagement party to make sure that this was indeed the right relationship for them. After some conversation, Lina decided that it was time for them to be sexually intimate. However, where to have sexual relations created a dilemma as they were both still living with their parents. Lina sought advice from friends to learn about options that did not involve the back seat of a parked car.

Amer arranged to pick Lina up after work to then find an apartment and have penile-vaginal intercourse for the first time. Lina was looking forward to going beyond oral sex with her new fiancée. Amer and Lina drove around a neighborhood that was outside of the areas where their families lived to avoid being seen by neighbors or family members. Amer found an apartment building that advertised short-term rentals and gave the door attendant 30JD (US$42). They spent the evening in the apartment and consummated their relationship. As of the writing of this chapter, they are happily married.

"FURNISHED APARTMENT FOR RENT"

Access to the Internet and social media sites such as Facebook has also been critical for enabling women and men to engage in physical intimacy in Jordan. The Internet has opened up opportunities for women and men to find apartments that they can rent by the hour/day. This provides women and men a clandestine place to be intimate, in a physical space, alone, with little to no paper trail. As Rand, twenty-three years of age, explained:

> It is a lot easier to find apartments online and give the landlords cash. If we go to hotels or if we use Airbnb, we have to use our credit cards and that is too risky because that will raise questions from our parents as to why we are renting an apartment by the day. They will know right away that we are engaging in sex and that will not be worth it.

Interlocutors discussed the different ways they were able to identify spaces they could rent in the neighborhoods of West Amman. This included listings on websites like expatriates.com, posts on Facebook groups such as "Apartments for rent," and driving through these neighborhoods for physically posted signs. Unmarried women perceive these daily short-term rental apartments as posing the least social risk: all financial transactions are in cash and most interactions occur between the door attendant and the male partner. Some facilities appear to signal that these apartments can be used for sexual purposes by disclosing in their ads that they do not rent apartments daily but only by the hour. Many of our interlocutors mentioned that these disclosures provide an additional layer of security because they are confident that they will not be reported by these facilities to authorities. Even with these arrangements, discretion is paramount and women still reported that it was important that they be "completely quiet" during their sexual encounters or risk being reported.

ONE WITH NATURE

Interlocutors discussed having friendships with women whom their parents or guardians trusted as essential for being able to date. Trustworthy friends often provided a cover for when women wanted to spend time with their sexual partners. Many of the women we spoke with discussed how they had to negotiate with their parents/guardians in order to get permission to "spend nights" with women friends. With this permission in hand, our interlocutors were then able to go to clubs, travel outside of Amman, and spend more significant time with groups of friends or sexual partners. As twenty-five-year-old Amina explained, "I would tell my parents that I would be joining a friend at her conference at the Dead Sea for the weekend as an alibi. We would bring all our friends together and rent a farm for the weekend which gave us the possibility to party with our friends and spend the night with our boyfriends . . ."

Our interlocutors emphasized the importance of traveling outside of Amman, to areas such as Madaba, the Dead Sea, Al-Salt, and Fuhais, to ensure that they weren't seen by members of their immediate and extended families or other social circles who could report back to their parents. Unmarried women explained that despite the level of planning, there still was significant risk. Indeed, our interlocutors relayed stories of neighbors or male guardians calling the police due to suspected inappropriate behavior. Consistent with the penalties outlined in a 2019 report by Amnesty International, women in our study feared significant social and criminal consequences if reported and convicted of "absence" (where a woman is absent from home without the permission of a male guardian) or adultery.

Sexual and Reproductive Health Services for Unmarried Women in Jordan

——————————————*Rania's story*——————————————

Rania, a twenty-six-year-old primary care provider, met Bakir at a house party. They hit it off and exchanged numbers. Rania and Bakir started dating and had penile-vaginal intercourse after a few dates. Shortly after they started to have sex, Rania noticed that her period was late. She called her friend who came to her home with a pregnancy test. The pregnancy test came back positive and Rania began to panic; she felt overwhelmed and questioned what this meant. She informed Bakir that she was pregnant and they decided that she would have an abortion.

Rania was afraid that if she went to anyone in the health sector, public or private, her work colleagues would find out that she had an unintended pregnancy outside of marriage. She did some research online to figure out her options and found information about medication abortion. Because of her profession, Rania was aware that in Jordan Cytotec, the brand name for a relatively effective solo abortifacient drug called misoprostol, was highly restricted and could only be obtained through hospitals. She knew it would not be an option to get the medication from the hospital she worked at.

In googling Cytotec, Rania found a Facebook page called "Misoprostol and mifepristone in Jordan." She spoke with Bakir and he decided to contact the owner of the page. Bakir requested eight pills and made an appointment with the individual who was selling them for 400JD (US$564). It was difficult for them to come up with such a large sum of money in such a short period. Rania did not want to disclose to their friends or families that she was having an abortion so Bakir had to ask for an advance from his employer. Rania ultimately took the misoprostol at home and had a successful termination.

Sexual and reproductive health services in Jordan have long been tailored to married women and few efforts have been undertaken to address the needs of adolescents, young adults, and unmarried women. Given the strong socio-cultural pressures surrounding marriage and female virginity, the Ministry of Health's hesitation to invest in programs to meet the comprehensive SRH needs of unmarried women is perhaps unsurprising. Although international nongovernmental organizations and some community-based organizations have recently created some youth SRH awareness programs, these programs focus primarily on puberty, nutrition, wellness, and the life course and are not specific to those who are, or might soon become, sexually active (Foster, Hammad, and El-Mowafi, 2019).

Empirical evidence shows that when comprehensive SRH services are unavailable, sexually active women are at increased risk of unintended pregnancy (Mbizvo and Zaidi 2010). Our interlocutors in Jordan spoke at length about their frustrations with the current SRH service provision for unmarried women. Unmarried women that we spoke with who had tried to access contraceptive services reported that they felt judged by providers and received inadequate information and counselling. Soumia, a thirty-one-year-old sexually active woman, went to an obstetrician/gynecologist (ob-gyn) to obtain an intrauterine device (IUD). The intake form assumed that any client receiving contraception would be married. As she explained, "Look at this!!! My husband's and father's name! When I gave the form back to the nurse and [she] saw that I crossed out the husband's and father's name cells, she asked me why I wanted to see the doctor if I was not married . . . I answered and told her it was none of her business."

As Rania's experience with an unintended pregnancy demonstrated, unmarried women also lack access to safe and legal abortion services. Under Jordan's Penal Code, abortion is only legally permissible when performed by a licensed physician and if the pregnancy endangers the life or health of the woman, resulted from rape, or involves a lethal fetal anomaly (Women on Waves 2020). Although these restrictions apply to all women and girls in Jordan, unmarried women are less likely than their married counterparts to be able to navigate the system and may have difficulty identifying a sympathetic private sector provider. As a consequence, there appears to be an unregulated market for misoprostol; several of our interlocutors mentioned using the Internet, and Facebook in particular, to identify unregulated distributors of Cytotec. Although it can be used safely and effectively to induce a first trimester abortion (World Health Organization 2012) and studies indicate that misoprostol can be distributed outside of clinical settings to increase access to safe abortion care (Foster, Arnott, and Hobstetter 2017), in Jordan the cost can be prohibitive. For unmarried women, who are already at heightened risk of unintended pregnancy because they lack access to contraceptive counseling and services, this can be especially devastating. However, just as unmarried women have been able to use technologies to identify potential sexual partners and explore their sexual desires, the Internet has also served as a valuable resource to expanding access to SRH information and services in the absence of brick-and-mortar resources.

Conclusion

Social media platforms, the Internet, and dating apps have changed the parameters within which women are able to navigate dating, hooking up, and casual sex in Jordan. Finding sexual and intimate partners through dating sites and social media platforms such as Bumble, Tinder,

WhatsApp, and ASKfm has provided women with a clandestine way to meet new partners and retain contact without exposing their behavior to family members who are likely to condemn and punish them.

Sexual and reproductive health services in Jordan remain targeted to married women, which leaves unmarried women wanting, especially with respect to information and care in the public sector. The legal implications for unmarried women who need or access SRH services combined with both externalized and internalized stigma create barriers for women in Jordan to advocate for their own sexual safety and SRH needs. Further, limited sexual education in schools and universities leaves women and girls in Jordan navigating their sexual agency with limited knowledge about contraception and sexual health. As Jordan's health system tries to respond to the changing needs in these communities, more research is needed to examine how unmarried women envision their SRH concerns and the challenges they encounter related to meeting their reproductive health needs.

ACKNOWLEDGMENTS

We would like to thank colleagues, friends, and all the women in Jordan who we spoke with on this topic—your earnestness is refreshing. Continue being the badass women that you are.

NOTES

1. "Misdemeanors Relating to Family Norms and Morals," Jordanian Penal Code No. 16 of 1960, Ch 2, sect. 2, articles 282–286

REFERENCES

"Abortion Law Jordan." 2022. Women on Waves. https://www.womenonwaves.org/en/page/4840/abortion-law-jordan.

Almasarweh, Issa S. 2003. "Adolescent and Youth Reproductive Health in Jordan: Status, Issues, Policies, and Programs." Washington, DC: POLICY Project, USAID.

Amnesty International. 2019. "Jordan: Imprisoned Women, Stolen Children: Policing Sex, Marriage and Pregnancy in Jordan," Amnesty International." October 23, 2019. www.amnesty.org/en/documents/mde16/0831/2019/en.

Cuthbert, Olivia. 2019. "Arab Women Fight Back against Online Sexual Harassment." Al Fanar Media. September 25, 2019. www.al-fanarmedia.org/2019/09/arab-women-fight-back-against-online-sexual-harassment.

DeJong Jocelyn, Rana Jawad, Iman M. Mortagy, and Bonnie Shepard. 2005. "The Sexual and Reproductive Health of Young People in the Arab Countries and Iran." *Reproductive Health Matters* 13, no. 25: 49–59.

Department of Statistics (DOS) and ICF. 2002. *Jordan Population and Family and Health Survey*. Rockville, MD: DOS and ICF.

———. 2013. *Jordan Population and Family and Health Survey 2013*. Rockville, MD: DOS and ICF.

———. 2018. *Jordan Population and Family and Health Survey 2017–2018*. Rockville, MD: DOS and ICF.

Economic Research Forum. 2016. *Labor Market Panel Survey 2016, JLMPS 2016*, survey ID # JOR_JLMPS_2016. Cairo: ERF. http://www.erfdataportal.com/index.php/catalog/139.

Foster, Angel M. 2014. "Young Women's Sexuality in Tunisia: The Health Consequences of Misinformation among University Students." In *Everyday Life in the Muslim Middle East*, edited by Donna Lee Bowen, Evelyn Early, and Becky Schulthies, 111–21. Bloomington: Indiana University Press.

Foster, Angel M., and Ieman M. El-Mowafi. 2018. *Evaluation of the 2013–2017 National Strategy for Reproductive Health in Jordan*. Amman, Jordan: Jordan Communication Advocacy and Policy.

Foster, Angel M., Majd Hammad, and Ieman El-Mowafi. 2019. *Gender-Based Violence and Sexual and Reproductive Health in the South of Jordan: Results from a Needs Assessment and Service Mapping Exercise*. Amman, Jordan: United Nations Population Fund.

Foster, Angel M., Grady Arnott, and Margaret Hobstetter. 2017. "Community-Based Distribution of Misoprostol for Early Abortion: Evaluation of a Program along the Thailand-Burma Border." *Contraception* 96, no. 4: 242–47.

Gausman, Jewel, Areej Othman, Iqbal Lutfi Hamad, Maysoon Dabobe, Insaf Daas, and Ana Langer. 2019. "How Do Jordanian and Syrian Youth Living in Jordan Envision Their Sexual and Reproductive Health Needs? A Concept Mapping Study Protocol." *BMJ Open* 9, no. 1. https://doi.org/10.1136/bmjopen-2018-027266.

Hu, Jane. 2019. "A Women Frustrated by Unsolicited Dick Pics Decided to Make Her Own Filters." *Slate*, September 10, 2019. https://slate.com/technology/2019/09/social-media-unsolicited-dick-pics-filter.html.

Khalaf, Inaam, Fathieh Abu-Moghli, and Erika Froelicher. 2010. "Youth-Friendly Reproductive Health Services in Jordan from the Perspective of the Youth: A Descriptive Qualitative Study." *Scandinavian Journal of Caring Sciences* 24, no. 2: 321–31. https://doi.org/10.1111/j.1471-6712.2009.00723.x.

Mbizvo, Michael Takura, and Shahida Zaidi. 2010. "Addressing Critical Gaps in Achieving Universal Access to Sexual and Reproductive Health (SRH): The Case for Improving Adolescent SRH, Preventing Unsafe Abortion, and Enhancing Linkages between SRH and HIV Interventions." *International Journal of Gynecology & Obstetrics* 110, no. 3–6: S3–6.

Nahhas, Roufan. 2018. "Jordan Sounds the Alarm over Rising Online Crimes." *Arab Weekly*, April 22, 2018. https://thearabweekly.com/jordan-sounds-alarm-over-rising-online-crimes.

North, Anna. 2019. "One State Has Banned Unsolicited Dick Pics. Will It Fix the Problem?" *Vox*, September 3, 2019. https://www.vox.com/policy-and-politics/2019/9/3/20847447/unsolicited-dick-pics-texas-law-harassment.

OECD Development Centre. 2018. *Youth Well-Being Policy Review of Jordan*. Paris: OECD Development Centre. www.oecd.org/dev.

Oswald, Flora, Alex Lopes, Kaylee Skoda, Cassandra L. Hesse, and Cory L. Pedersen. 2019. "I'll Show You Mine So You'll Show Me Yours: Motivations and Personality Variables in Photographic Exhibitionism." *Journal of Sex Research* 57, no. 5: 1–13.

Salem, Rania. 2012. "Trends and Differentials in Jordanian Marriage Behaviour: Marriage Timing, Spousal Characteristics, Household Structure and Matrimonial Expenditures." Working paper No. 668, Economic Research Foundation Working Paper Series. Dokki, Giza: ERF. https://erf.org.eg/publications/trends-differentials-jordanian-marriage-behavior-marriage-timing-spousal-characteristics-household-structure-matrimonial-expenditures.

Sieverding, Maia, Nasma Berri, and Sawsan Abdulrahim. 2018. "Marriage and Fertility Patterns among Jordanians and Syrian Refugees in Jordan." Working paper No. 1187, Economic Research Foundation Working Paper Series. Dokki, Giza: ERF". https://erf.org.eg/publications/marriage-and-fertility-patterns-among-jordanians-and-syrian-refugees-in-jordan.

UNWomen, and REACH. 2017. *Jordanian and Syrian Refugee Women's Labour Force Participation and Attitudes towards Employment*. Amman: UNWomen. https://jordan.unwomen.org/en/digital-library/publications/2017/3/jordanian-and-syrian-refugee-womens-labour-force-participation-and-attitudes-towards-employment.

World Health Organization. 2012. *Safe Abortion: Technical and Policy Guidance for Health Systems*, 2nd edition. Geneva: World Health Organization. https://www.who.int/reproductivehealth/publications/unsafe_abortion/9789241548434/en.

CHAPTER 2

Gay Sex Apps and Normative Masculinity among Queer Men in Beirut, Lebanon

MATHEW GAGNÉ

Michael and Mano—two best friends I got to know over the course of my fieldwork into the digitally mediated intimate lives of queer men in Beirut—shared a profession, sense of humor, and bond over drag and fashion.[1] I met Mano early on in my fieldwork. After some banter over Grindr one afternoon, I invited him to share a dessert at a coffee shop near his work. Upon entering the trendy Urbanista café in the Gemmayzeh neighborhood of Beirut, I noticed how his tall, voluptuous body carried queer swagger that seemed in excess of the norms of masculine demeanor in Beirut, a gait he shared with Michael.

Over our brownie, Mano guided me through some of the gender norms among queer Beiruti men, specifically how the idealized masculine body plays out within men's online sexual chatter through apps like Grindr and Scruff. Men valorized those with pictures of muscular, often hairy, bodies and a dominant sexual language. Among queer men in Beirut, *rujula* (manliness) is idealized as being fit, well-groomed, and muscular, one who does not obsess over looks and has a silent yet assertive demeanor (Moussavi 2008, 110).

With his sardonic sense of humor, he told me he felt too fat and femme to land in the muscular zone that seemed to gain attention within the visual aesthetics of sex apps. He was having less sex than he wanted, which he said was due to rejection for his bigger body and flamboyant gesticulations that did not conform to idealized masculinity.

A few weeks later, Mano introduced me to Michael while at Bardo, a popular queer restaurant-cum-weekend dance bar. We stood in the corner of the outdoor area and spoke about Michael's frustrations around sex and love in Beirut. He had only had one four-month affair in the two years since moving to Beirut to join his retired Lebanese parents after growing up in the United States. Michael's search for a relationship over sex apps often left him disappointed, which he attributed to the effects of normative Lebanese masculinity over gay sex and pleasure. Men like Michael and Mano expressed a frustration that amid a sense of expanded intimate possibilities precipitated by sex apps, they still had difficulty finding what they were looking for.

Like many other men, Michael and Mano express a central experience in the digitally mediated sex lives of queer men in Beirut: the redoubling of Lebanese heteronormative masculinity within queer male desires. Social constructs like masculinity are often absorbed into sexual desires and normalized as innate and unwavering characteristics of the individual rather than manifestations of learned social prejudice and hierarchies, especially in sex apps (Greene 2008, 25; Berlant 2012, 6). As scholars of gay sex apps have shown, the interface-driven categories are often based on normative models of gender and selfhood, reifying rather than opening up queer desires and sexualities (Race 2017, 54; Roth 2014, 2121–24). As I show, digital interfaces transfigure embodied masculinity into easily communicable and definable words and aesthetics, embedding masculinity within the design and operations of digital information. In this chapter, I explore how queer masculinities in Lebanon are refracted through informational and technical processes and practices, sometimes reifying and other times challenging homonormative masculinity in Beirut.

Throughout my fieldwork—conducted intermittently over twenty months between 2013 and 2016—men often expressed frustration toward the idealization of masculine bodies.[2] It seemed to many as if the norms of heteronormative masculinity overdetermined their sexual possibilities, playing too big a role. The accosting frequency of phrases like "muscular men only," "only manly men/real men," "be a man," "no feminine," or "no queeny" within sex apps felt, to many, like painful cuts to the feeling of sexual possibility and exploration. For some of those men who took to sex apps to cultivate queer relationships, these phrases precluded the potential to create something different from the overabundance of hetero-sexual cultural symbols and practices that pervade Lebanese public spaces and cultures. For others, those norms were the foundation of their sexual desires and choices.

Within sex apps in Beirut, there is an air of exaggerated masculinity, where profiles are rife with words and images that give the impression that everyone embodied heteronormative masculinity. This, sociologist Ghassan Moussawi (2008, 95) suggests, is a strategy for facing a politic of shame that works upon queer bodies to shape them into masculine bodies that can pass in heteronormative time and space, while marginalizing those men who do not fit this ideal (see also McCormick 2006; Merabet 2014). Robinson (2016) defines heteronormativity as a system and ideology that naturalizes heterosexuality as superior, while homonormativity is an ideology that nonnormative sexualities ought to fit into heteronormative systems. Cenk Özbay calls this "exaggerated masculinity," where men embody a version of masculinity that attenuates the "risks that same-sex sexual activities pose for the reproduction of their masculine selves" (2010, 645). While he developed this concept in relation to heterosexual-identified men working as sex workers among the queer clubs of Istanbul, it can be applied to men in Beirut, who also seek to minimize the public risks of queerness through masculinity. The cultural imperative toward compulsory heterosexuality among queer men drives their adoption of the norms of heterosexual masculine embodiment among their desires and pleasures, giving them a homonormative quality (Donaldson 1993; Moussawi 2008, 3–5).

In the study of queer masculinities, exaggerated masculinity is often seen as a form of reckoning with social marginality and heavy norms of class, nation, and race (Lambevski 1999, 402; Padilla 2007, 30–32; Özbay 2010, 646). In addition, it is associated with distinguishing one's self from the feminized forms of queer masculinity associated with the influence of the West on historical, authentic forms of localized heterosexual masculinities (Özbay 2010, 647; McCormick 2011, 80).

In this chapter, I explore how hegemonic Lebanese masculinity feels within the sex lives of queer men in Beirut. In contrast to literature detailing the construction of Lebanese masculinity through class, sect, and heterosexuality (Hanssen 2006; Merabet 2014; Allouche 2019), I explore its production through sexual desire and possibility, and its negation. What comes to matter about the role of heteronormative masculinity among Lebanese queer men is how it produces and precludes sexual desires and possibilities.

Gay sex apps have produced a sense of possibility for overcoming the limits of law and conservative society in the intimate lives of gay men. Yet, plenty of men deployed the norms of Lebanese masculinity over the apps, creating a new form of discursive and aesthetic production of heteronormative masculinity. The words and images that have become popular and conventional online constitute a renewed, yet modified, application of heteronormative limits within queer possibilities for men. What does it mean to take normative Lebanese masculinity as an affective problem, a feeling of exclusion, rather than a discursive form of normalization?

To answer this question, I first explore how digital media and sex apps have normalized certain ways of talking about sex, desire, and masculinity among queer men in Beirut. I wish to highlight the role of technology as affective rather than discursive. That is, while I first attend to the words and aesthetics men use online, I later turn to exploring the emotional impacts of these forms of Lebanese masculinity on some of my closest interlocutors. I argue the norms of Lebanese masculinity come to matter *within* the sex lives of queer men not through discursive means but by the affects they create among men.

Men often debated how hegemonic aesthetics and ideals of Lebanese masculinity ought to intercede into the affective space of sexual pleasure and desire. It was a question of how queer men re-inscribe social norms among themselves, to the point that sexual pleasure, for many men, feels undermined by the deliberate reproduction of marginalizing social norms like heteronormative masculinity. While these tensions might seem to be unresolved in the affective lives of many men, I end the chapter by discussing how some interlocutors create intimate connections through sexual pleasure that unsettle and rearrange the norms of masculinity.

Global Technologies and the Tense Place of Gay Sex in Beirut

In the digital age, gay sex in Beirut feels like a rather ordinary pleasure that is part of everyday life, even if everyday life also includes legal, familial, and social risk. Early on in my fieldwork, I had a random conversation with a man on Grindr by the profile name "Always Horny." Our conversation quickly turned to sex when he asked me what I was looking for. Wanting to not predetermine any possible outcome, I equivocated, and said I was open to possibilities. He criticized me for trying to be "creative" in my approach to sex apps by looking for something more than sex. When I asked him if he would ever be open to more than sex, he responded, "I try to be happy in my life [and] sex is one of my happy times." Digitally mediated gay sex comes with new ideas of happiness, pleasure, and self-control over one's desire despite the preponderance of oppressive forces in Lebanon and beyond, such as raids and arrests, the forced cancelation of events like Beirut Pride, or everyday acts of homophobic violence against queer people, asymmetrically targeting lower- and working-class men, trans people, migrant workers, and Syrian refugees (Mansour 2017, 198; Moussawi 2018, 175). In fact, as part of a string of assaults on queer life, in May 2019, the Lebanese Ministry of Telecommunications officially blocked Grindr for making romantic and sexual connections among queer men accessible (although other sex apps remained available).[3] However, the sense of gay sex's relative liberty is swiftly undercut by events that viscerally remind men of the state's force in regulating sex.

With the popularity of apps, gay sex in Beirut has come to inhabit a tense place between a sense of personal freedom over desire and pleasure and the persistent socio-political regulation of sexual and intimate realms. Since the end of the Lebanese civil war in 1990, Beirut has seen new queer spaces and the proliferation of queer activist networks, including feminist politics and sexual health (Merabet 2014). These activist organizations advanced a queer politic that went beyond queer visibility based on lifestyle and sexual desires to challenging social structures from an intersectional "anti-sectarian, anti-racist, and anti-xenophobic" approach (Makaram 2011, 105; Naber and Zaatari 2014). To many men—specifically, those with class and masculine privilege to move through social space and political institutions with relative ease—Beirut feels permissive, as if gay sex permeates the city, thanks to the presence of a few bars, NGOs, and advocacy groups working on issues of gender and sexuality, some media representation, and court rulings challenging penal code 534 criminalizing sex deemed against nature.[4]

In fact, the history of sex apps in Beirut reflects the gradual expansion of gay sex and pleasure in Beirut. In the mid-1990s, with the rebuilding of Lebanon's decimated telecommunications infrastructure (Jamali 2003, 34–35), Lebanese men and women began using various queer-themed chatrooms and message boards, like Internet Relay Chat (IRC) and GayLebanon.com, to connect (Abou Chakra 2007, 185–87). Beiruti queer activist Ghassan Makarem claims that men's early Internet usage was to make "acquaintances for sex and sometimes politics." Here, the "sometimes politics" refers to the men and women who, through these chatrooms, came together and organized what is touted as the first public anti-homophobia event in Beirut: I Exist, held in 2000 (Makarem 2011, 102).

Gradually, new forms of technology emerged, with each iteration changing the ways men talk about and feel sex. The advent of Web 2.0 in the early 2000s saw the rise of new websites of user-generated content whose interfaces incorporated images and visual aspects impossible within chatrooms where men could only describe sexualized bodies through words. In websites like Manjam.com and GayRomeo.com, profile pictures are prominently displayed and men communicate more directly and privately, and share images of themselves, which created a culture of desire and sexual arousal centered on the visuality of body parts within images.

Around 2011, mobile phone apps replaced websites as the popular technology for men to connect. Smartphones, along with apps, became more accessible and affordable due to the introduction of new prepaid packages that bundled telecommunications services and reduced prices, the commercial launch of 3G services, and the construction of new underwater cables that increased Lebanon's bandwidth capacity, therefore increasing speed and data caps—not to forget the opening of the Lebanese Apple App Store in 2010.[5] The first users to migrate to gay sex/dating apps were upper- and middle-class men who could afford the high costs of devices and network fees, a class-based segmentation of queer men that has gradually flattened without disappearing entirely as smartphones and apps have become more accessible.

Sex apps untethered gay sex from the weight of a desktop computer, giving users increased mobility and access to sex, as if encounters happen faster and with fewer social steps (Yeo and Fung 2018, 5–6). Men now approach their sex lives through the media ideology (Gershon 2010, 18) that sexual desire and pleasure can be accessed quickly whenever the individual is free with an empty space in which to have sex.

Within the constraints of social and legal forces, men have found expanded sexual possibilities and pleasures through the mobility and privacy of sex apps that quickly connect hundreds of men. Take, for instance, a moment I shared with Nadir, a friend and interlocutor. On Christmas day 2014, Nadir and I were lounging on my couch; the television was on while he played on his phone. His typically disheveled jet-black hair was further tousled by the cool Mediterranean winds wafting in through the open patio doors of my fourth-floor apartment. Nadir interrupted the silence with, "I made a new rule: to focus only on my fuck buddies." He explained that he would invest his energies into developing sexual relationships with a set of men over time rather than meeting new men. "I violated it twice yesterday. Seems like everyone is horny on Christmas Eve," he laughed, relishing the juxtaposition of abundant gay sex with religion—a source of power that marginalizes queerness in Lebanon. The night before, while chatting on Grindr and Scruff, he had invited over two guys at different times for sex.

Men felt that the risks of being queer in public have been attenuated by the privacy of sex apps as a virtual space housed on private hand-held devices that they can reach into to find sex and pleasure in those moments between heteronormative routine obligations. Nadir reminded me on several occasions that sex apps have created the impression that gay sex transcends the normative boundaries of the law over sex and intimacy. One day, Nadir and I were strolling past the police station in the Gemmayzeh neighborhood of West Beirut when he pointed to an apartment building just around the corner. With a coy smile he said, "I once got a blow job on the roof of that building. I met the guy in front of the police station and we went up to the top to find a place." Another time, Nadir, while at a work event in public health, wrote on Facebook, "going on Grindr while sitting next to ISF [Internal Security Forces] personnel at a workshop is priceless!" He saw his sexual communications in proximity to security personnel—the forces that maintain sexual normativity through law and prosecution—as delightfully taunting. Nadir's queer sexual desire expressed over sex apps outpaced the power of the police who, under more public circumstances, may have harassed or arrested him for gay sex. His comment conveys a sense shared by many queer Lebanese men that sex apps have extended gay sex beyond the power of the security forces by disseminating sex among a network of men, private spaces such as homes and hotels, and technologies.

Although sex apps are seen as having privatized men's sex lives beyond the reaches of state power, they are not without risk. Entrapment online is a risk, prompting warnings about safety online (Arab Foundation for Freedom and Equality 2014; Long 2015a, 2015b; Suchy 2019). In Lebanon, such incidences of entrapment rarely happen or are rarely reported to the police. But in 2018, a court ruled against two men for entrapping and robbing two other men over a sex app (Lebanon 24 2018). Authorities were increasingly and illegally searching mobile phones. Lebanon's Cybercrimes Bureau grants authorities free reign to collect information from internet technologies like cell phones and social media to be used in a range of investigations, from the threat of terrorism to cases concerning sex and intimate life, despite the violations this poses to Lebanon's privacy law (Qasqas 2015; Khatib and Deaibess 2017; Alami 2018). Sex apps have kept pace with these events, too. When I entered Lebanon, Scruff and Grindr automatically displayed warnings to users about the risk of imprisonment for gay sex and encouraged users to turn off their GPS location data so they could not be located on a map. To increase privacy and security, Grindr, which is globally recognizable because of all the media attention it gets, released a new feature in winter 2018 enabling users to change the appearance of the app icon so that it is not recognizable, in case someone unwittingly or maliciously looked at another's screen.

Sexual Pleasures and Information

Sex, to many men, is the logical outcome of sex apps. Mano, responding to my question about the seeming absence of seduction and flirtation in digitally mediated sex, reinforced their status as sex apps: "This is just how it is done, it is about getting off, fucking, sticking a dick in an ass." He said this to me offhandedly while we, along with Michael, were walking from his parked car toward Circus, a short-lived gay club located in a refurbished basement theater in Beirut's Hamra district. Around this time, I was thinking about the ethnographic differences between love and sex, and how communication shapes these differences. Michael understood my question differently and also wondered why men have developed this sex-centric logic over one that could have been about exploring romantic possibilities through open exchange and flirtatious conversation.

Nadeem, a digital app designer who understands sex apps in a technical sense, explained the logic of sex apps as for sex. Nadeem said to me when describing why he uses sex apps for sex and not general social connection that could become many things, "If I want information about the world, I'll go to Twitter, if I want to see what my friends are doing, I'll go to Facebook. If I want to read an article, I'll go to my internet browser's reading list. And to talk to friends, I'll go to WhatsApp." Amid these distinct ways of connecting with people, he uses sex apps to connect sexually with strangers. Drawing on his training in user experience (UX) design, Nadeem explained the differences between these apps by how they order information within their interfaces. He pointed out that Twitter's interface, with its cascade of tweets, focuses on words, hyperlinks, and hashtags, while Facebook focuses on what users are doing, reading, thinking, and feeling. Sex apps, however, provide an interface that displays pictures of people and details about their height, weight, and body type, and not "showing what they are doing, reading, thinking, posting, but how they look. They display pictures and a few words, not much else," he instructed me, mobilizing his design anthropology sensibilities to suggest that sexual affects are partially generated through interface design.

Sex emanates from the interface: so many bodies, sexy words, scenarios, profile names, allusions to genitals. All kinds of sex were present: penetrative sex, oral sex, rough sex, romantic sex, group sex, quick sex, kinky sex. These types of sex were signified in just as many digital forms: pictures accentuating sexualized body parts like bulging crotches, tight chests, muscular legs. Profile names like Sex Now, Hot Top, and Al-manyak (the fucker) stir sexual affects and encourage imaginaries of sexual possibilities.

Men talk about sex a lot over digital media, like the kinds of bodies and sex acts they desire, when and where to have sex, and what they hope might happen in their intimate lives. As Nadir once told me, "Sex is highly negotiable. People go into details of what they want to do and what they expect, where to cum, how to fuck, what position, do you want to do it on the floor or on the bed—they go into so many details about sexual pleasure. They want to make sure that what they expect or the pleasure they are gonna get out of it is guaranteed." Sex apps have produced a genre of sexual sociality that is textual and visual, where sex is communicated and felt as men trade words and images to create mutual desire and negotiate sexual possibilities (Race 2015, 255).

Technology's connection to social life is affective. In addition to its material form producing a tactile, erotic—even "orgasmic"—stimulation (Simondon 2012, 3), it is also a sensation that connects "the hand, the mind, and the social body" (Dobres 2001, 49). That is, the affective, mental, and relational aspects of technology are intertwined. Mobile phones are affective technologies first because touching, hearing, and carrying them is a somatic experience, but more importantly, because they are invested with emotional qualities in what we want them to do for us, but also in what they do (Lasén 2010). Men trade information to feel attraction, desire, and pleasure. In digital sex cultures, information creates sensations—or an intensity, to use a term from Brian Massumi (2002)—upon the body that fuel sexual possibilities (Keilty 2017, 68).

THE DATA OF IDEALIZED LEBANESE MALE BODIES

In profiles and private conversations, men used visual aesthetics and words to make male bodies appear masculine according to hegemonic norms of muscularity and sexual virility. One Grindr user displaying a picture of himself in a tank top at the gym, flexing a well-defined bicep, wrote, "what should I do with my big, veiny, curved, very thick, uncut dick?[6] I am very masculine, toned body, manly, very discreet, I have fetishes. A long list of them." His material body—and its lustful qualities—is produced through information patterns: the sequence of data that turns his material body into a model of masculine sexual pleasure. The app user, like many men, submits his body to objectification through a series of adjectives that become an image of a masculine man.

In a culture of discretion where few men displayed face pictures in their profiles, they opted instead for cropped images of body parts often made to appear muscular, such as rounded shoulders and pectoral muscles with popping lines, the lower body with flexing hamstrings, or the abdominal muscles of a gym-fit body. Men used lighting techniques and angles to capture and accentuate the lines of the flexing male body. Displaying only one part of the body can give the impression to viewers that the entire body might be muscular, and desirable. The normativity of this information is profound enough that men started to measure the desirability of their physical bodies by whether they could truthfully describe their own bodies according to these linguistic terms and visual cues. In fact, many men went to the gym, and performed work on their actual bodies just to achieve the norms of the aesthetically valuable bodies depicted within online queer male spaces (Hakim 2016, 86).

Within men's profiles, masculinity was communicated through information about musculature, body hair, voice, and gait. Like one profile with the name "here for you," where the user wrote, "Topless perfect muscled body. Be a man . . . come in. Have a beard, don't be feminine, be a man have sex like a man body hair is a plus muscled fit athletic slim is a plus.. fake profiles =block.. ur pic is the key in Lebanon for a visit." In this example, two notable qualities of the masculine body are emphasized and normalized: muscularity and body hair.

A user with the name Jon wrote in his Scruff profile, "not into (smooth, feminine, queenies, and boys) and (Asians) and (chubby men) [sic]. The same goes if your body is smooth and you shave your chest/facial hair, beard is a must. Also, if you don't see yourself as a man then you are on the wrong page." Under "what I am looking for," he wrote, "Muscular, manly, Arab versatile men for NSA [no strings attached] fun." The high erotic value of gym-fit bodies has long been a feature of queer spaces in Beirut, where scantily clad muscular male bodies gain more attention (Merabet 2014, 63), but in sex apps it is expressed through both words and images.

Under the umbrella of "Arab," this user emphasizes two main qualities of the masculine body: muscularity and body hair. Historically, a well-defined musculature became characteristic of "*effendi* masculinity" that emerged as a colonial brand of Egyptian masculinity, spreading within the region during the nineteenth and twentieth centuries through magazines and film (Jacob 2011, 4). The physical male strength of these bodies symbolized the future and the past of the beleaguered Arab nations after their weakening from colonialism (90).

Hair, too, has historically played a role in the production of masculinity in the region (Daoud 2000; Najmabadi 2005). Ze'evi traces this version of masculinity in the Ottoman Empire through a Galenic medical model that saw the body as regulated by a series of humors and elements. A male's highly sexed disposition—with a humoral balance of hot and dry—was manifested as a body that is hairy, muscular, relatively short and sturdy, with a low voice, fleshy arms, stubby fingers, and big testicles (2006, 27).

To some men, however, Arab masculinity is thick, sturdy, unkempt, and beyond the pale of obsessive bodily concern. These men rejected the gym-conditioned body as a culturally masculine ideal. For instance, a user displaying an image of a muscular shoulder in a tank top with the screen name "DakarMazbout" (roughly translated as exact/perfect/absolute man; the colloquial term *dakar* referring to a masculinity that is strong and virile, and embodied in a masculine gait, countenance, and voice) wrote: "rejaal bil share3 [sic], sharmout bil takhet [a man in the streets, a whore in the sheets] - this is how I would describe my boy. Bisexual guy who is enjoying life on both sides. P.s Women obsessed with muscular bodies stay away. Befhamoun bs ma t2arbo [*sic*] [I understand you, but don't approach]." His comment speaks to a cultural imperative that gay men (and women) separate a respectable public demeanor from a private, sexual self. Another user wrote an aggressive rejection of these norms and considered those who only wanted men in these categories as abnormal. His name: "BearBottom." His picture was of the upper right side of his chest and his armpit. His profile read: "No place/bottom/im hairy and NOT fit or muscled. GET OVER IT. Couples: fuck you all. Escorts: fuck you all. Hairy haters: go fuck girls, they are hairless by nature. Muscled plastic bodies: get a life and a brain. For normal men and bear top cut lovers: u are welcome. Thanks." His acrimony suggests a history of having been excluded as a possible lover due to idealized masculine embodiment.

Queer Arab male bodies have been recast through the Western-derived category of "the bear" (McCormick 2011, 72–73). This figure emphasizes a natural, hairy, perhaps slightly unkempt, sometimes heavyset, other times muscular, but always thick male physique who stands in contrast to the gay male physical ideal of the smooth, muscled man (Hennen 2008, 96, 110–11). In Lebanon, "bears" have hybridized versions of Arab masculinity that play on orientalist depictions and homoerotic desires with global gay male physical types (McCormick 2011, 79, 85; see also Boone 1995; Massad 2007). The "bear" conforms to heteronormative standards of masculinity as sturdy, hairy, with masculine (i.e., unfeminine) gait and gestures while embodying their queerness (McCormick 2011, 73, 88).

MASCULINITY AND PENETRATION

Online, masculinity was often signified through acts of sexual penetration, especially through the signification of rough, dominant penetration. Take, for instance, the profile I saw of a couple looking for sex. In the free space, they wrote that they are "75 percent top and 25 percent kissing and cuddling," a befuddling categorical distinction that needs to be broken down to understand the relationship between gendered sexual pleasure and language. The "75 percent top" ratio performs a virile heteronormative masculinity that assumes that penetration and emotion/attachment are distinctly gendered sex acts. Their top-ness suggests a sexual performance that is rough, penile-centric, and focused on the bottom's pleasure from the inserted penis. Penile penetration as a signal of authentic masculinity can be traced to pre-colonial sexual categories where he who penetrates retains his masculinity while he who is penetrated is ascribed a problematic masculinity (Legrange 2000, 170–71). In the Galenic medical model in the Ottoman Empire, penetrated men were considered to have imbalanced humors and be in need of medical intervention (Ze'evi 2006, 22). While the categories of hetero- and homosexual had not been invented yet, being the penetrator legitimatized a proper masculinity, while men's desire to be penetrated was culturally and medically problematized.

Traces of this model appear in the anonymous couple's profile because they retain their masculinity through their 75 percent top-ness while leaving open the possibility of sentimental forms of sexual connection. In some ways, their top-ness is not even about penetration but about a form of masculine power in a sexual encounter, which I often saw among those men who identified themselves as tops but insisted upon nonpenetrative sex. The materiality of the penis is a site of the reproduction of heteronormative masculinity and sexual virility among queer men through the idea of penetrative pleasure (Hage 2006, 120–123). In fact, while top/bottom and active/passive sexual binaries are global, queer men in Beirut often used the unique category of "manly bottom" to refer to someone who embodies masculine traits but prefers the "passive" role.

THE FRAUGHT FEELING OF NORMATIVE LEBANESE MASCULINITY

All these demands placed on men to appear according to the embodied norms of Lebanese masculinity produced a frustrating sense of struggle in their intimate lives. Intesar, an interlocutor I came to know over the longue durée of my fieldwork, struggled with sex apps, often seeking the desire of those who never gave him attention. He often spoke with desire of the hairy muscled men he couldn't attract. Intesar didn't consider himself conventionally attractive but chased those he saw as such with little success. "I like the normative body. I get into it. I want to disrupt the perceived ranking system. But I am not sure how," he told me one day while sitting in my garden. He felt the pressure of a sexual economy that valorizes and rewards men embodying norms of Lebanese masculinity with affirming sexual attention. It was an economy where fragmented body parts are vested with degrees of erotic value exchanged as pieces of information. He called this "pocket-sized beauty," referring to the cascades of images of topless, muscular men in sex apps, housed on devices kept in our pockets. Intesar often felt sour over his online interactions because he did not have the kind of body that granted him a sense of control over the kinds of attention he wanted.

One night, he recounted a conversation he had over the global grid of Scruff with an older, muscled man in the United Kingdom. Intesar saw this man's muscles as embodying a problem between his desire for them and his perceived inability to capture the man's attention and access his body for pleasure. At first, the UK man was not giving Intesar much attention. Intesar was scrappy and sarcastic with him, trying to gain the upper hand in the conversation through his words, but still the man in the UK paid him little attention.

The man's profile indicated that he is top but would bottom for a big dick. Intesar decided to reverse the man's limited attention by appealing to his desires. Intesar told him that he likes his sexual partners muscular and hairy anyway, conveying to the man in the UK that he was not hairy enough for Intesar. Then Intesar lied, claiming that his penis was 8.5 inches, large by any standard.

Suddenly the guy sent four messages in a row, explaining that his body is actually very hairy, but he shaved it to make the muscular lines on his torso more visible. Intesar relished how the man's standoffish veneer melted at the mention of a large dick, as he attempted to appeal to Intesar's desire so he could see a picture of Intesar's dick. In this erotic exchange, Intesar gained power through (false) information about his penis, whose value to the UK man led him to exchange information about his chest and muscles in line with what Intesar values.

Many interlocutors felt frustrated by these exclusions and the feeling that such a list prevents flexibility in one's desire that might lead to connections beyond these exclusions. Nadir, in fact, wrote a blog piece dissuading men from normalizing desires based on certain skin tone, body type, hirsuteness, masculine gestures and embodiments, height, or weight: essentially those instances of "NO" on sex apps that exclude possible lovers based on an idealized set of bodily criteria. He called this the "a lot of hate when all we want is head" phenomenon, to describe the feeling of closure and negativity that excludes people even before a connection is made.

Yet, the overarching problem of normative masculinity was the sense that it restrains queer sociality, keeping it beholden to a set of cultural norms that bear down upon queerness. After Rashid—a young man who initially started using sex apps to casually meet men and explore relationship possibilities when he moved from his home in the Bekaaʻ valley to Beirut for school—encountered the force of sex over sex apps, he developed a bold sexual language. His profile read, "straight acting? You won't look so straight with my cock in your mouth." He told me that his content deliberately speaks to a part of Beiruti "gay society" with the tendency toward a gender normativity that marginalizes effeminate men.

To Rashid, gendered divisions among men are a microcosm of social structuring in Lebanese society. He said, "This quality of gay society is not moving forward. Society is putting queers aside and labeling them as deviant, and they are doing the same to one another. These types of negative things are not healing queers. We are judging each other by looks when society is judging us, we are judged by society, and judging each other, but at the end of the day, we are judged the same by mainstream society." Rashid emphasized his frustration about the reproduction of heteronormative masculinity in queer male sociality by telling me that he has penetrated the kinds of self-professed manly men who deride nonhetero, feminine-conforming men, adding, "There is no difference between him [the manly bottom] and the effeminate twink [typically defined as a young, skinny, hairless gay man] when they both look the same sucking dick, or with my balls in their mouth." Seemingly, sucking dick is the great social equalizer, especially where plenty of queer men wanting to maintain the connection between masculinity and heteronormative sexual penetration often repudiated the masculinity of those taking the passive role in sex.

Michael, too, challenged the politics of masculinity. His playful profile content read, "I want a queen on the streets and a man in the sheets." This statement, he told me, confused some men, a few even asking him, "I'm a man in the sheets, but not a queen in the streets, is that okay?" From this ambiguity, he explained his content to Mano and me, "What I am saying is I want someone that is super comfortable with their sexuality and it doesn't matter if they put on heels and a wig . . . just be gay. It's fine. We all have homo traits and the whole macho attitude turns me off. If I am in bed, and the guy is being super macho with me, it's a bit of a turn off. I want him to be an average Joe." His larger point was that these terms perform an idealized set of behaviors and traits bound to cultural models that overdetermine how men act to appear to conform to the norms of Lebanese masculinity.

Conclusion: Pleasure, Possibility, and Expanding
Queer Connections beyond Social Norms

Sex, to many men, is about the pleasure of possibility and the potential for pleasure. Sex creates and expands social life through the intersubjective negotiation of pleasure that can lead to new emotions, experiences, and collectivities (Warner and Berlant 1998; Dean 2009; Allen 2011). Yet, the debates my interlocutors had were about the basis of that pleasure, and what kinds of norms surround or determine pleasure. This debate, in fact, recapitulates a debate within scholarly literature concerning sex, which is widely cast within broader social relations of gender, class, ethnicity, and nation (Weiss 2011; Stout 2014; Race 2017). It is beholden to it, already part of it. At the same time, sex can invent new possibilities that rearrange the social and create new conditions of possibility for marginalized bodies, desires, and pleasure (Foucault 1984; Muñoz 2009). What seems like a contradiction is rather a productive tension between sex's imbrication with the social and its capacity to rearrange it. Among men in Beirut, this tension was the debate over the degree to which norms of masculinity ought to be the basis of sexual pleasure.

Nadir, in fact, advocated for a sexual ethic that included flourishing queer connections based on pleasure and mutual satisfaction rather than the satisfaction of criteria relating to normative masculine bodies. After being in a five-year monogamous relationship in his twenties, Nadir veered into experimentation with relationships that incorporated intimate bonds with multiple lovers—ranging from one-night stands and ongoing casual sexual relationships to friendships that included sex. Nadir wanted to bypass the social limits upon queer male sex in Beirut via many kinds of intimacies through mutually negotiated pleasures. Amid one-time encounters, he often had a roster of lovers with whom he negotiated different kinds of relationships, from close sexual friendships to strictly sexual encounters. For about two years, Nadir had casual sex with a man I knew by a letter. Initially, they agreed to meet for a quick sexual encounter, and it was only to be oral sex. "But then during sex" Nadir says, "we just went 'oooohh, you like this, I like this,' and then we developed a thing where we have been seeing each other for a while, exploring other methods of BDSM [bondage, discipline, sadism and masochism]." They had negotiated something very specific to happen, yet it moved beyond that once they were physically together, exemplifying how Nadir created relationships based on mutually negotiated pleasures.

One day early into my fieldwork, before meeting one of Nadir's men-of-interest, he turned to Dina (a mutual friend) and declared, "You are about to witness a Grindr-only phenomenon where you learn the person's name once you shake hands and never actually know it before." Dina did not look surprised. She had been around plenty of men using these technologies and was familiar with the ritual. I, however, was a bit surprised because I had never noticed this effect before. I always asked people for their names, especially if I was providing them with my phone number. It was how I was used to using these technologies among men in Toronto and elsewhere. In combing through my experiences in Beirut until that point, I realized I was always the first person to initiate exchanging names. In this ritual, names and other markers of social identity matter less than possible sexual pleasures as a condition of being together.

The pleasures of sex resonated in a conversation between Nadir and his friend and lover Saad one day while we were careening through the streets of Beirut. From the back of Nadir's work van, Saad said he wanted to meet men of certain quality of character and decent employment, which is tacitly a formulation of one's classed and gendered social position. He wanted a sex life that flowed from interpersonal bonding and sentimentality, between the physical and social pleasures of sex. He admittedly carried a cultural precept that sex ought to be had out of interpersonal bonds and unique connections and having sex for the sake of physical pleasure and lust was illegitimate. The difference here was that lust, to many men, is driven by physical instincts that differentiated possible lovers based on bodies, whereas a bond was an orientation of care, compassion, and emotion toward an individual selected as special among the rest for their personality and uniqueness.

Nadir challenged him, "Who cares if they are quality; so long as they get your dick up, have fun." For Nadir, sex for the sake of pleasure was enough to find value in an encounter. The point for Nadir was not to evaluate the potential for sexual pleasure based on a set of abstract criteria such as the embodied norms of masculinity but just based on whether there was the potential for pleasure.

Nadir, like other men, enlivened the affective dimensions of a sexual politic where pleasure and desire mark a queer horizon of (potential) relationality. The challenge to norms of intimacy was the liberty to have sex and to be queerly associated, to form a social milieu based on a sexual connection that was more personable compared to sex based on the satisfaction of idealized criteria of Lebanese masculinity. This was not simply enacting a politic of the freedom to choose one's lover despite Beiruti social, legal, and state structures that have marginalized queer relationships, but a politic of letting each unique encounter between individuals give life to subjective and social potentialities.

ACKNOWLEDGMENTS

I received a Social Science and Humanities Research Council of Canada doctoral fellowship that supported this research. I'd like to thank the editors, L. L. Wynn and Angel M. Foster, for their invitation to contribute and Naisargi Dave for her countless comments.

NOTES

1. I identify my interlocutors using pseudonyms.
2. The Research Ethics Board (REB) at the University of Toronto approved this research. I recruited participants through casual conversation and relationship building. I arrived in Beirut and quickly began chatting with men online through the apps. Gradually, I developed research relationships both online and offline. Given the fraught nature of informed consent in ethnography, I established consent through relationship building. I made clear to men that I was a researcher studying their sex lives, and that they could always refuse to participate, or ask me not to include our friendships and interactions within my data. Some men were clear in the desire to not include our interactions in the data. Online, men were often forthcoming in their participation and excited about the research. I interpreted nonresponse as nonconsent. I was very attuned to how people communicate consent through indirect verbal and nonverbal means. Furthermore, I often reminded my interlocutors that the stories they shared as friends were being included in the research and that they could refuse anytime. I asked for written consent when participants sat for formal interviews.
3. Why did the government block Grindr after nearly a decade of it being accessible in Beirut while leaving other kinds of sex and dating apps accessible? I have no concrete answer. For many activists, this was just another in a series of events targeting queer people and Grindr was the target because it is the most recognizable of gay apps beyond users (Hall 2019; Redd 2019; Traboulsi 2019).
4. In recent years, the judiciary has dismissed these cases for various reasons, including ruling that homosexuality is not against nature especially when practiced in private, or, in the cases where trans women are on trial, ruling that trans women are women therefore the law does not stand (Rainey 2014; Reid 2017; Frangieh 2019; Assaf 2019).
5. Last accessed December 2017 from the Lebanese Telecommunications Regulatory Authority at http://www.tra.gov.lb/Market-Data-Facts-and-figures (last updated in 2011); see "The iPhone App Store Comes to Lebanon," *Qifa Nabki* (blog), February 21, 2010, https://qifanabki.com/2010/02/21/the-iphone-app-store-comes-to-lebanon.
6. His circumcision status is simultaneously arousing sexual description and a possible indication of his Christian religious background since Christians and Muslims can be differentiated based on circumcision.

REFERENCES

Abou Chakra, Chirine. 2007. "Gaygle ton ami! Usages et rencontres des homosexuels Bey-routhins sur internet." In *Société de l'information au Proche-Orient: Internet au Liban et en Syrie*, edited by Yves Gonzalez-Quijano and Christophe-Henri Varin, 181–200. Beirut: Centre d'études pour le monde arabe moderne, Université Saint-Joseph.

Alami, Mona. 2018. "Lebanon's Shrinking Freedom of Expression." *Arab Weekly*, July 29, 2018. https://thearabweekly.com/lebanons-shrinking-freedom-expression.

Allen, Jafari S. 2011. *¡Venceremos?: The Erotics of Black Self-Making in Cuba*. Durham, NC: Duke University Press.

Allouche, Sabiha. 2019. "The Reluctant Queer." *Kohl: A Journal for Body and Gender Research* 5, no. 1: 11–22.

Arab Foundation for Freedom and Equality. 2014. "Avoiding Entrapment after an Online Chat." November 14, 2014. http://www.afemena.org/avoiding-entrapment-after-an-online-chat.

Assaf, Claude. 2019. "A Landmark Decision, a Lebanese Military Tribunal Decriminal-izes Homosexuality." *L'orient le jour* April 4, 2019. https://www.lorientlejour.com/article/1164847/in-a-landmark-decision-a-lebanese-military-tribunal-decriminalizes-homosexuality.html.

Berlant, Lauren. 2012. *Desire/Love*. New York: Punctum Books.

Boone, Joseph A. 1995. "Vacation Cruises; or, The Homoerotics of Orientalism." *PMLA* 110, no. 1: 89–107.

Daoud, Hassan. 2000. "Those Two Heavy Wings of Manhood: On Moustaches." In *Imagined Masculinities: Male Identity and Culture in the Modern Middle East*, edited by Mai Ghous-soub and Emma Sinclair-Webb, 251–67. London: Saqi Books.

Dean, Tim. 2009. *Unlimited Intimacy: Reflections on the Subculture of Barebacking*. Chicago: University of Chicago Press.

Dobres, Marcia-Anne. 2001. "Meaning in the Making: Agency and the Social Embodiment of Technology and Art." In *Anthropological Perspectives on Technology*, edited by Michael Brian Schiffer, 47–76. Albuquerque: University of New Mexico Press.

Donaldson, Mike. 1993. "What Is Hegemonic Masculinity?" *Theory and Society, Special Issue: Masculinities* 22, no. 5: 643–57.

Foucault, Michel. 1984. "Friendship as a Way of Life." In *The Foucault Reader*, edited by Paul Rabinow, 135–40. New York: Pantheon.

Frangieh, Ghida. 2019 "Beirut Court of Appeal: Sexual Orientation Is Not Punishable." *Legal Agenda*, May 28, 2019. https://english.legal-agenda.com/beirut-court-of-appeal-sexual-orientation-is-not-punishable.

Gershon, Ilana. 2010. *The Breakup 2.0: Disconnecting over New Media*. Ithaca: Cornell University Press.

Green, Adam Isaiah. 2008. "The Social Organization of Desire: The Sexual Fields Approach." *Sociological Theory* 26, no. 1: 25–50.

Hage, Ghassan. 2006. "Migration, Marginalized Masculinity and Dephallicization: A Leba-nese Villager's Experience." In *Sexuality in the Arab World*, edited by Samir Khalaf and John Gagnon, 107–29. London: Saqi Books.

Hakim, Jamie. 2016. "'Fit Is the New Rich': Male Embodiment in the Age of Austerity." *Soundings: A Journal of Politics and Culture* 61, no. 1: 84–94.

Hall, Richard. 2019. "Lebanon Blocks Grindr in Latest Attack on LGBT+ Community." *Independent*, May 28, 2019. https://www.independent.co.uk/news/world/middle-east/grindr-lebanon-ban-lgbt-rights-dating-app-gay-a8933556.html.

Hanssen, Jens. 2006. "Sexuality, Health and Colonialism in Postwar 1860 Beirut." In *Sexuality in the Arab World*, edited by Samir Khalaf and John Gagnon, 63–84, London: Saqi Books.

Hennen, Peter. 2008. *Faeries, Bears, and Leathermen: Men in Community Queering the Masculine*. Chicago: University of Chicago Press.

Jacob, Wilson Chacko. 2011. *Working Out Egypt: Effendi Masculinity and Subject Formation in Colonial Modernity, 1870–1940*. Durham, NC: Duke University Press Books.

Jamali, Dima. 2003. "Post-War Telecommunications Reform in Lebanon: Trends and Challenges." *Info* 5, no. 2: 34–44.

Keilty, Patrick. 2017. "Embodied Engagements with Online Pornography." *Information Society* 32, no. 1: 64–73.

Khatib, Lina, and Bassem Deaibess. 2017. "Lebanon's Cybercrime Arrests Threaten State's Credibility." *Middle East Eye*, January 13, 2017. https://www.middleeasteye.net/opinion/lebanons-cybercrime-arrests-threaten-states-credibility.

Lambevski, Sasho A. 1999. "Suck My Nation—Masculinity, Ethnicity and the Politics of (Homo)sex." *Sexualities* 2, no. 4: 397–419.

Lasén, Amparo. 2010. "Mobile Media and Affectivity: Some Thoughts about the Notion of Affective Bandwidth." In *Mobile Media and the Change of Everyday Life*, edited by Joachim R. Höflich, Georg F. Kircher, Christine Linke, and Isabel Schlote, 131–53, Frankfurt am Main: Peter Lang.

Lebanon 24. 2018. "Daniel and Louay Were Lured through a Gay Dating App . . . Here Is the Full Story." [In Arabic.] *Lebanon 24* December 12, 2018. https://www.lebanon24.com/news/lebanon/536645/
استدرجوا-دانيال-ولؤي-عبر-تطبيق-لتعارف-مثلي-الجنس-

Legrange, Frédéric. 2000. "Male Homosexuality in Modern Arabic Literature." In *Imagined Masculinities: Male Identity and Culture in the Modern Middle East*, edited by Mai Ghoussoub and Emma Sinclair-Webb, 156–75. London: Saqi Books.

Long, Scott. 2015a. "Internet Entrapment in Egypt: Protect Yourself!" [In Arabic.] *A Paper Bird* (blog), June 12, 2015. https://paper-bird.net/2015/06/12/egypt_internet_entrapment.

———.2015b. "Entrapped! How to Use a Phone App to Destroy a Life," *A Paper Bird* (blog). Sept. 19, 2015. https://paper-bird.net/2015/09/19/entrapped-how-to-use-a-phone-app-to-destroy-a-life.

Makarem, Ghassan. 2011. "The Story of HELEM." *Journal of Middle East Women's Studies* 7, no. 3: 98–112.

Mansour, Nisrine. 2017. "Visualizing the (In)Visible: The Queer Body and the Revolving Doors of the Lebanese Queer Subculture." In *Arab Subcultures Transformations in Practice and Theory*, edited by Tarik Sabry and Layal Ftouni, 196–221. New York: I. B. Tauris.

Massad, Joseph A. 2007. *Desiring Arabs*. Chicago: University of Chicago Press.

Massumi, Brian. 2002. *Parables for the Virtual: Movement, Affect, Sensation*. Durham, NC: Duke University Press Books.

McCormick, Jared. 2006. "Transition Beirut: Gay Identities, Lived Realities." In *Sexuality in the Arab World*, edited by Samir Khalaf and John Gagnon, 243–60. London: Saqi Books.

———. 2011. "Hairy Chest, Will Travel. Tourism, Identity, and Sexuality in the Levant." *Journal of Middle East Women's Studies* 7, no. 3: 71–97.

Merabet, Sofian. 2014. *Queer Beirut*. Austin: University of Texas Press.

Moussawi, Ghassan. 2008. *On the Shaming of Gender: Compulsory Heterosexuality and the Construction of Non-Heterosexual Masculinities in Beirut*. MA Thesis, American University of Beirut.

———. 2018. "Queer Exceptionalism and Exclusion: Cosmopolitanism and Inequalities in 'Gay-Friendly' Beirut." *Sociological Review* 66, no. 1: 174–90.

Muñoz, Jose Esteban. 2009. *Cruising Utopia: The Then and There of Queer Futurity*. New York: NYU Press.

Naber, Nadine, and Zeina Zaatari. 2014. "Reframing the War on Terror: Feminist and Lesbian, Gay, Bisexual, Transgender, and Queer (LGBTQ) Activism in the Context of the 2006 Israeli Invasion of Lebanon." *Cultural Dynamics* 26, no. 1: 91–111.

Najmabadi, Afsaneh. 2005. *Women with Mustaches and Men without Beards: Gender and Sexual Anxieties of Iranian Modernity*. Berkeley: University of California Press.

Özbay, Cenk. 2010. "Nocturnal Queers: Rent Boys' Masculinity in Istanbul." *Sexualities* 13, no. 5: 645–63.

Padilla, Mark. 2007. *Caribbean Pleasure Industry: Tourism, Sexuality, and AIDS in the Dominican Republic*. Chicago: University of Chicago Press.

Qasqas, Omar. 2015. "Fighting Cybercrime in Lebanon." *The New Arab*, January 21, 2015. https://www.alaraby.co.uk/english/features/2015/1/21/fighting-cybercrime-in-lebanon.

Race, Kane. 2015. "'Party and Play': Online Hook-Up Devices and the Emergence of PNP Practices among Gay Men." *Sexualities* 18, no. 3: 253–75.

———. 2017. *The Gay Science: Intimate Experiments with the Problem of HIV*. New York: Routledge.

Rainey, Venetia. 2014. "Landmark Ruling Rubbishes Anti-Gay Law in Lebanon." *Daily Star*, March 5, 2014. https://www.dailystar.com.lb/News/Lebanon-News/2014/Mar-05/249261-landmarkruling-rubbishes-anti-gay-lawin-lebanon.ashx#axzz2v8zsB9YB.

Redd, Benjamin. 2019. "Mystery Surrounds Grindr Ban, Users Worried." *Daily Star*, May 18, 2019. https://www.dailystar.com.lb/News/Lebanon-News/2019/Jan-22/474640-mystery-surrounds-grindr-ban-users-worried.ashx.

Reid, Graeme. 2017. "Lebanon Edges Closer to Decriminalizing Same-Sex Conduct." *Human Rights Watch*, February 2, 2017. https://www.hrw.org/news/2017/02/02/lebanon-edges-closer-decriminalizing-same-sex-conduct.

Robinson, Brandon Andrew. 2016. "Heteronormativity and Homonormativity." In *The Wiley Blackwell Encyclopedia of Gender and Sexuality Studies*, edited by Nancy A. Naples,

Angela Wong, Maithree Wickramasinghe, and Renée Hoogland, 1–3. Hoboken, NJ: John Wiley & Sons.

Roth, Yoel. 2014. "Locating the 'Scruff Guy': Theorizing Body and Space in Gay Geosocial Media." *International Journal of Communication* 8: 2113–33.

Schüll, Natasha Dow. 2012. *Addiction by Design: Machine Gambling in Las Vegas*. Princeton, NJ: Princeton University Press.

Simondon, Gilbert. 2012. "On Techno-Aesthetics," translated by Arne De Boever. *Parrhesia*, no. 14: 1–8.

Stout, Noelle M. 2014. *After Love: Queer Intimacy and Erotic Economies in Post-Soviet Cuba*. Durham, NC: Duke University Press.

Suchy, Clara. 2019. "Tackling Safe Sexting, Online Dating." *Daily Star*. March 9, 2019. https://www.dailystar.com.lb/News/Lebanon-News/2019/Mar-09/478379-tackling-safe-sexting-online-dating.ashx.

Traboulsi, Karim. 2019. "#GrindrLebBan: Lebanon Partially Blocks Gay Dating App." *New Arab*, January 22, 2019. https://english.alaraby.co.uk/news/grindrlebban-lebanon-restricts-online-gay-dating-app.

Warner, Michael, and Lauren Berlant. 1998. "Sex in Public." *Critical Inquiry* 24, no. 2: 547–66.

Weiss, Margot. 2011. *Techniques of Pleasure: BDSM and the Circuits of Sexuality*. Durham, NC: Duke University Press.

Yeo, Tien Ee Dominic, and Tsz Hin Fung. 2018. "'Mr Right Now': Temporality of Relationship Formation on Gay Mobile Dating Apps." *Mobile Media Communication* 6, no. 1: 3–18.

Ze'evi, Dror. 2006. *Producing Desire: Changing Sexual Discourse in the Ottoman Middle East, 1500–1900*. Berkeley: University of California Press.

CHAPTER 3

Better Out than In

The Importance of Withdrawal in Sex and Family Planning in Turkey

KATRINA MACFARLANE

Withdrawal—also known as coitus interruptus, or more colloquially, pulling out—is one of the oldest and most widely used forms of family planning. With references in the religious texts of Judaism, Christianity, and Islam (Potts and Campbell 2002), the origins of withdrawal are documented as far back as 2,500 years ago. Withdrawal, the practice of removing the penis from the vagina prior to ejaculation, is still practiced widely as an important family planning method today; the United Nations (UN) reported forty-seven million users worldwide in 2019 (United Nations DESA 2019a). Studies have demonstrated that the failure rates for withdrawal and condoms are similar (18 percent and 17 percent, respectively) (Kost et al. 2008) and that with perfect use, 4 percent of withdrawal users would become pregnant within a year of use (Hatcher et al. 2007, 338).

In sexual and reproductive health scholarship, contraceptive methods are typically categorized in two broad categories: non-biomedical, more commonly referred to as "traditional," methods of contraception, and biomedical, or "modern," methods of contraception. Not surprisingly, withdrawal was widely practiced well before the advent of biomedical contraceptives, which were developed and became more readily available during the twentieth century. Particularly after the introduction of the oral contraceptive pill (OCP) and the intrauterine device (IUD) in the 1960s, many people who wanted to prevent pregnancy shifted to using biomedical interventions. Some national governments actively promoted the use of biomedical contraceptive methods, and certain regions have seen a remarkable uptake with simultaneous declines in the use of non-biomedical methods. Western European countries report rates of withdrawal use among reproductive-aged women at less than 1 percent and an overwhelming preference for biomedical over non-biomedical contraceptive methods (United Nations 2019a). In contrast, although Turkey introduced a robust national family-planning program in the 1960s and saw a subsequent rise in the use of biomedical contraceptive methods, use of withdrawal also increased and has remained remarkably stable since the 1980s, with only a minor decline in the last several years (HUIPS 2019). A similar pattern is mirrored across some other Eastern European and Western Asian countries that still show a strong inclination toward withdrawal as a primary pregnancy prevention method (United Nations DESA 2019a).

The continued use of "traditional" contraceptive methods in some regions might suggest that people lack knowledge about "modern" methods. Indeed, the very use of the terminology *traditional* and *modern* establishes a hierarchy between the two classes of methods and assigns a positive value judgment to modern methods, suggesting that they are a more evolved or sophisticated choice, while traditional methods are outdated or a relic of the past. Within that, there may also be assumptions that those using traditional methods are doing so because they don't know any alternative, and a preference for these methods stems only from a lack of knowledge of or access to biomedical methods. By painting some methods as modern and thus implying these methods are the optimal choice, it is also suggestive that those with more knowledge or education would invariably opt for modern methods, which I will argue is not necessarily the case. As the current nomenclature reinforces the notion that modern methods are a more preferable alternative in the current era, I argue that a revision in terminology is necessary, and for the remainder of this chapter, I will refer to traditional methods—including withdrawal and calendar methods—as non-biomedical methods, and modern methods—including OCPs and the IUD—as biomedical methods.

And while there is a positive association between education level and the use of biomedical methods in Turkey (Koç 2000), I argue that there are other reasons why many Turkish couples continue to use withdrawal and why it remains a popular choice. A lack of knowledge of biomedical options, for instance, does not appear to be the issue. Turkish women have near-universal knowledge of contraception. The 2018 Demographic and Health Survey (DHS) of Turkey demonstrates that nearly all women (>97 percent) knew of at least one biomedical method of contraception. In addition, the use of biomedical contraceptive methods has steadily climbed over the last three decades, from 31 percent of married women using a biomedical method in 1988 to 49 percent in 2018. Yet all the while, the use of withdrawal has remained relatively steady and persists as the single most common form of contraception used; according to the most recent DHS, 20 percent of currently married women were using withdrawal as their most effective family-planning method. Further, more than half of married women (58 percent) reported that they had ever used this method. Because premarital sex is still highly stigmatized in Turkey, reported contraceptive use is typically lower among *all* women as compared to *currently married* women; however, overall trends in contraceptive use are similar. Of all women, 13.5 percent report withdrawal as their current method, making it the most common form of family planning ahead of male condoms (12.8 percent) and the IUD (9.2 percent). This suggests that withdrawal is a particularly salient strategy, for both married and unmarried Turkish women. The use of withdrawal is also prominent among Turks of all ages; married fifteen- to nineteen-year-olds have a reported usage of 17.2 percent, making withdrawal the most popular form of contraception among married Turkish adolescents, and it is consistently ranked as the most common form of contraception ever used among all women across all age cohorts. One might imagine that this inclination toward withdrawal indicates an overall reliance on or preference for non-biomedical methods more generally, but this does not appear to be the case. Fewer than half of all Turkish women even reported knowledge of the rhythm (calendar) method and less than 1 percent use the rhythm method as their most effective method, irrespective of age and marital status (HUIPS 2019).

I argue in this chapter that modern Turkish women and men are continuing to use and choose withdrawal—a traditional method—for myriad reasons. Some people are indeed choosing this method contemporaneously and not simply using it because it is their only option; opting for withdrawal can very well be a modern decision. Despite its importance for family planning for millions of couples around the world, relatively little research has focused on withdrawal. This chapter explores some of the reasons behind the persistent popularity of withdrawal among Turks. Its continued use in a context where almost all women are aware of at least one biomedical method of contraception and national programs have emphasized and provided these methods for decades suggests that some people are making deliberate choices to use withdrawal. The literature frames the practice of withdrawal solely as a method of contraception when it represents more than that in reality; it can be an important part of sex, and its relative importance or desirability to different people is colored by cultural norms and understandings of sex and pleasure. Withdrawal is indeed a method of contraception, but it may be equally important for sexual pleasure or what it signals (or does not signal) to a partner about intimacy and trust. Choosing to use withdrawal, or not to use it, is far from a decision about just contraception; it is a decision about sexual practices and pleasure, social and religious acceptability, and partnership dynamics.

My interest in this fascinating dynamic first became piqued when I was living and working in Istanbul in the early 2010s. My day-to-day observations, interactions with friends and colleagues, and regular engagement with Turkish news and popular media shaped my thinking about the use of and satisfaction with withdrawal. In this chapter, I combine long-term participant observation and community residence with a formal review of peer-reviewed and grey literatures, in both English and Turkish. I also draw from twenty-five formal interviews that I conducted in 2015 with key informants and women living in Turkey as part of my master's degree in interdisciplinary health sciences (MacFarlane et al. 2017; MacFarlane et al. 2016). Although that project specifically focused on abortion, participants also spoke about broader issues related to sexual and reproductive health and their own contraceptive practices. We recruited in-depth interview participants by advertising the study on social media and through local research and nonprofit organizations in Istanbul. We identified relevant key informants who worked in sexual and reproductive health and reached out to them based on publicly available information online. For key informants, we also employed snowball sampling, where we asked early participants to pass on information about the study to any colleagues who might be interested in participating. We obtained verbal consent prior to conducting each interview and reminded participants that they could discontinue participation at any point. We protected participant confidentiality by removing any personally identifying information in final publications. Prior to completing this work, we obtained ethics approval from the Social Sciences and Humanities Research Ethics Board (REB) at the University of Ottawa.

Withdrawal—Yesterday, Today, and Tomorrow?

Prior to the 1900s, people had to rely exclusively, and with varying degrees of effectiveness, on non-biomedical methods of contraception. Withdrawal, along with douching and herbal remedies, were some of the methods historically used to prevent pregnancy. This was very much the case in then Ottoman territory; use of withdrawal was well documented in places such as Istanbul during the late nineteenth century. At the turn of the century, Istanbul had a total fertility rate (TFR) of 3.88, far below not only the rest of Turkey but also much of Europe (Duben and Behar 1991). During this period, women in Istanbul who had successfully limited their family sizes consistently explained that their husbands had "been very careful." Duben and Behar assert that "being careful" has long been a euphemism for withdrawal practices. They point out that according to women in Istanbul in the early twentieth century, the affordability, ease, and practicality of withdrawal motivated use (1991). Thus, a preference for smaller family sizes was evident in urban Turkey a century ago and was achieved, in part, by practicing withdrawal, while the TFR remained high throughout the rest of the country during the late Ottoman era.

The early twentieth century gave way to enormous sociopolitical changes in what is now modern-day Turkey. Founded in 1923, the Republic of Turkey in its earliest days continued to emphasize the pronatalism that was a mainstay in the declining years of the Ottoman Empire. High fertility was desirable to Turkish leaders in the 1920s and 1930s to help repopulate after massive losses in consecutive wars—the Balkan War, the First World War, and the Turkish War of Independence (Gürsoy 1996). The state developed pronatalist propaganda, prohibited both abortion and contraception, reduced the legal age of marriage, and provided financial remuneration for having more children, all in an effort to encourage larger families (Benezra 2014). By the early 1960s, the national TFR was 6.2 children per woman (United Nations DESA 2019b). Although the use of biomedi-cal methods of contraception was still prohibited during this era, evidence suggests that couples continued to use non-biomedical methods to prevent pregnancy (Ortayli et al. 2005).

By the 1960s, it became apparent that unfettered population growth, particularly with the population boom following World War II, would hinder Turkey's economic and development goals. This, paired with an increased incidence of abortion in the late 1950s, shifted the political nee-dle such that the state introduced anti-natalist policies with the aim of decreasing the TFR (Benezra 2014). Turkey introduced an expansive fam-ily-planning program that included biomedical contraceptives in the mid-1960s. The 1965 Law on Population Planning legalized the sale and distribu-tion of contraceptives as well as educational materials about contraception (Huntington et al. 1996). During this effort, IUDs were the primary con-traceptive method provided to women and, while there was some increase in the uptake of OCPs and the IUD, the primary method responsible for the increase in ever-use of contraception between 1963 and 1968 was with-drawal (Özbay and Shorter 1970). By 1973, the rate of biomedical contra-ceptive use in Turkey had increased from 1 percent to 3 percent. Mean-while, withdrawal use had more than doubled to about 24 percent. This rate of withdrawal use continued apace in the 1980s and remained the sin-gle most commonly used method across all ages of Turkish women in the early twenty-first century (HUIPS 2014).

This historical trajectory of withdrawal use in the Turkish landscape is of significance to its contemporary use. Withdrawal has long been viewed among Turks as an accessible and reliable approach to pregnancy preven-tion and has been a major driver of decreases in the country's TFR over the last century. Given this context, it is not altogether surprising that it is still valued as a method today. The very things that made it so popular a century ago—accessibility, cost, discretion, lack of side effects, male involvement in family planning, hygiene, and cleanliness—remain ever pertinent in the collective imagination. Further, the rollout of the family-planning pro-gram in the 1960s took a top-down, state-sponsored approach and did not necessarily serve the needs and wants of Turkish women (Benezra 2014). The national program also strongly emphasized biomedical methods, and specifically the IUD, and this push may not have resonated with individu-als who had well-defined preferences and reasons to opt for a non-biomed-ical method of family planning, such as concerns about the side effects of biomedical methods. In modern day Turkey, the political discourse around contraception has become contentious, which may also be influencing people's decisions about and access to family planning. The state has become more hostile toward access to abortion and contraception, and the current sociopolitical context may also in part be contributing to why withdrawal— a free, discreet, and easy option—continues to be a leading choice for Turks of all backgrounds.

The Role of Withdrawal in Broader Family Planning Strategies

Withdrawal is the most effective form of contraception used among one-fifth of married couples in Turkey today. However, withdrawal may not always be the primary method of contraception that people are using; it is often used in concert with other methods or strategies. Withdrawal is an important piece of the puzzle in how Turks think about family planning, and it is used in tandem with a range of other biomedical and non-biomedical methods including male condoms, the calendar method, oral contraceptive pills, and emergency contraception. Whether women use withdrawal as a second or "back-up" method or whether they used it when other methods such as condoms are undesirable, Turkish women described using withdrawal as part of an overall contraceptive strategy.

For example, women talked about using withdrawal as a strategy in lieu of condom use. When asked if she had ever used withdrawal, one interviewee shared, "Yes. When we didn't use condoms that's what we did." Others used withdrawal as part of their strategy alongside the calendar method; they would not use any form of contraception during less fertile times and would use withdrawal during the fertile window around ovulation rather than abstaining altogether. This aligns with research indicating that a majority of Turkish women who were using contraception were using withdrawal, either alone or in combination with another method, as their strategy (Bulut et al. 1996); this phenomenon of using withdrawal as a component of a broader strategy alongside other methods is also mirrored in other contexts (Jones, Lindberg and Higgins 2014; Higgins and Wang 2015).

Other women that I interviewed used withdrawal exclusively. This was most notably the case among married women, with some indicating that this was their husband's preference and that their husbands may not be open to biomedical contraceptives. The way that some women talked about it suggested that they characterized withdrawal as quite distinct from other types of contraception.[1] When asked about whether she had ever used birth control, one married woman explained, "No, never. My husband doesn't want it. . . . He is using withdrawal, he trusts himself. He doesn't accept anything else."

Withdrawal also seemed to be a factor in whether or not some women chose to use emergency contraception (EC). When she experienced an unplanned pregnancy, one woman explained during our interview, "Well, the thing was that it was the first time we had slept with each other and we were so drunk and everything. I didn't even think about anything like that [EC]. And also because he said that he pulled out." In many of my conversations with Turkish women, withdrawal was almost assumed or was the default method used, even in circumstances like first-time encounters. And if withdrawal was used, this was sufficiently protective for many people; overwhelmingly my interlocutors thought of withdrawal as effective and reliable. This is consistent with what Whittaker and colleagues (2010) have documented in other contexts; withdrawal is a normalized and accepted aspect of sexual behavior, particularly among young people. The normalization of this practice is important. Withdrawal, like any coital-dependent method, cannot be siloed as just a contraceptive; the practice of withdrawal is very much a part of sex itself. Thus the perceptions of what withdrawal means not just for pregnancy prevention but for pleasure and intimacy as well are an integral part of understanding why people continue to opt for this as their chosen method. Depending on the user, withdrawal may be viewed as either positively or negatively impacting connection, intimacy, and pleasure during sexual encounters. Studies in other contexts indicated that 21 to 29 percent of young adults felt it was a hassle to use condoms every time they had sex (Frost, Lindberg and Finer 2012), and withdrawal can be seen by some as a more pleasurable alternative to barrier methods like condoms (Jones et al. 2009). Withdrawal has also been reported as a preferred method among users who eroticize safe sex practices, because using withdrawal in tandem with other methods made people feel especially safe (Jones et al. 2009). Another study found that people tend to dislike barrier methods like condoms for a host of reasons relating to pleasure—because they increase physical discomfort, interrupt "sexual flow," and impede the ability to have physical closeness and skin-on-skin contact—and women worried condoms might hinder their male partner's pleasure (Higgins and Hirsch 2008); some of these concerns around pleasure may be mitigated by using a method like withdrawal instead.

This broad acceptance of withdrawal is not limited to young people. It also appears to be an important approach to pregnancy prevention at the other end of the spectrum, when Turkish women approach menopause. Although use of all contraceptive methods drops substantially from the forty to forty-four to the forty-five to forty-nine age cohorts, from 79.8 percent to 59 percent respectively, much of that drop is due to a decreased use of biomedical methods. Indeed, use of withdrawal remains relatively high among Turkish women aged forty-five to forty-nine (HUIPS 2014). A 2007 study of 202 Turkish women in Istanbul found that 38.8 percent of peri-menopausal women aged forty-five to fifty-nine were using withdrawal at the time of the study (Şahin and Kharbouch 2007). Many women (80.2 percent) reported not knowing when to terminate contraception use as they entered menopause; withdrawal served as a good stopgap for women who wanted to be cautious. Similarly, a multivariate analysis found that married Turkish women aged forty and older who wanted to limits births were more likely to use withdrawal than modern contraceptive methods; the authors reasoned that as the risk of pregnancy decreases for a couple, the likelihood that they will use withdrawal increases (Erfani and Yüksel-Kaptanoğlu 2012).

Even among those for whom withdrawal was not the first or preferred choice, it was still an important tool; it is often used as a "switching" or "transitional" method. Following childbirth or other moments of life transition or when experiencing delays in getting a biomedical contraceptive method, Turkish women reported using withdrawal temporarily for its very flexibility—it is free, not dependent on a medical provider, and requires no additional planning or preparation. As in other studies, current and ever users also reported using withdrawal as a backup to, or in tandem with, other methods such as the IUD, oral contraceptive pills, and the calendar method (Ortayli et al. 2005).

Finally, given the overall cultural attitudes toward abortion, its legal status, and its relative importance in the family planning landscape in Turkey, it may also be that Turks find using withdrawal in conjunction with abortion care as a suitable option within an overall family planning and fertility control strategy. The prevalence of abortion in Turkey even prior to legalization in 1983 was relatively high. According to the 1983 Turkish Population and Health Survey, 37 percent of Turkish women reported having had at least one abortion (HUIPS 1987). Evidence suggests that abortion has long been considered commonplace and thought of as morally permissible or morally neutral in Turkey. In the late 1980s, Gürsoy (1996) found that 57 percent of women surveyed thought abortion was permissible without restriction to reason and only 9 percent of participants thought abortion was unacceptable in all cases. My Turkish interlocutors, interviewees, and friends commonly noted this as well. Many younger women reported that among their mothers' and grandmothers' generations abortion was so common that it was almost as if everyone had had one. As one Turkish woman explained, "But I think we have this support system in our family . . . you have always had this woman's solidarity in the family. . . . I know from my mother's generation, my mother, probably my aunts, they all had abortions."

One study on abortion in Turkey found that of the women that had been using a family planning method when they became pregnant, over two-thirds were using non-biomedical methods and the vast majority were using withdrawal. In this study, most of the women who had obtained abortion care (88 percent) expressed a desire to use contraception following their abortion (Huntington et al. 1996). Although earlier studies suggested otherwise (Goldberg and Toros 1994), a more recent demographic health survey does suggest withdrawal discontinuation is often the result of a withdrawal failure. The 2013 Turkish DHS found that withdrawal use dropped from 37 percent prior to induced abortion to 14 percent after induced abortion (HUIPS 2014). Nonetheless, this family planning strategy relies on withdrawal working in tandem with abortion care. Furthermore, 14 percent is not an insignificant proportion of women who report that they will continue to use this approach to family planning following an induced abortion. These data collectively suggest that using withdrawal until the method fails, and often even after failure, is an approach being used by Turks. Whether that is their first choice or not is unknown, but this is certainly how some Turks approach family planning, and withdrawal is instrumental in this broader strategy.

But Why Withdrawal . . . Still?

THE STATUS QUO AND SEXUAL NORMS

The persistent use of withdrawal among Turkish women of all walks of life is likely due in part to the generational and traditional dimensions of contraception. Because withdrawal has been an integral part of Turkish life for a long time, these preferences may be transmitted through families and friend groups and transcend generations. A study of the knowledge of and attitudes toward family planning among Turkish university students found that women knew more than men and were more likely to obtain information about family planning from family and friends (Aygin and Fidan 2012). When it comes to contraception, where knowledge is also heavily influenced by education and socioeconomic status, withdrawal is a very familiar choice for many.

Turkish women often anecdotally shared that they have discussed contraception and abortion fairly openly with their mothers, sisters, aunts, and cousins. And family planning choices are greatly impacted by early exposures and decisions; once a woman has used withdrawal as her first method, she is much more likely to opt for that method later on. Indeed, Cindoğlu and colleagues (2008) demonstrated that Turkish women were 5.4 times more likely to use withdrawal as their chosen method of family planning if that had been their first type of contraceptive method used. Particularly for families of a lower educational background or socioeconomic status, practicing withdrawal may seem like a clear choice because that is what they and their families have always done. Further, misconceptions about or negative experiences with biomedical contraceptive methods may also be crossing generations. Some men had heard negative experiences from their mothers about their experiences with biomedical methods and turned away from these methods with their partners. Ortayli and colleagues shared a quote from one male participant in their study, "Don't want that coil thing. My mother used the coil; she had women's disease because of that. I don't want my wife to use it"(2005, 168).

Where Turkish men learn about contraception and whom they discuss it with also becomes relevant when considering the cultural aspects of contraceptive choice. One study demonstrated that Turkish men typically learn about biomedical methods through their wives, while they learn about withdrawal through friends or word of mouth (Ortayli et al. 2005). Although men are less likely to talk about family planning with each other than women are, the fact remains that if and when they do, withdrawal is typically what Turkish men will share information about.

Regional cultural influences also seem to influence withdrawal use. For instance, longer-term residence in Istanbul meant that women were less likely to practice withdrawal, something researchers attribute to the "modernizing" influences of the region and also to having more exposure and access to services (Cindoğlu, Sirkeci, and Sirkeci 2008). This aligns with previous qualitative work with Turkish men and women who recognized their migration into Istanbul as a key event for learning more about contraception and for women's empowerment (Cebeci Save et al. 2004). Even so, my interlocutors and interviewees residing in Istanbul also seemed to acknowledge the broader cultural importance and prevalence of withdrawal in Turkey. When I asked one married woman in her thirties living in Istanbul if she was using any kind of contraception with her husband, she said, "No, um, they call it the withdrawal method. . . . It's very popular in Turkey." Withdrawal seems to represent the status quo of contraception for many and continues to be almost be considered a default method of family planning in Turkey.

"IT IS THE WAY OF THE PROPHET"

Religious influences may play a role in the continued acceptance of and preference for withdrawal among contemporary Turks. The Qur'an itself does not specifically reference contraception generally or withdrawal specifically. However, there are several hadith, sayings of the Prophet Muhammad, that suggest he viewed the practice of withdrawal favorably (Atighetchi 1994). Withdrawal, known as 'azl within the context of Islamic law, was understood to have been practiced during the Prophet's lifetime. The overarching understanding on the subject suggests that withdrawal is not forbidden in part because of the very omnipotence of God; if conception were God's will, then it would be so regardless of whether withdrawal was used or not (Atighetchi 1994). Musallam (1981) writes, "There is a remarkable unanimity among Muslim jurists concerning [the permissibility of] this technique ['azl]."

Given that there is no one central authority in Islam, the position of the various schools of Islamic jurisprudence on contraception are varied and nuanced. However, there is general consensus among Islamic jurists and scholars that Islam permits the use of non-permanent methods of contraception within a marital relationship (Maguire 2003, 115). The importance of female consent in 'azl and in the broader practice of family planning has long been considered by Islamic authorities, and more recent fatwas (religious opinions or rulings) indicate that the use of family planning should be agreed upon by both spouses (Atighetchi 1994).

In Turkey, the Department of Religious Affairs has historically supported family planning measures (Gürsoy 1996). However, although most Turks are accepting of family planning in general, qualitative research indicates that some Turkish men and women reported that they preferred withdrawal because it is permitted in Islam and that it was the way of the Prophet (Cebeci Save et al. 2004). A later study suggested that Turkish women were significantly more likely to rely on withdrawal if their husbands believed that some family planning methods were against religion compared to women whose husbands were broadly accepting of contraception. Religious sect also seems of importance, with Alevi women significantly less likely to practice withdrawal than Sunni or other Muslim women (Cindoğlu, Sirkeci, and Sirkeci 2008).[2]

LITERACY, EDUCATION AND SOCIOECONOMIC STATUS

Previous work demonstrates that as Turkish men and women attain higher levels of education, they are more likely to use contraception in general (Vural et al. 1999). However, educational attainment is also tied to more specific patterns in contraceptive use and although withdrawal is practiced across all demographics in Turkey, one study found that with every year of education that women received, the incidence of withdrawal use decreased (Cindoğlu, Sirkeci, and Sirkeci 2008). Other studies echo this and have found that married illiterate women were twice as likely to use withdrawal than those who had more than a primary education (Yanikkerem, Acar, and Elem 2006). Although Cindoğlu, Sirkeci, and Sirkeci (2008) found that with every year of education, men were slightly more likely to practice withdrawal, a later study did indicate a correlation between more education and less withdrawal use among male partners as well (Sirkeci and Cindoğlu 2012).

Households of a higher socioeconomic status were also less likely to practice withdrawal, as were those living in urban areas. Cindoğlu, Sirkeci, and Sirkeci (2008) contend that women with greater economic resources are able to procure biomedical contraceptive methods more readily and are thereby less likely to rely on withdrawal.

PARTNERSHIP AND GENDER DYNAMICS

A study of married women using withdrawal in Manisa, a large city in Turkey's Aegean region, found that nearly one-third of women (31.2 percent) used this method because it was their husband's preference (Yanikkerem, Acar, and Elem 2006). This reason was second only to viewing the method as reliable, thus demonstrating how important male preference is in selecting withdrawal. However, the findings on this are ultimately mixed. While some studies have demonstrated that decision-making around withdrawal is largely guided by the husband (Cindoğlu, Sirkeci, and Sirkeci 2008; Buldurucu and Yazici 2015), in another study the majority of Turkish couples reported that they made the decision to practice withdrawal jointly, and withdrawal was viewed as highly acceptable to both Turkish women and men (Yanikkerem, Acar, and Elem 2006). Among some couples who had previously used condoms and were now pulling out, discontinuation of condom use was sometimes due to unwillingness of the man to continue using barrier methods (Yanikkerem, Acar, and Elem 2006). The negotiation between condom use and withdrawal, and how each practice affects pleasure, seems to be relevant in a couple's decision to practice withdrawal or not.

Male involvement in family planning was also an important aspect of choosing withdrawal, although this was not necessarily guided by the desire for control or power within the relationship. On the contrary, Yanikkerem, Acar, and Elem (2006) point to joint contraceptive decision-making in Turkey and indicate that spouses often negotiate their contraceptive use as a unit. Turkish men were motivated to be involved and use withdrawal and often described taking on the burden of family planning as a signal of respect and love for their spouse (Ortayli et al. 2005). Particularly when weighing the possible negative side effects of modern contraception, Turkish men believed that they were protecting their wives and their health and safety by using withdrawal. Ortayli et al. (2005) felt that male involvement and responsibility was actually one of the key aspects of withdrawal use and strongly underlies this preference among many couples.

EASY, ACCESSIBLE, FREE—AND NO SIDE EFFECTS

Yanikkerem, Acar, and Elem (2006) found that commonly cited reasons among couples in Manisa for using withdrawal were that it was easier to use than other methods, had fewer side effects, and was free. These same findings are supported by an earlier study done by Ortayli and colleagues (2005) that found the time and money associated with procuring biomedical contraceptive methods made withdrawal a very desirable option for Turkish men.

Once participants completed their research questionnaire, Yanikkerem, Acar, and Elem (2006) provided education about biomedical contraceptive methods and offered a supply of the chosen method, but the researchers found that the majority of women (57.6 percent) wanted to continue using withdrawal. Even after learning more about their options, more women than not felt strongly about carrying on with withdrawal. Upon further probing, misconceptions about oral contraceptive pills, condoms, and IUDs emerged. In particular, some women thought that oral contraceptive pills could lead to a host of negative long-term health consequences, including cancer and infertility. Other women focused on amenorrhea being undesirable, as not bleeding would lead to headaches, weakness, and fatigue. Misconceptions around biomedical methods were commonplace and persisted even after receiving additional information. This aligns with what previous studies have shown: concerns about adverse side effects were a major reason that Turkish women and men opted for non-biomedical methods (Bulut et al. 1997; Ortayli et al. 2005). Bulut and colleagues (1997) contended that withdrawal may offer a "refuge" from the health effects of biomedical methods because they were of such apparent concern to the women in Istanbul who participated in their study. Literature documenting withdrawal practices in Turkey highlight that concerns about side effects, both real and perceived, are a key factor in the decision-making of both Turkish men and women.

Pulling Out for Pleasure, Intimacy, and Bonding

An overwhelming majority of Turkish women (83.6 percent) reported that they enjoyed sexual intercourse while using withdrawal as their chosen method (Yanikkerem, Acar, and Elem 2006). According to this same study, more women were pleased with withdrawal as a method (84.4 percent) than their male counterparts were (69.9 percent). Interestingly, the permissibility of withdrawal in Islamic jurisprudence and theological reasoning was in part rooted in female sexual pleasure. The woman is entitled to sexual pleasure and given that withdrawal could interrupt or reduce her pleasure, she must consent to the practice (Maguire 2003, 115). And while a more recent study indicated that a majority of Turkish couples report that their sex life is negatively impacted by using withdrawal, 31.3 percent report no difference and 8 percent even report a net positive impact on their sex lives (Buldurcu and Yazici 2015). Though there is little research on the potentially positive effects of withdrawal on sexual pleasure, there is broader evidence that some methods of contraception are eroticized and pulling out may be more appealing to users than other methods for reasons around kink and sexual pleasure.

Perceptions on how withdrawal impacts sexual pleasure have been shown to influence men's contraceptive behaviors and their current use of withdrawal. Among Turkish men interviewed by Ortayli and colleagues (2005) who were current users, many acknowledged that withdrawal resulted in decreased sexual pleasure, but felt that using condoms decreased pleasure even more. Studies in other contexts echo this finding and have shown that people who felt that condom use would decrease their pleasure were significantly more likely to use withdrawal (Higgins and Wang 2015). A US-based study found that, at best, people seem to have net neutral feelings about condoms but do not eroticize their use or experience any sexual benefit from using them. At worst, however, men reported a host of impacts on their pleasure and sensation, and some women reported pain and discomfort from condom use. Participants in this same study who talked at length about the negative impacts of condom use on pleasure overwhelmingly preferred other methods, specifically withdrawal (Fennell 2014). On the other hand, Turkish men who felt that their decrease in pleasure using withdrawal was significant tended to be never-users or former users of withdrawal (Ortayli et al. 2005). That it was less pleasurable did not seem limited strictly to physical sensation, but was also intertwined with the added anxiety and uncertainty of being able to time their withdrawal. Some of these men also raised the issue of their partners' sexual pleasure and found withdrawal problematic for this reason (Ortayli et al. 2005).

But Turkish users' perceptions of withdrawal actually come down to more than just physical sensation; withdrawal seems to be of importance in signaling trust and intimacy between partners. One participant from the study by Ortayli and colleagues explained the rationale behind choosing withdrawal. "You know the woman, she is clean [sic]. There is intimacy.

You cannot use condoms, she would feel offended. Still you do not want to take the risk [of pregnancy]. So you withdraw" (2005, 169). In a US-based study, some participants also viewed condoms as decreasing intimacy and withdrawal was sometimes deemed a preferable alternative (Whittaker et al. 2010). Arteaga and Gomez (2016) found in their qualitative work that some participants described the enhanced intimacy achieved with withdrawal, in particular describing a certain feeling with withdrawal that you cannot achieve with condom use.

The use of withdrawal was not linked only to this feeling of intimacy, however; it also held implications about the degree of trust between partners. One participant in this same study reported that her male partner said he had used withdrawal with her because she looked like she could be "trusted" and she then hesitated to insist on condom use because that may make her seem "untrustworthy" (Arteaga and Gomez 2016, 629). Much like our Turkish male participant above, who was worried that using a condom would offend his female partner, the use—or non-use—of withdrawal seems to carry an unspoken connotation: that withdrawal use is reserved for those we trust and that condom use is relegated for those we don't. This aligns with previous research suggesting that people feel that insisting on condom use may risk harming the relationship (Umphrey and Sherblom 2007) and may imply that an individual is untrustworthy or promiscuous (Canin, Dolcini, and Adler 1999). Particularly in Turkish culture where premarital sex is so heavily stigmatized, the implications of condom use and what it signals to partners may be even more pronounced, thus contributing to preferences for withdrawal.

Finally, research from Turkey indicates that some women also preferred withdrawal because they felt it was more *temiz*, or clean, than other options (Angin and Shorter 1998). This suggests that perceptions around hygiene and cleanliness may also impact pleasure and influence preferences for withdrawal.

Conclusion

The reasons that withdrawal is still so commonplace in Turkey are many. This chapter offers a starting point in exploring some of these reasons, but there remains a dearth of literature regarding why this method is still so commonly used among Turkish couples; in particular, there is an absence of work on the intersection of sexual pleasure and contraceptive choice among Turkish women and men. This is not too surprising considering how stigmatized sex remains in Turkish culture; however, further work on this subject is needed to fully understand the strong preferences for withdrawal, given that this preliminary exploration offers up that sexual norms, intimacy, trust, and sexual pleasure all seem to be factors in decisionmaking. This method offers a lot that is particularly desirable in the Turkish context and will likely continue to play an important role in the reproductive lives of Turks in the years to come. Particularly in a political climate that has become increasingly hostile toward abortion, family planning, and reproductive rights (MacFarlane et al. 2016), withdrawal may indeed become more important than ever as it is not clinician- or product-dependent and Turkish people may be facing more challenges and stigma accessing reproductive health care.

The last two decades have seen a return to religious conservative values among the Turkish political leadership. The AKP (Adalet ve Kalkınma Partisi, Justice and Development Party), came to power in 2002; this political party has repeatedly condemned abortion, family planning, and Caesarean sections, and as part of its pronatalist efforts has publicly urged women to have a minimum of three children (MacFarlane 2017). In 2012, then prime minister Tayyip Recep Erdoğan threatened to enact legal restrictions on abortion. Although Turkey's abortion law has since remained unchanged, there is evidence suggesting that the provision of abortion without restriction as to reason in public hospitals has been radically diminished (O'Neil 2017). Erdoğan also publicly indicted the use of contraception in 2014 and again in 2016, claiming that its use was treasonous and that Muslim families should not use interventions to control or limit birth (Tharoor 2016). Given all of this, and a cultural return to more traditional and religious norms, withdrawal may be the best or only option for many. The strong underlying preference for withdrawal among Turks, for all the reasons enumerated in this chapter, paired with the current sociopolitical context may render withdrawal particularly salient in the years to come. Using withdrawal may very well be the only method that feels safe or accessible, particularly for young people, unmarried people, low-income people, and other marginalized groups. Dayi (2019) writes,

> In terms of sexual and reproductive health care, the closing down of the directory for AÇSAP and most of its centers—which had specialized in providing sexual and reproductive care, including contraception, abor-

tion, and counseling and education on sexual and reproductive health—and their replacement by FHCs [family health centers] and community health centers (TSMs) affected women's access to contraception, family planning counseling, and abortion. (62)

Premarital sex has always been highly stigmatized in Turkey and the recent political discourse only stands to hurt unmarried women trying to access contraception and abortion. One participant in a study by Angin and Shorter (1998) in the late 1990s highlighted the precarity then of seeking contraception as an unmarried woman:

> I had decided to use pills but did not go to a gynecologist. There is the risk of discovery of the relationship by other people. As a single person this is very dangerous . . . I know, since my mother searches everything that belongs to me. If you live in such an environment . . . really it is not very easy for a single woman. When you go to public hospitals or clinics, and if you are an unmarried woman, you should be very cautious when getting a medical service. Nobody in your close community should know this. Everything should be done in a very secret way. For a man, it is very easy to go to a pharmacy and buy condoms. (560)

Angin and Shorter thus determined that the only real choices available to young and unmarried people are condoms or withdrawal. More recent studies have found that unmarried women in particular continue to face tremendous stigma and mistreatment when seeking abortion and sexual and reproductive health care services (MacFarlane et al. 2016).

More work is needed to understand the nuances behind selecting withdrawal, as well as the things that prevent Turkish women and men from accessing other methods. Current popular opinion, which is typically dismissive of withdrawal and other non-biomedical methods, creates barriers to understanding why people are continuing to use this method with such fervor. Particularly for a method like withdrawal that has been shown to be as effective as condoms with perfect and typical use (Hatcher et al. 2007), efforts focused on better understanding the reasons why people continue to use it and what the impacts of real time sociopolitical change may be on people's reproductive choices would be valuable. Further, for couples who are intent on using withdrawal, providing the tools for them to practice the method more successfully or in tandem with other methods is warranted; withdrawal takes practice and some work suggests that couples get better at using it over time, thereby increasing reliability (Yanikkerem, Acar, and Elem 2006). But given the longstanding importance of withdrawal in Turkey, its cultural and religious acceptability, its lack of side effects, its positive associations with sexual pleasure and intimacy, and the ownership that couples feel in practicing it, it is safe to say that withdrawal in Turkey isn't going anywhere anytime soon and will remain an important part of the sexual landscape.

ACKNOWLEDGMENTS

I would like to thank my Turkish colleagues, friends, and peers who spoke so openly with me about these topics and a huge thank-you to my Turkish interpreters and translators who made this work possible—Deniz, Elvin, and Barış. Another big thanks to Mona, Sarah, Sam, and Sean for being a sounding board and for their many edits on this manuscript. This work was funded in part by a research grant from Mitacs. Finally, I would like acknowledge that this work was carried out independently of the Guttmacher Institute and this contribution does not necessarily reflect the views of the Institute.

NOTES

1. There is also evidence in the literature (Potts & Diggory 1983; Jones et al. 2009) that people don't think of withdrawal as a "real" method of contraception and therefore don't report it or that people view it as a "practice" rather than contraception. Some of my interviews were consistent with these findings.
2. Alevis are a non-Sunni Muslim religious minority that make up 15 to 25 percent of the Turkish population. Although Alevism shares some tenets with Shiʻism, Alevism is a distinct religious sect with unique practices and beliefs.

REFERENCES

Angin, Zeynep, and Frederic C. Shorter. 1998. "Negotiating Reproduction and Gender during the Fertility Decline in Turkey." *Social Science and Medicine* 47, no. 5: 555–64.

Arteaga, Stephanie, and Anu Manchikanti Gomez. 2016. "'Is That a Method Birth Control?' A Qualitative Exploration of Young Women's Use of Withdrawal." *Journal of Sex Research* 53, no. 4-5: 626–32.

Atighetchi, Dariusch. 1994. "The Position of Islamic Tradition on Contraception." *Medicine and Law* 13, no. 4: 717–28.

Aygin, Dilek, and Fatma Fidan. 2012. "Evaluation of Knowledge, Attitude and Behavior of

Turkish University Students Regarding Family Planning." *Revista Eletronica de Enfermagem* 14, no. 3: 464–72.

Benezra, Belin. 2014. "The Institutional History of Family Planning in Turkey." In *Contemporary Turkey at a Glance*, edited by Kristina Kamp, Ayhan Kaya, E. Fuat Kayman, and Özge Onursal Beşgül, 41–56. New York: Springer VS. https://link.springer.com/content/pdf/10.1007%2F978-3-658-04916-4.pdf.

Buldurcu, Sinem, and Saadet Yazici. 2015. "Reasons for Couples to Prefer Withdrawal Method." *Sağlık Bilimleri ve Meslekleri Dergisi* 2, no. 2: 156–66.

Bulut, Ayşen, Nuray Yolsal, F. Kayaturk, Hacer Nalbant, J. Mozan, Veronique Filippi, Tom Marshall, and Wendy Graham. 1996. "Contraceptive Methods Used in Istanbul and Factors Affecting Method Choice and Continuation." *Nufusbil Derg*, no. 17-18: 3–19.

Bulut, Ayşen, Veronique Filippi, Tom Marshall, Hacer Nalbant, Nuray Yolsal, and Wendy Graham. 1997. "Contraceptive Choice and Reproductive Morbidity in Istanbul." *Studies in Family Planning* 28, no. 1: 35–43.

Canin, Lisa M., Margaret Dolcini, and Nancy E. Adler. 1999. Barriers to and Facilitators of HIV-STD Behavior Change: Intrapersonal and Relationship-Based Factors. *Review of General Psychology* 3, no. 4: 338–71.

Cebeci Save, Dilşad, Tuğrul Erbaydar, Sibel Kalaca, Hande Harmancı, Sanda Calı, and Melda Karavuş. 2004. "Resistance against Contraception or Medical Contraceptive Methods: A Qualitative Study on Women and Men in Instanbul." *European Journal of Contraception and Reproductive Health Care* 9, no. 2: 94–101.

Cindoğlu, Dilek, Ibrahim Sirkeci, and Rukiye Fusun Sirkeci. 2008. "Determinants of Choosing Withdrawal over Modern Contraceptive Methods in Turkey." *European Journal of Contraception and Reproductive Health Care* 13, no. 4: 412–21.

Dayi, Ayşe. 2019. "Neoliberal Health Restructuring, Neoconservatism and the Limits of Law: Erosion of Reproductive Rights in Turkey." *Health and Human Rights Journal* 21, no. 2: 57–68.

Duben, Alan, and Cem Behar. 1991. *Istanbul Households: Marriage, Family and Fertility 1880–1940*. Cambridge, UK: Cambridge University Press.

Erfani, Amir, and Ilknur Yüksel-Kaptanoğlu. 2012. "The Use of Withdrawal among Birth Limiters in Iran and Turkey." *Studies in Family Planning* 43, no. 1: 21–32.

Fennell, Julie. 2014. "'And Isn't that the Point?': Pleasure and Contraceptive Decisions." *Contraception* 89, no. 4: 264–70.

Frost, Jennifer, Laura D. Lindberg, and Lawrence B. Finer. 2012. "Young Adults' Contraceptive Knowledge, Norms and Attitudes: Associations with Risk of Unintended Pregnancy." *Perspectives on Sexual and Reproductive Health* 44, no. 2: 107–16.

Goldberg, Howard I., and Aykut Toros. 1994. "The Use of Traditional Methods of Contraception among Turkish Couples." *Studies in Family Planning* 25, no. 2: 122–28.

Gürsoy, Akile. 1996. "Abortion in Turkey: A Matter of State, Family, or Individual Decision." *Social Science and Medicine*, 42 no. 4: 531–42.

HUIPS (Hacettepe University Institute of Population Studies). 1987. "1983 Turkish Population and Health Survey." Ankara: Hacettepe University Institute of Population Studies, T.R. Ministry of Development and TÜBİTAK.

———. 2014. "2013 Turkey Demographic and Health Survey." Ankara: Hacettepe University Institute of Population Studies, T.R. Ministry of Development and TÜBİTAK.

———. 2019. "2018 Turkey Demographic and Health Survey." Ankara: Hacettepe University Institute of Population Studies, T.R. Ministry of Development and TÜBİTAK.

Hatcher, Robert A., James Trussell, Anita L. Nelson, Willard Cates, Felicia H. Stewart, and Deborah Kowal. 2007. *Contraceptive Technology*, 19th ed. New York: Ardent Media.

Higgins, Jenny A., and Jennifer S. Hirsch. 2008. "Pleasure, Power, and Inequality: Incorporating Sexuality into Research on Contraceptive Use." *American Journal of Public Health* 98, no. 10: 1803–13.

Higgins, Jenny, and Yu Wang. 2015. "Which Young Adults Are Most Likely to Use Withdrawal?: The Importance of Pregnancy Attitudes and Pleasure." *Contraception* 91, no. 4: 320–27.

Huntington, Dale, Ayse Akin Dervisoglu, John M. Pile, C. Bumin, and Barbara Mensche. 1996. "The Quality of Abortion Services in Turkey." *International Journal of Gynecology and Obstetrics* 53, no. 1: 41–44.

Jones, Rachel K., Julie Fennell, Jenny A. Higgins, and Kelly Blanchard. 2009. "Better Than Nothing or Savvy Risk-Reduction Practice?: The Importance of Withdrawal." *Contraception* 79, no. 6: 407–10.

Jones, Rachel K., Laura D. Lindberg, and Jenny A. Higgins. 2014. "Pull and Pray or Extra Protection?: Contraceptive Strategies Involving Withdrawal among US Adult Women." *Contraception* 90, no. 4: 416–21.

Koç, Ismet. 2000. "Determinants of Method Choice in Turkey." *Journal of Biosocial Science* 32, no. 3: 329–42.

Kost, Kathryn, Susheela Singh, Barbara Vaughan, James Trussell, Bankole Akinrinola. 2008. "Estimates of Contraceptive Failure from the 2002 National Survey of Family Growth." *Contraception* 77, no. 1: 10–21.

MacFarlane, Katrina A., Mary L. O'Neil, Deniz Tekdemir, Elvin Çetin, Barış Bilgen, and Angel M. Foster. 2016. "Politics, Policies, Pronatalism, and Practice: Availability and Accessibility of Abortion and Reproductive Health Services in Turkey." *Reproductive Health Matters* 24, no. 48: 62–70.

MacFarlane, Katrina A., Mary L. O'Neil, Deniz Tekdemir, and Angel M. Foster. 2017. "'It Was as if Society Didn't Want a Woman to Get an Abortion': A Qualitative Study in Istanbul, Turkey." *Contraception* 95, no. 2: 154–60.

MacFarlane, Katrina. 2017. "C-Sections as a Nefarious Plot: The Politics of Pronatalism in Turkey." In *Abortion Pills, Test Tube Babies, and Sex Toys: Emerging Sexual and Reproductive Technologies in the Middle East and North Africa*, edited by L. L. Wynn and Angel M. Foster, 122–34. Nashville, TN: Vanderbilt University Press.

Musallam, Basim F. 1981. "Why Islam Permitted Birth Control." *Arab Studies Quarterly* 3, no. 2: 181–97.

Maguire, Daniel C. 2003. *The Case for Contraception and Abortion in World Religions*. New York: Oxford University Press.

O'Neil, Mary L. 2017. "The Availability of Abortion at State Hospitals in Turkey: A National Study." *Contraception* 95, no. 2: 148–53.

Ortayli, Nuriye, Ayşen Bulut, Metin Ozugurlu, and Muhtar Çokar. 2005. "Why Withdrawal? Why Not Withdrawal?: Men's Perspectives." *Reproductive Health Matters* 13, no. 25: 164–73.

Özbay, Ferhunde, and Frederic C. Shorter. 1970. "Turkey: Changes in Birth Control Practices, 1963–1968." *Studies in Family Planning* 1, no. 51: 1–7.

Potts, Malcom, and Martha Campbell. 2002. "History of Contraception." In *Gynecology and Obstetrics*, vol. 6, edited by J. J. Sciarra, 1–23. New York: Lippincott, Williams and Wilkins.

Potts, Malcom, and Peter Diggory. 1983. "Traditional Methods." In *Textbook of Contraceptive Practice*, 2nd ed., 74–83. Cambridge, UK: Cambridge University Press.

Şahin, Nevin H., and Sema B. Kharbouch. 2007. "Perimenopausal Contraception in Turkish Women: A Cross-Sectional Study." *BMC Nursing* 6, no. 1. DOI: 10.1186/1472-6955-6-1.

Sirkeci, Ibrahim, and Dilek Cindoğlu. 2012. "Space, Agency, and Withdrawal: Birth Control Choices of Women in Turkey." *Healthcare for Women International* 33, no. 7: 614–30.

Tharoor, Ishaan. 2016. "Muslim Families Should Not Use Birth Control Says Turkey's Erdogan." *Washington Post*, May 31, 2016. https://www.washingtonpost.com/news/worldviews/wp/2016/05/31/muslim-families-should-not-use-birth-control-says-turkeys-erdogan.

Türk, Rukiye, Füsun Terzioğlu, and Lut Tamam. 2019. "Attitudes of Couples Towards Withdrawal Method in Birth Control." *Cukurova Medical Journal* 44, no. 3: 794–803.

Umphrey, Laura, and John Sherblom. 2007. "Relational Commitment and Threats to Relationship Maintenance Goals: Influences on Condom Use." *Journal of American College Health* 56, no. 1: 61–67.

United Nations DESA (Department of Economic and Social Affairs, Population Division). 2019a. *Contraceptive Use by Method 2019 Data Booklet*. New York: UN DESA.

——— 2019b. "World Population Prospects 2019." Population Dynamics. UN Department of Economic and Social Affairs. https://population.un.org/wpp/DataQuery.

Vural, Birol, Fisun Vural, J. Diker, and Izzet Yücesoy. 1999. "Factors Affecting Contraceptive Use and Behavior in Kocaeli, Turkey." *Advances in Contraception* 15, no. 4: 325–36.

Whittaker, Paul G., Rebecca D. Merkh, Dare Henry-Moss, and Linda Hock-Long. 2010. "Withdrawal Attitudes and Experiences: A Qualitative Perspective among Young Urban Adults." *Perspectives on Sexual and Reproductive Health* 42, no. 2: 102–9.

Yanikkerem, Emre, Hatice Acar, and Emel Elem. 2006. "Withdrawal Users' Perceptions of and Experience with Contraceptive Methods in Manisa, Turkey." *Midwifery* 22, no. 3: 274–84.

CHAPTER 4

Queer Sociality in the Gulf in the Early 2000s

A Continuum of Outness and Silence Mediated by Class Privilege

SAFFAA HASSANEIN

L. L. WYNN

In 2002, Joseph Massad published a seminal article, "Re-Orienting Desire: The Gay International and the Arab World." In it, he followed in the footsteps of scholars like Edward Said (1978), Rana Kabbani (1986), and Malek Alloula (1986) who have described how Western writing on the Middle East—both academic portrayals and popular travel literature— has excessively focused on the region's sexuality and portrayed it as the essential antonym to Western sexuality, an ever-shifting foil of otherness that serves to define self. Massad argued that when Western societies were themselves sexually conservative, Western writers portrayed the Middle East as a hotbed of men having sex with men and female homoeroticism in the harem. However, with the advent of gay rights in the West, por- trayals of the queer Middle East flipped to present an image of repression, with homosexual acts undefined as such and unmoored due to the lack of a liberating connection to international gay activism, a trend which has characterized Western representations of Middle Eastern sexuality more broadly (see the introduction to this volume).

Massad analyzed writings by what he calls the "Gay International" as a body of literature that simultaneously generated a portrait of a repressed Middle Eastern homosexuality and issued a call for liberation. "The larger mission" of this literature, Massad wrote, was "to liberate Arab and Muslim 'gays and lesbians' from the oppression under which they allegedly live by transforming them from practitioners of same-sex contact into subjects who identify as homosexual and gay" (2002, 362).

Such writing, Massad argued, was characteristic of a "a type of anthropology that fails to problematize its own mythical idealized self, that continues to view the other as all that the self does not contain or condone" (370). This implicitly created a Western *us* of the audience and author against the Middle Eastern *other* that this literature objectified and described. Portrayals of "a permissive polysexual West and a repressive heteronormative Middle East," Epps (2008, 117–18) tells us, are both "politically motivated fantasies," and as Ann Stoler (1995, 195) has argued for a whole array of European literature through the colonial period and beyond, "the history of Western sexuality must be located in the production of historical Others."

Massad wasn't (only) describing a literal change in sexual practices in the Middle East tracking against the changing sexual mores of the West. He was describing a shift in representational practices and their politics. But he also showed how the activist organizations of the "Gay International" were themselves generating a more rigid theorization of sexuality in Middle East activism and politics. He argued that the result was both the textual and real-life destruction of diverse queer Middle East sexualities in favor of constrained, narrow definitions of sexuality, pleasure, and identity politics—"the creation not of a queer planet but rather a straight one" (2002, 385).

Massad's seminal article triggered a modest flourishing of what Adi Kuntsman and Noor Al-Qasimi (2012, 2) called "queering Middle East studies." This trend is characterized by attempts to theorize and conduct research on Middle Eastern sexualities, both queer and otherwise, outside of an Orientalist paradigm, the proliferation of Arab and other Indigenous voices in this scholarship, and an attentiveness to a multiplicity of desires, pleasures, and sexual practices that go far beyond the homo/hetero binary that Massad had critiqued. Further, the queering of Middle Eastern studies rejects oppositions of traditional versus modernizing, "narratives structured by the fantasy of rescue, and the old colonial project of saving the natives from themselves" (Kuntzman and Al-Qasimi 2012, 4). Kathryn Babayan and Afsaneh Najmabadi (2008) noted a scholarly trend away from using the term "homosexuality" to focusing instead on "same-sex practices and desires" in the region to express the range of sexualities and queer identities beyond Western political movements of what Kuntsman and Al-Qasimi (2012, 4) call the "queer-as-liberation model."

The challenge, Kuntsman and Al-Qasimi (2012, 5) tell us, is to develop a critical queer scholarship of "non-Western or non-white queerness, without reaffirming whiteness and the Eurocentre as an epistemic center" and without mapping out a geography of West and East as a simplistic set of dualisms: "liberal and backward, queer and heteronormative." The other part of the challenge of writing about a queer Middle East is to show a critical awareness of the transnational political economy of representations that generates an audience for portrayals of Middle Eastern sexuality (Wynn 2018, 201–9).

Paul Amar and Omnia El Shakry (2013) are among a group of scholars who have articulated an agenda for a critical queer scholarship of the Middle East (also see Shakhsari 2013; Jacob 2013; Al-Samman and El-Ariss 2013; Nasser-Eddin, Abu-Assab, and Greatrick 2018). They have called for an approach that goes beyond sexual identity politics and narrowly framed gay and lesbian studies to examine an array of queer desires and forms of embodiment, the relationship between hegemonic heteronormativity and marginal practices and subcultures, and how all of these are situated in particular historical moments and political economic structures. As a critical theoretical posture, queerness "invokes the indeterminacy and dubiety, rather than the foundational stability, of a range of categories, including identity and locality" (Amar and El Shakry 2013, 333).

While there is a growing body of literature on queer men in the Middle East, the literature on queer women in the region was scant over a decade ago, when Samar Habib (2007) wrote a historical treatise on the topic, and apart from rare exceptions such as Noor Al-Qasimi (2011, 2012) and Sara Mourad (2013), remains so today. This is in spite of the fact that Habib (2007, 22) has presented historical evidence dating back to medieval times of what she calls an "Arabian epistemology of sexuality" that recognizes women's sexual desire for other women and that even, contra Foucault, sees homosexuality as a category of identity in the pre-modern Arab world as well as in contemporary Arab literature.

Taking up these calls for a critical queer scholarship of the Middle East and addressing this lacuna in literature about queer women in the region, we offer an account of queer sociality and pleasure in the Arabian Gulf (the United Arab Emirates, Saudi Arabia, and Bahrain) in the early 2000s, with a focus on queer women. We do this through a reflexive memoir approach that echoes Everett Zhang's (2005) exploration of his own recollections of desire during the Mao era in China. Zhang productively used autoethnography to excavate sexual histories and memories of a time now past.

We are further inspired to undertake this project in response to two academic texts on queerness in the region. The first is Massad's, which perplexingly made the sweeping claim that "in reality there is no evidence of gay movements anywhere in the Arab world *or even of gay group identity* outside of the small groups of men in metropolitan areas such as Cairo and Beirut" (2002, 373; emphasis ours). This assertion is sharply at odds with our own understandings of lesbian and other queer subcultures across the Gulf during that era. We are not sure if the cities of Dubai, Manama, Jeddah, and Riyadh constitute "such as" areas in Massad's framing, but even before the spread of social media's digital connectedness and the resulting elaboration of a transnational queer imaginary in the Gulf (Al-Qasimi 2011, 289–90), there were thriving queer communities and gay and lesbian group identity in the Gulf in the early 2000s.

The second text, by Lorenz Nigst and José Sánchez García (2010), is one of the very few academic texts focusing specifically on queer women in the Gulf. Nigst and Sánchez García undertake a digital ethnography of how people in Gulf countries describe the phenomenon of *boyat* (plural; singular: *boya* or *boyah*), tomboys who dress or in other ways physically comport themselves like men and who may or may not also be lesbians. Nigst and Sánchez García remind us that the definitive labeling of the sexual practices and desires of *boyat* is much less important than understanding what it means to perform transgressive gender norms publicly. The authors analyze Gulf online discussions of the phenomenon, from those who identify themselves as *boyat* to those who describe finding *boyat*'s behavior and appearance disturbing to those who call for remedial measures, either punishment for these women's moral transgressions or therapeutic treatment for their assumed psychological problems.

Amid Nigst and Sánchez García's otherwise excellent research and analysis is this peculiar statement: "their [the *boyat*'s] approach follows the forms of conceiving of gender similar to how it has appeared in Western contexts since the 1970s" (2010, 16). Thus in their writing, they frame a contemporary Gulf cultural phenomenon and social movement as a variation on a Western past. To riff on the title of Valerie Traub's (2008) analysis of representations of Middle East sexualities, "The Past Is a Foreign Country," we might add that the idea that *the foreign country is a past* continues to underpin much writing about sexuality and social movements in the Middle East.

Moreover, while Nigst and Sánchez García provide a valuable overview of Gulf commentary on the *boyat* phenomenon and an analysis of how it disturbs local gender norms, their digital ethnography is also characterized by a high degree of speculation about where homosexual activity comes from (one answer they offer is from gender segregation itself) and what cross-dressing means to the *boyat* themselves. With recurring phrases that frame their analysis in terms of guesswork, such as "in all probability" (2010, 30), the authors theorize about *boyat* without actually being able to say much about what *boyat* say about themselves and about their sexual practices. In many ways, Nigst and Sánchez García's account of *boyat* in the Gulf is admirably in keeping with Wilson Chacko Jacob's description of queerness beyond sexual practice or identity: "a queer space of being that sits at strange and disruptive angles to various hegemonies" (2013, 349). Yet the actual lives, motivations, activities, and desires of *boyat* in their account remain remarkably opaque, only available for imagination and speculation.

Thus, in a spirit of productive engagement with the authors who have set out an agenda for a critical queer studies of the Middle East, we contribute this reflexive memoir of *boyat* and other queer people in the Gulf in the early 2000s. It is a preliminary attempt to generate a phenomenological account of queer sexuality, homosociality, and allyship in the Gulf.

Autoethnography, especially of times long past (Zhang 2005), poses particular challenges to ethical research practice and methodological accounting. Memories are partial, fragmented, and biased, and thus must be approached with a degree of skepticism. Furthermore, recollections from many years ago are not available for bureaucratic scrutiny and ethics review. It is for this reason that, in Australia at least, academic memoir is not subject to review by human research ethics committees in the same way that prospective human research is. Nevertheless, we have carefully considered the ethics of human research and representation in penning this chapter. To protect people's privacy, we have carefully changed names and redacted other information that might reveal the identities of those described in this memoir. And in the spirit of Massad's critique of an academic literature that is too fixated on tidy categorization, we decline to provide information about the authors' own sexualities, other than to situate ourselves firmly in the position of allies. But in keeping with anthropological ethics of representation which acknowledge the relevance of positionality and the way that knowledge is always embodied, we begin by specifying something of our own backgrounds. Hassanein is a Saudi-Australian scholar, artist, and activist who was raised in Jeddah, later studied in the United States, and then worked in Dubai before moving to Australia to pursue her PhD. Wynn is an American-Australian anthropologist who was raised in the United States, later worked in Jeddah for two years, and then undertook ethnographic research in Cairo for a total of nearly four years.

In presenting our recollections here, we acknowledge of all the ways that these are partial and biased, not least because they are memories of events of over a decade ago. Nevertheless, despite all the limitations of memory, these three vignettes from the Gulf capture a set of rich social phenomena at a particular historical moment. They are valuable for what they tell us about how lesbian sociability sometimes mimics and sometimes rejects heterosexual masculine norms, how communities of queer people and allies socialized, and how class privilege enables queer sex in the Gulf. What all the vignettes illustrate is that lively underground queer communities certainly did exist in the Gulf at the start of the millennium and these queer Gulf communities were neither exclusively public with their sexual practices and desires nor did they always keep them hidden. Instead, their sexual identities and practices existed on a continuum of revelation and secrecy, shaped by transnational networks of straight and queer allies as well as kinship and class privilege.

──────*Salwa's Story: Emulation of Toxic Masculinity*──────

Layla was a Saudi woman from the city of Ta'if. She moved to Dubai in her mid-twenties to work for a multinational corporation. When she was there, she started dating Hala, who was from Qatar and had moved to Dubai where she worked in a media company. Layla was very femme. She had recently traveled to Kuwait for breast implant surgery and on her return to Dubai she felt very feminine and enjoyed the attention her new breasts were bringing her.

One of the people in Hala's extended social circle was her ex-girl-friend, Salwa. Salwa was a middle-class Saudi woman who had the blue eyes, light skin, and light brown hair of some Saudis of Turkish heritage. She was raised in Jeddah and then moved to Dubai in her twenties to work for a multinational corporation with colleagues from all over the Arab world and Europe. Even those who didn't know what Salwa's sexual preferences were assumed that she was gay because she embraced a masculine aesthetic. She was, as Layla described it, "butch. She dressed like a boy and talked like a boy." She wore baggy jeans and a baggy t-shirt, she had acne, and she wore her short hair in a tiny, tight ponytail. She also had a reputation for pursuing women who were ultra-femme in appearance and for lov-ing the challenge of trying to seduce a straight woman.

One day, Hala and Layla were standing together in a group of friends. Salwa approached Hala to chat but excluded Layla from the conversation. Then she glanced over at Layla, who was wearing a low-cut top that showed off her new breasts and turned back to Hala. Pointing at Layla, she asked Hala, "How do you let your girlfriend go out like this?"

Upset and uncomfortable, Layla looked at Salwa and retorted, "She is standing right here." Later she commented that she had felt disrespected by the way Salwa talked about her in the third per-son right in front of her, but she also felt "weirdly flattered" by the attention and the way Salwa's comment implied that she was too attractive for public viewing. Reflecting later on the encounter, she commented:

At the time, I couldn't put my finger on why I wasn't comfortable with her talking about me. I hated that she was talking about me like I wasn't present, but I couldn't break down the sexism and the misogyny in that sentence. Why would my girlfriend "let me" go out? Was she implying that Hala was the man in the relationship and I was meant to be the woman because Hala was more butch than me? Now I understand what bothered me, but at the time I was so confused. Hala was being told to control me. But why would she have the authority to tell me what to wear and what not to wear? We were on equal footing. She's a woman; I'm a woman. I wasn't dating a man for exactly that reason. So why should another woman tell me what to wear?

That "control your woman" narrative, Layla observed, mapped a conventional toxic heterosexual relationship dynamic onto a lesbian relationship.

Because Salwa's experience of masculinity has always been toxic, she took on the masculine role in her pursuit of women and embraced that toxic masculinity. That was part of what I was fleeing when I left my husband. I liked the dynamic of being on equal footing with a woman. I liked the fact that I could never get pregnant. When I went home with Hala that night, I said to her, "This is ridiculous." I was upset about having to defend my boobs. I said, "You don't buy a Ferrari to park it in the garage." And because Hala had gone with me to Kuwait to get my boobs done, she said to me, "But I have one-third ownership over this Ferrari." She hadn't paid for anything, but she supported me through that time. She was joking, but there was an underlying seriousness to it.

————————*Noora's Story: Queer-Ally Communities in Dubai*————————

Noora grew up in a poor working class family in Oman. Her parents were both intellectuals and activists. Her sister Rana was a brilliant high achiever; her brother tried to control Noora in his position as the patriarchal leader of the family. Noora was able to leave the country to work and travel because her mother and father enabled it, but her brother was conservative regarding gender norms and objected to his parents allowing his unmarried sister Noora to live alone in Dubai. When she visited her family in Oman, he would try to control her excursions; if, for example, she went out late at night, he would yell at her when she came home. Their mother would admonish him to leave his sister alone.

Noora was dating Khalida, a Saudi woman who had recently divorced her husband, and Noora always worried that Khalida wasn't really a committed lesbian. Noora thought that for Khalida dating a woman was an act of post-divorce rebellion and that she might eventually go back to men. Men were always hitting on her at the clubs where they would go out, and Noora was jealous of any straight man who approached her. To placate her, Khalida only socialized with gay male friends, with one exception: Sami.

Sami was a straight Palestinian-Lebanese man who sometimes cut himself. Khalida had met him at work before she ever knew Noora, which perhaps explained why Noora didn't act jealous over Khalida's friendship with him. Whenever they would go out together in a group of friends, Khalida would pretend Sami was her boyfriend, holding his hand and hugging him. She did this not to hide her own sexuality; after her divorce, she was very open and excited about being lesbian, even disclosing this to her ex-husband. But she displayed physical affection with Sami because it prevented strange men in clubs from hitting on her, which always triggered Noora's jealousy. Sometimes she would hold Sami's and Noora's hands at the same time. Noora even "allowed" Khalida to go out alone with Sami if she wasn't available to accompany them, which she did not tolerate her doing with any other man.

One night, Khalida met Ali, a Kuwaiti man, at a club. He approached, complimented her on her beauty, and asked where she was from. They bonded over their nationalities; Saudis and Kuwaitis felt a strong sense of cultural closeness and rivalry, even compared to other Gulf Arabs, so it gave them something to talk about amid all the Emiratis and other expatriates around them. Although Ali appeared very masculine, Khalida assumed that he was gay from his flamboyant gestures. In order to head off conflict with her girlfriend, Khalida grabbed Ali by the hand and brought him over to Noora, where she introduced him, saying, "This is Ali, he's gay, and he's from Kuwait." Ali immediately understood that Noora was her girlfriend and was jealous; he didn't express any surprise when she introduced him as gay without it having even been a prior topic of conversation.

Ali was a very good-looking man from a rich family in Kuwait, and he never had one steady boyfriend but was always jumping from one man to another. His friends joked that he had a crush on half the men in Dubai and had a particular penchant for white, Western boys. He never dated Emirati men and proudly declared amongst his circle of friends that he was "a bottom." While other gay Arab men in their circle felt there was something effeminate and shameful in admitting to being penetrated, Ali owned it with pride. He used to say, "I take it up my bum and I love it." When Sami wasn't available, Ali would pretend he was Khalida's boyfriend when they were out at clubs.

These were some of the dramas of Dubai's thriving underground gay and lesbian scene. It was a close-knit community of gay men, lesbians, social misfits, and trustworthy allies. They all socialized in the same clubs and went to the same after parties at the farms, lavish apartments, or yachts of people in their community. They spent most of their time at The Club. The Club was in Deera, an untrendy part of Dubai close to the airport, in a nondescript, windowless, isolated building with a parking lot almost as large as the building itself. Inside, the lighting was dark and the decor minimal, with a DJ booth, a dance floor, and box-shaped stools for people to sit on. People from a wide variety of nationalities partied at The Club: South Africans, Europeans, Australians, and South Americans. Americans were rare. The venue was local knowledge and a well-kept secret among the local queer community, who only talked about it in front of other queers or allies. It was run by two Iranians who had lived in Dubai all their lives. With no cover charge and free drinks, The Club seemed to be their gift to the gay community, a safe space for them to socialize. Perhaps it was also an opportunity to market and set trends since the owners, who also owned several clothing stores and galleries, launched new stores and held fashion shows at The Club. With a stable contingent of attendees, it felt safe and underground and wasn't on the radar of the police.

Some of the local men who participated in this scene had wives and kids and were influential government officials and they dressed conservatively in conventionally masculine garb. They also had sex with men, though most were reserved and measured in their public displays of affection. Other locals were single and flamboyantly gay, wearing clothing that was glamorous, revealing, and slightly feminine, which clearly signaled their queerness. Everyone knew who was dating whom and who was cheating on their partners and wives. There was an unspoken code of silence whereby people in the community protected each other's secrets.

─────────*Leena's Story: Dating a Lesbian Royal*─────────

According to Leena, Dubai was a lesbian playground. After she split up with her first girlfriend, she dated and had sex with seventeen different lesbian, bisexual, and curious women she knew in Dubai. Then, one night, drunk and horny in a club in Dubai, Leena noticed a woman in a loud group of people who looked like they were having lots of fun. When they crossed paths in the bathroom, Leena heard the woman speaking with her friend in a distinctive accent. Leena herself was from Dammam in Saudi Arabia and asked them in Arabic if they were from the Gulf. They were surprised, assuming from Leena's blonde hair that she wasn't Saudi. She offered her phone number to Nour, the woman who had caught her eye. They started texting and flirting.

Over weeks of transnational flirting (Nour had flown home to her country), Leena learned that Nour's parents lived in London and inferred from her mannerisms that she came from a privileged background. She became even more certain of this after they all went out to dinner together in a group of friends and Nour paid for everyone's dinner in cash. It wasn't until much later in their relationship that she thought to ask about Nour's family name during a conversation where they were discussing Nour's unique accent, which stood out as distinctive, even amongst her city's natives. Nour simply replied, "I come from the Family," and Leena realized that she was talking about the royal family of that country.

Reflecting on the dress and comportment of Nour many years later, Leena described what Nigst and Sánchez García and the social commentators they analyze might recognize as a *boya*, but which Leena, fluent in English and an international lexicon of queer self-presentation, simply called a dyke.

Imagine an Arab princess. Who do you see? Perhaps Jasmine from Aladdin? Or is it someone in a ball gown or someone covered in black from head to toe and wearing a tiara over her veil? Well, no. When I met Nour for the first time she was wearing a pair of Diesel black jeans, a plain, loose-fitting, basic black t-shirt, Converse high tops, and her long hair was tied back with a black hair band. She walked like a dyke, talked like a dyke, and had no makeup on. Tall, big, and beautiful, with a mischievous smile.

After weeks of flirtatious texting, Nour flew to Dubai to see Leena and invited her to the hotel where she was staying, where they shared their first kiss before partying with Nour's Gulf friends who were visiting for the weekend. A few weeks later, Nour invited Leena to come to her country for a visit. Leena was reluctant to meet her family and asked if they could meet somewhere where they could have some privacy and get to know each other. Nour suggested that they meet at her family's beach house in Bahrain where, she assured Leena, they would have complete privacy. Leena took a week's leave from work and flew to Bahrain.

When Nour told her that her driver would meet me at the airport, Leena expected he would be a Southeast Asian man. Instead, she was greeted by a tall, well-groomed, handsome man who appeared to be of African descent, elegantly styled in a pristine white *thobe* (the long, white robe that Gulf men wear) and full male headdress of *shimagh* and *-eqal*. She was surprised and slightly distressed at the thought of a Gulf man knowing about her romantic rendezvous with Nour. He insisted on carrying her luggage and ushered her to the car, a black BMW with black-tinted windows that was parked illegally in a no stopping zone right outside the airport. When he opened the door for her, Nour was sitting inside. After he started driving, Nour leaned in to kiss Leena, who was taken aback and whispered, "The driver!" Nour told her to not worry about him and Leena noticed that as soon as they started kissing, he turned his rear view mirror to the side so that he couldn't see them. After more reassurances from Nour, Leena climbed into her lap and they kissed the whole drive home, listening to Adele songs.

When they got there, Leena was surprised at the luxury of the house. Nour had a whole bedroom suite to herself and in her closets there were three neat rows of Converse shoes. Her t-shirts and pants were hung in a color-coded arrangement. After Nour gave Leena a tour of the house, Nour's friends—the same ones she had been partying with in Dubai—arrived with booze, food, music, brownie mix, and hashish oil. Leena recalled that the next five days were a haze where night and day blurred together in a hedonistic tableau of having sex with Nour, eating hash brownies, dancing, laughing, sleeping, and feeling intoxicated with love.

On the last night she was there, Leena asked Nour if she had seen her lubricant. Nour replied, "The house help must have moved it." Leena was terrified that this meant that they knew about their sexual relationship, but Nour reassured her, "Don't worry. No one says anything. They see the booze and the hash too. They have actually come three times already to clean the house. It's okay, babe. It's not a big deal."

Their relationship was a loving and committed one and lasted four years. It was also no secret from the staff who worked for Nour's parents, her two younger sisters, and all of Nour's close friends. Another time when they were in the car with her Gulf driver, Nour ordered him to pull over and get out of the car. He stood by the side of the road while Nour and Leena had sex in the car.

Although Nour made no effort to hide her sexual relationship from domestic staff, friends, or her younger siblings, her parents and elder sister (who was a kind of authority figure in the family) did not know. They thought that Leena was simply Nour's best friend. The end came when Nour and Leena had loud sex in the family house on the first day of Ramadan (the month during which observant Muslims abstain from food, drink, and sex during daylight), and Nour's oldest sister overheard and told her parents. They ordered Leena's bags to be packed and sent her away. For a time after that, Nour and Leena stayed in secret contact through a cell phone that Nour mailed to Leena, but their connection eventually faded.

Outness, Silence, and Privilege

In the first vignette, Layla reflects on how one of the pleasures she found in an intimate relationship with another woman was the potential for egalitarianism between partners; she saw her relationship with Hala as an opportunity to steer clear of the misogyny and sexism she had experienced in her relationship with her husband. Her critique of Salwa's comment was that it reproduced and maintained the types of controlling behavior she saw as characteristic of the conventional relationships between Gulf men and women, only mapped on new gendered dynamics. Layla saw that as a key moment in her development of a critical awareness of the ways that women contributed to maintaining patriarchy and the oppression of other women.

The second vignette sheds light on the thriving underground subculture of queer Emiratis, expatriates, and straight allies in Dubai in the early 2000s. A large community of people socialized in both commercial dance clubs and more private venues where they were at less risk of being raided by the police. Their self-presentation ran the gamut from conventionally masculine and feminine to women who wore masculine clothing and men who were flamboyantly effeminate. Some of the married men who also had sex with men avoided advertising their queerness by dressing conservatively when they were in public clubs, while others were more open about it, and would even talk openly about their sexual preferences amongst allies. Khalida, a Saudi woman who was new to dating and having sex with women, was open with people in her circle about her sexual preferences, but she sought allies in both straight and gay men whose public affection helped her to discourage the advances of straight men who were strangers. The wealth, social status, and government positions of some group members helped to protect the less wealthy who were part of this scene, and all were aware of the threat of the police. Yet, in Khalida's telling, consciousness of the state's politics of sexuality took a back seat to the small social dramas and pleasures of an insular, hedonistic, transnational community. They felt safe enough to express themselves sexually and enjoy those little social dramas as if they were in a country where homosexuality was not criminalized.

Nigst and Sánchez García (2010, 32) write, "If most Arab lesbians would not dare to say their name or to come out in public or to proclaim their identity, then the most salient characteristic of the *boyat* is that they make public their condition." We agree that there is something very striking and distinctive about the *boyat* phenomenon and the way that these "tomboys" trouble normative expectations of feminine expression and comportment. The ambiguity over whether their nonnormative personal presentation denotes similarly nonnormative sexual preferences is very powerful. It simultaneously troubles observers, protects the women, and gives their displays its disruptive force.

But Nigst and Sánchez García's framing seems to assume a simple dichotomy of public and private sexual identities. However, all of the vignettes we have presented, and the final one in particular, show that the publicness of queer Gulf women's and men's sexual activities and desires runs on a continuum and that continuum is shaped by kinship and class privilege. No simple divide distinguishes those who are "out" from those who are "in the closet" (to use the English-language colloquialisms). Queer Gulf people can simultaneously be out to some people—particularly if they are not kin and if they are of a lower social status—and actively hide their sexual activities from or decline to discuss their identities or experiences with others. A number of scholars, including Massad (2002) and Moussawi (2020), have argued that for queer people in the Middle East, and indeed all over the world, power is not only to be found in a politics of public outness; there is also power, safety, and care for kin in people's decisions to cloak their sexuality in silence and ambiguity.

Conclusion

In this chapter, we have tried to take up other scholars' call for a robust queer studies of the Middle East with a memoir of scenes of queer sociality in the Gulf in the first years of the new millennium. Adding to these scholars' critiques and agendas, we believe the critical queer Middle East studies of the present and future will prominently feature voices from the region, rather than presenting mainly Western voices writing for Western audiences about Eastern sexualities. Rather than making broad generalizations, it will focus on the specificity of individuals' experiences, in keeping with Lila Abu-Lughod's (1991) call for anthropologists to "write against culture." It will avoid writing about Middle East and North African societies and political movements as if they are belatedly enacting scenes from some Western past. This scholarship will analyze social groups and movements first and foremost as things-in-themselves. It will bring up Western social groups, movements, and histories not to tacitly establish a comparative universal evolution of social/political movements, but rather to show the specifics of how global ideologies circulate and how local individuals and groups interpret and engage with them (Shakhsari 2013, 342). It will recognize the complex interplay of vulnerability and privilege in both queer communities, and how privacy and public outness may coexist on a continuum, rather than as mutually exclusive opposites.

REFERENCES

Abu-Lughod, Lila. 1991. "Writing against Culture." *Recapturing Anthropology: Working in the Present*, ed. Richard Fox, 137–62. Santa Fe, NM: School of American Research.

Alloula, Malek. 1986. *The Colonial Harem*. Translation by Myrna Godzich and Wlad Godzich. Introduction by Barbara Harlow. Minneapolis: University of Minnesota Press.

Al-Samman, Hanadi, and Tarek El-Ariss. 2013. "Queer Affects: Introduction." *International Journal of Middle East Studies* 45, no. 2: 205–9.

Al-Qasimi, Noor. 2011. "Ladies and Gentlemen, Boyahs and Girls: Uploading Transnational Queer Subjectivities in the United Arab Emirates." In *Circuits of Visibility: Gender and Transnational Media*, edited by Radha Hegde, 286–302. New York: New York University Press.

———. 2012. "The 'Boyah' and the 'Baby Lady': Queer Mediations in Fatima Al Qadiri and Khalid al Gharaballi's WaWa Series (2011)." *Journal of Middle East Women's Studies* 8, no. 3: 139–42.

Amar, Paul, and Omnia El Shakry. 2013. "Introduction: Curiosities of Middle East Studies in Queer Times." In "Queer Affects," ed. Hanadi Al-Samman and Tarek El-Ariss, special issue, *International Journal of Middle East Studies* 45, no. 2: 331–35.

Babayan, Kathryn, and Afsaneh Najmabadi, eds. 2008. *Islamicate Sexualities: Translations across Temporal Geographies of Desire*. Cambridge, MA: Harvard University Press.

Epps, Brad. 2008. "Comparison, Competition, and Cross-Dressing: Cross-Cultural Analysis in a Contested World." In *Islamicate Sexualities: Translations across Temporal Geographies of Desire*, edited by Kathryn Babayan and Afsaneh Najmabadi, 114–60. Cambridge, MA: Harvard University Press.

Habib, Samar. 2007. *Female Homosexuality in the Middle East: Histories and Representations*. New York: Routledge.

Jacob, Wilson Chacko. 2013. "The Middle East: Global, Postcolonial, Regional, and Queer." *International Journal of Middle East Studies* 45, no. 2: 347–49.

Kabbani, Rana. 1986. *Europe's Myths of Orient*. Bloomington: Indiana University Press.

Kuntsman, Adi, and Noor Al-Qasimi. 2012. Introduction to "Queering Middle Eastern Cyberscapes," eds. Adi Kuntsman and Noor Al-Qasimi. Special issue, *Journal of Middle East Women's Studies* 8, no. 3: 1–13.

Massad, Joseph A. 2002. "Re-Orienting Desire: The Gay International and the Arab World." *Public Culture* 14, no. 2: 361–85.

Mourad, Sara. 2013. "Queering the Mother Tongue." In "Doing It: Methodological Challenges of Communication Research on Sexuality," special section of *International Journal of Communication*, no. 7: 2533–46.

Moussawi, Ghassan. 2020. *Disruptive Situations: Fractal Orientalism and Queer Strategies in Beirut*. Philadelphia, PA: Temple University Press.

Nigst, Lorenz, and José Sánchez García. 2010. "Boyat in the Gulf: Identity, Contestation, and Social Control." *Middle East Critique* 19, no. 1: 5–34.

Nasser-Eddin, Nof, Nour Abu-Assab, and Aydan Greatrick. 2018. "Reconceptualising and

Contextualising Sexual Rights in the MENA Region: Beyond LGBTQI Categories." *Gender and Development* 26, no. 1: 173–89.

Said, Edward. 1978. *Orientalism*. New York: Pantheon Books.

Shakhsari, Sima. 2013. "Transnational Governmentality and the Politics of Life and Death." *International Journal of Middle East Studies* 45, no. 2: 340–42.

Stoler, Ann. 1995. *Race and the Education of Desire: Foucault's History of Sexuality and the Colonial Order of Things*. Durham, NC: Duke University Press.

Traub, Valerie. 2008. "The Past Is a Foreign Country?: The Times and Spaces of Islamicate Sexuality Studies." In *Islamicate Sexualities: Translations across Temporal Geographies of Desire*, edited by Kathryn Babayan and Afsaneh Najmabadi, 1–40. Cambridge, MA: Harvard University Press.

Wynn, L. L. 2018. *Love, Sex, and Desire in Modern Egypt: Navigating the Margins of Respectability*. Austin: University of Texas Press.

Zhang, Everett. 2005. "Rethinking Sexual Repression in Maoist China: Ideology, Structure and the Ownership of the Body." *Body and Society* 11, no. 3: 1–25.

CHAPTER 5

Hexes and Exes

Post-Breakup Curses in Fez, Morocco

SHANNON HAYES

Dating multiple partners prior to marriage has become a standard part of the courting process for many Moroccans. However, expectations around virginity continue to disproportionately impact women, particularly when sexually active partners choose to end their relationship. In order to protect their reputations in these cases, some young women of Fez use various forms of *siḥr*, or magic, solicited from supernatural practitioners around the city to secure the fidelity or silence of their male partners.[1] These female practitioners—referred to as *shawafat* (sing. *shawafa*)—are believed to be able to manipulate the intangible (e.g., love and desire) through the use of sympathetic magic. Sympathetic magic uses objects or imagery to represent a person and intention and in these scenarios is used to inflict impotence, keep a partner enamored, or prevent a partner from seeing other women altogether. Regardless of its actual frequency, rumors of *siḥr* heavily influence dating culture, exacerbate men's anxieties around marriage, and feed into a perception that women have control over the courting process.

In Fez, dating culture is strongly impacted by the norms enforced by *hshouma*, or shame. As Habiba Chafai describes, *hshouma* is constantly invoked in childrearing and throughout adolescence as a way to dictate appropriate attitudes, practices, and morals for men and women (2017, 828). Although dating is commonplace in the city, its practice is heavily impacted by the threat of discovery. Women may change men's names to those of women in their phone contacts, and couples often select date locations outside of their neighborhoods to avoid detection. Fez itself is divided into distinct neighborhoods of traditional and contemporary architecture as a result of its French colonial history. Clustered houses and tight alleys of the medina (the traditional downtown area) may be risky for young couples who can be seen from the towering windows. However, in the more open Ville Nouvelle (the modern part of town), mixed-gender cafés and large parks provide perfect escapes for a romantic rendezvous.

Dating before Marriage

Although premarital sex and issues around virginity have been studied at length in Morocco, dating is just beginning to receive attention in the literature. "Dating" covers a wide range of activities in Morocco; my interlocutors defined dating as an activity that involves emotional intimacy and time with someone of the opposite sex in a way that is explicitly labeled as dating. For example, texting a partner without ever meeting may be considered dating if the involved individuals *choose* to label it as such. That said, premarital relationships are nothing new in Morocco and they are becoming more commonplace as a phase of the courting process.

Demographic shifts play a significant role in lengthening what scholars have called "waithood," the liminal period between adolescence and marriage where "young people remain financially dependent on their families . . . and they must live by the rules and morality of their parents" (Singerman 2007, 6). For example, the fertility rate has steadily dropped over the years, while the average age at first marriage has increased. In the 1970s, there was an average of seven children per woman in Morocco. In 1995, the rate had dropped to three, then again to 1.8 by 2010 (Bakass, Ferrand, and Depledge 2013, 38). The increased period of time between marrying and childbearing has increased the potential for nonreproductive marital intimacy—one of the foundations of companionate marriage. In Morocco, the decrease in the total fertility rate also correlates with a rise in the age of first marriage; for women this has increased from 17.5 to 26.2 years of age between 1960 and 2004. Laura Menin investigates how these demographic shifts began to manifest in dating culture across Morocco. The image of the "modern couple" was perpetuated in magazines, advertisements, and foreign films beginning in the 1960s and 1970s (Menin 2015, 897).

Moroccan youth are still expected to move toward marriage regardless of their dating habits, but economic realities make marriage impossible for many young Moroccans who are underemployed or unemployed. In 2012, levels of unemployment for youths aged fifteen to twenty-four were three and a half times higher than the unemployment rate of the total labor force (Serajuddin and Verme 2012, 5). Although unemployment impacts both men and women, Serajuddin and Verme's World Bank report focuses on the feelings of relative deprivation and anxiety held by men in the context of a society that legally requires men to provide for their wives and families. These anxieties are particularly salient when discussing employment in mixed-gender settings, where men performed gendered roles in a certain way in front of women. For example, in dating, anxieties associated with lack of resources or stable employment may become more salient in spite of romantic love and a desire for choosing one's own spouse. It is not uncommon for breakups to occur as a result of a man's profession, lack of employment, or inability to afford a certain lifestyle.

Love, Magic, and Love Magic

Love and magic have long been intertwined in literature, religious movements, and proverbs around the world. From the more overt Neo-Pagan religions in the Americas and Europe to famous texts such as *One Thousand and One Nights*, love continues to be viewed as a distinct state of being wherein one is "enchanted" by a lover's qualities or appearance and remains faithful as long as this state of being persists. Men are "bewitched" by women into cheating on their wives and women put men "under their spell" through flirtation.

Two similarly intertwined tropes emerge from this conflation of magic and love: the witch and the whore. While there has been no scholarly work on the connection between these archetypes within Morocco, Jose Machado Pais has published on a similar phenomenon in Portugal, exploring the Mothers of Bragança movement as a response to Brazilian immigration (2011). In an area still grappling with the sexual repression of early twentieth century rule, female Brazilian immigrants—some of whom worked in brothels—were seen as a direct threat to the stability of marriage as an institution. In order to preserve their relationships, Portuguese women began accusing Brazilians of bewitching their husbands into cheating. The husbands happily corroborated the story, as it allowed them to express their virile masculinity in the form of visiting prostitutes while preserving commitments to their wives and miraculously escaping blame.

MAGIC IN MOROCCO

In Morocco, folktales, shrines, and ritual practices do play a role in love and marriage for some. Perhaps the most famous example of these practices is visiting the Oudayas Castle outside Rabat. Each day, women from across Morocco visit the castle's marriage well to aid them in a variety of romantic endeavors (Sachdev 2014). To summon luck in finding a husband, visitors drink a mixture of rose water and water from the well. To reverse sexual stagnation or treat infertility, women leave their underwear on the grounds and light candles for the *jinn*, or spirits. Returning to traditional or magical methods of treating infertility is not uncommon, especially after resources for modern procedures, such as in vitro fertilization (IVF), have been exhausted.[2]

Working to explain the prevalence of such practices in Morocco, Mohamed Chtatou brings together various theories on the origin of modern day "Moroccan Islam" and its allowance of herbal medicine, saint worship, and appeals to magicians for physical and social ailments (2016, 2017). For Chtatou, the rituals of Sufism and Maraboutism—encouraged by the Moroccan government and monarchy in order to prevent Islamism—have precipitated the more mystical elements of the culture. In 2012, the Pew Forum on Religion and Public Life confirmed Chtatou's description in a survey of over thirty-eight thousand Muslims in countries around the world. In the chapter on additional beliefs, the Pew Forum showed that among the thirty-nine countries surveyed, Morocco ranks highest for belief in *jinn*, with 86 percent believing in these spirits and 78 percent believing in what Pew labeled "witchcraft."[3] In Egypt, just 69 percent of Muslims surveyed believe in *jinn* and a mere 16 percent believe in witchcraft.

In Moroccan folklore, these *jinn* tend to take on animal attributes. With her hoofed goat's legs, Aisha Kandisha is one of the most notable of these spirits and remains the main character of stories intended to scare young boys (Mernissi 1987, 42). Fatima Mernissi's *Beyond the Veil* describes this character at length in relation to men. Mothers warn their sons of the demon's seductive guises and deploy the threat of a visitation to stop negative behaviors. Aisha Kandisha is seen as representing the duality of the feminine: beautiful and haggish, able to seduce and to take away men's masculinity if given the chance. Douglas and Susan Davis show that this threat can become a reality, describing the potential for women to become possessed by the chaotic spirit (1995, 227). If a woman is not careful, a lengthy exorcism may be required to return her to normal.

Regarding witchcraft, the use of magic in the form of love spells is not uncommon among young women and their mothers in Morocco. In 2012, two local women with Morocco World News went undercover and visited several *shawafat* in and around Rabat to discover who these supernatural practitioners and their clientele were (Rhanem 2012). Despite my host mother's and teachers' insistence that *siḥr* is an old and dying practice, the majority of these *shawafat* were in their mid-twenties. Upon talking to women in the waiting area, the reporters found that many mothers sought to discover the future marriage possibilities for their daughters by requesting a divination, whereby the *shawafa* sees the future of the solicitor. The article aimed to be a warning against visiting these women, who are portrayed as ripping off their customers with fake spells and predictions. In terms of pricing, lower-grade candle spells may cost around 50 dirhams (US$5), a *kouboul* (a talisman that makes its wearer loved by all) 300 to 500 dirhams (US$30–50), and herbs for *bukhoor* (incense) anywhere from 20 to 1000 dirhams (US$2–100) based on the type of herb and if the solicitor is from out of town.

Returning to the idea of the witch and whore archetypes, it is important to consider the global implications of stories about witchcraft and folk practices. In 2011, Saudi Arabia began allowing Moroccan women to enter the country and work as domestic servants (Dockery and Marghich 2018). Since then, there have been several publicized incidents of sexual assault and physical abuse of Moroccan women within their employers' homes. News coverage of these events mention a growing anxiety among Saudi women that their husbands are being seduced by Moroccan maids, putting the Saudi women in a place of precarity within the household. In her blog post "Search for the Shawafa," Peace Corps volunteer Colleen Daley details rumors that Saudi women think Moroccans are taking this a step further and bewitching Saudi men (2012). Rumors like this not only impact the reputation of Moroccan women on the global scale, but reinforce local assumptions that women are to be regarded with suspicion, especially at the beginning and end of a relationship.

Methodological Notes

In 2018, I conducted research on romantic relationships over a three-month period in Fez, Morocco. Prior to launching my research, I applied for and obtained research ethics approval from my institutional review board (IRB) to ensure that confidentiality and safety were integrated into the design of my interview protocol. Once approved, I conducted semi-structured interviews about dating culture with nine men and sixteen women between the ages of eighteen and twenty-eight using the snowball method of recruitment. Each participant provided oral consent for the interview and was given the opportunity to revoke consent after the interview concluded. Immediately after each interview, I immediately transferred all recordings to a password-protected folder and deleted the files from the recording device.

The participant group featured a variety of occupations, educational backgrounds, relationship statuses, and language proficiencies. I asked participants if they preferred for me to conduct the interview in Arabic; however, all but two chose to do the interview in English. The interviewees described a wide variety of relationship experiences and current relationship statuses. About half of the participants were single at the time of the interview and the other half were in relationships. Two participants stated their intentions to propose to their female partners within six months; both subsequently did so.

I chose to focus on younger, unmarried Moroccans in order to explore stories of dating (or deciding not to date) in contemporary Fez. The city is rapidly changing, with new opportunities to meet and date created every year, such as the new Medina Social Club that brings young, single tourists and young Fassis together for events. To better access these spaces, I also spent significant time observing and participating in various leisure activities with local friends and interlocuters around the city, as well as my extended host family. To avoid discomfort and the risk of being overheard, I had participants choose the locations for their interviews and invited them to bring a companion for support if desired. I use pseudonyms for my participants and have masked or redacted identifiable information.

Presence of Siḥr *in the Fez Dating Scene*

While my interview script did not originally include a question about *siḥr*, the first three participants all cited instances of this magic in the form of curses as important to understanding the perils of dating in Fez. After hearing these stories, I began asking each participant about *siḥr* and all twenty-five agreed that this practice exists in Fez. Curses were most frequently cited as a method of exacting revenge against an ex-boyfriend. This revenge can manifest in several ways: the inability to maintain future relationships, especially when one approaches an engagement; the inability to "see" other women besides the spell-caster; *thaqāf,* meaning complete impotence or impotence during sexual encounters with women other than the spell-caster; and physical or mental illness after attempting to break up with a partner. When asked, most young Moroccans have stories about a friend-of-a-friend or distant cousin who has fallen victim to such a curse. For Salma, a twenty-three-year-old PhD student, a curse struck closer to home and impacted her brother's chances of marrying for years. After a particularly bad breakup, he began to experience seizures. Finally, after many failed visits to local doctors, he consulted a *fqih*, or an Islamic scholar, and was diagnosed and healed of his curse for a few hundred dirhams. While *fqih* are traditionally Qurʾanic reciters and teachers, my interlocuters pointed to their involvement in removing curses for young men using forms of magic considered permissible in Islam.[4] Although the price is steep for those in Fez's lower and middle classes, a man's family may be more than willing to pay in order to ensure a future marriage. While several participants mentioned similar stories about the consequences of this magic, many described cases of its failure and of catching young women in the act of preparing a curse. Such revelations invariably lead to a breakup and amplified the distrust of women already felt by many young men in Fez.

Khadija, a twenty-three-year-old woman living on campus in Fez, had both heard about and personally witnessed *siḥr* while visiting her close male friends in Casablanca. She described the two brothers as particularly popular and attractive and noted how often she worried for their safety as a result. Once, after the eldest of the two brothers and his girlfriend had been sleeping together for a few weeks, he noticed she started wiping up his semen after intercourse. When they broke up shortly afterward, he found himself unable to get an erection during sex with other women. Again, a brief visit to a religious scholar at the local mosque and a few hundred dirhams cleared him of the ailment.

According to my interlocutors, the most common—and supposedly most effective—method for enacting these curses is to gather body fluids, primarily semen, from the object of the enchantment. As a result, men who have regular sex with multiple partners may be particular about cleaning themselves after intercourse. This was certainly the case for the brothers mentioned above. Shortly after hearing about this incident, Khadija caught a woman stuffing wet tissues into her bag after spending the night at the brothers' apartment. Realizing that she was caught, the young woman fled and never spoke to either of them again.

Although this method has remained consistent for decades given the stories described by Davis and Davis (1995), the usual clientele of *shawafat* appears to have changed. Instead of relying on magic to retain a husband who is suspected of straying, younger women in contemporary Morocco visit *shawafat* to attract a love interest or curse an ex-boyfriend. In 1996, Deborah Kapchan had local interlocutors record conversations that married Moroccan women have about such topics when they are alone. The reasons for seeking magic then had more to do with keeping a husband and preventing cheating, but they still relied on the semen-covered cloth, a nearby *shawafa*, and a payment exchange (1996, 236).

For those who have not been physically involved with the object of their ire or affections, less expensive forms of *siḥr* can be purchased. Within this category my interlocutors discuss three courses of action: using an object such as a photo or piece of clothing for curses, fortune-telling for potential outcomes related to marriage, and using *toukal*, magic that is ingested via food or drink by the object of the curse. As Oussama, a twenty-eight-year-old man working in the medina, put it, magic is everywhere and one must be careful to avoid it: "It could be something in the food or something when you're walking if you tap on it with your foot, or if they have a piece of your hair." Participants like Oussama who live or spend significant time in the medina tended to have more detailed stories about these methods. Although I have no exact explanation for this correlation, it may indicate a higher number of *shawafat* living in the older parts of the city. Aissa describes exactly how photographs are used to ensure that a partner reciprocates one's feelings: "Sometimes it's pictures. We lock a picture: pierce a picture and add a lock to it and throw it in the deep waters of the sea . . . it guarantees you a husband, the object of the picture."

According to Aissa, *Lailat al-Qadr*, the twenty-seventh and most holy night of Ramadan, is considered the most potent time to use *siḥr* on the object of one's affections because of its magical and historical significance.

Using the English terms for the holidays, Aissa jokingly calls this night a combination of Halloween and Valentine's Day. Men who fear the use of *siḥr* against them on a night when the veil between *jinn* and humans is thinnest are increasingly sweet to their female partners, purchasing elaborate gifts and taking them out for expensive dinners to avoid such a fate. Each of the men interviewed mentioned the increasing toll of economic expectations that they believe women have for marriage. In a city where youth unemployment remains high, men certainly cannot afford the apartment and car, let alone lavish gifts to prevent the threat of a curse.

MAGIC FOR MITIGATING RISK

As shown in both the interviews and the literature, the majority of these curses are solicited by women who have already had sexual intercourse with their partners. Although older generations of Moroccans are beginning to accept dating as a legitimate path to marriage, gendered expectations around virginity still persist and inform social dynamics around love and dating. This pressure leads young people to engage in practices specifically chosen to avoid "breaking" the hymen while still fostering intimacy and pleasure for both partners (Dialmy 2002).

Any anxieties that women have about losing their virginity prior to marriage pale in comparison to the thought of their family discovering this fact. Kaoutar, a university student living with her divorced mother, calls this akin to "losing everything" and points to this threat as the reason that women turn to curses. In these cases, women want insurance that the partner they have intercourse with will one day be their husband. An alternative to *siḥr* in the above situation is to restore the hymen retroactively, not by magic, but with hymenoplasty. Hymenoplasty is a procedure in which one reconstructs a torn hymen (or creates the facsimile of a hymen using vaginal tissue), typically with a dissolvable suture, to ensure bleeding on the wedding night and the first conjugal sexual encounter. Hymenoplasty is performed around the world, but there is no standard method for the procedure. In Morocco, these surgeries are generally only accessible to the middle and upper class, costing between 5,000 and 6,000 dirhams (US$500–600) per operation (Dialmy 2002, 81).

Curses, even on the pricier end of the spectrum, are a far more accessible—and less invasive—option for Moroccan youth. However, similar to hymenoplasty, these solutions remain rooted in gendered notions of sexuality and bodily autonomy. Although older men may visit *fqih* for assistance with promotions or workplace success, the Moroccans I interviewed generally viewed magic as a woman's art and a reason for some men to distrust young women. Both the men and women I interviewed were hyperaware of this divide. Halima, a nineteen-year-old university student, summarized the issue, saying, "It's a stereotype of Morocco in general. Because they think girls are evil. They think girls do curses on the guys to get them or so the guys don't see anyone besides them. . . . People our age believe in that." This stereotype is a difficult one to parse out, as it contains both gendered and classed elements. Those who described curses called this practice "outdated" and "dangerous." Several participants argued that *sihr* is a dying practice but later added that they know someone who fell victim to an enchantment while in high school or university. Participants also connected the use of *sihr* to being "uneducated" and "not good in their mentality," even as they cited instances of the phenomenon in private and public schools in urban centers throughout Morocco. Popular opinion suggests that if someone knew the spiritual risks associated with this magic, they would avoid the practice altogether. Therefore, those who use *sihr* must be ignorant of the spiritual and social ramifications. On the other hand, it requires a certain amount of disposable income to purchase *sihr* on one's behalf, and reputational costs must also be accounted for. Given this, affluent families may be both more able and more willing to pay a *shawafa* in order to protect their family name and ensure a successful marriage.

Given the discussion around this recourse for women, there is a clear dissonance between public denouncement of *sihr* and its nevertheless apparently widespread use as a legitimate tool for fulfilling the goals of securing a successful relationship. In her investigative study of witchcraft in Morocco, Alisa Sachdev attempted to explain the popularity of *shawafat* by comparing their services to those of therapy (Sachdev 2014). According to the author, with the high rate of unemployment and the widening gap between adolescence and the average age of first marriage, women want to ensure that the time they have put into long-term relationships is not wasted when disagreements or infidelity causes a breakup. For those who cannot afford multiple counseling sessions, seeing a *shawafa* once to repair a relationship and ensure its longevity is an appealing alternative.

My research demonstrated that women also use *sihr* to regain control over their precarious positionality in relationships, especially those that involve premarital sex. Using curses as a way to secure a partner or condemn them to a fate of impotence or singledom gives women who have been treated poorly—often to the detriment of their reputation—a way to feel in control. Additionally, curses may be used to minimize risks by securing a partner's fidelity or silence, thus securing the woman's future marriage and protecting her reputation. However, the narrative about women being witches "out to get" men reinforces and is reinforced by stereotypes about Moroccan women as well as local historical productions through storytelling and rumors. Moroccan men already face pressures to marry that primarily manifest through familial control over their spending and mobility. *Siḥr* poses a threat to existing and future relationships regardless of a man's economic ability to marry. The possibility of being cursed makes men feel that they lack control over their romantic futures, whether or not they ever fall victim to one.

RUMORS, FEAR, AND POWER

Stories of friends and family members falling prey to curses inform us in two ways. When examined as a social phenomenon, they highlight the ways women seek to circumvent barriers to marriage while staying within cultural norms around premarital sex. However, these stories can also demonstrate the power and potential of rumors to influence social behaviors. Rachel Newcomb argues that the deployment of rumor can be a strategy for identity reinforcement in Fez: "Individuals use rumor to comment on aspects of social life that are changing rapidly or are threatened by the presence of alternative discourses" (2004, 95). Rather than assessing the accuracy of the rumors themselves, Newcomb focuses on what truths the rumors seek and what work rumors do when Moroccans choose to share them. Anika Wilson's work on witchcraft in Malawi uses the same interpretive framework, seeing rumors as both a revelation of these structural tensions and of the collective anxieties of listeners (2012, 153). For dating culture, rumors about curses and bad breakups shape how youth are socialized by warning of potential relationship outcomes. In Fez, it is a common rumor that women often break up with men over their lack of sufficient income, the fact that they work for the private sector rather than the more stable and respected public sector, or because they have the "wrong" kind of degree. There may be a genuine desire to marry, but the state of the economy prevents young men from being eligible to do so. Stories of curses exacerbate these economic anxieties, which may undermine ideals for a successful, companionate marriage by preventing a man from marrying the person of his choice, or worse, forcing him to marry a woman he does not choose.

However, for women, curses represent the ability to control dating in a way that secures their future. It seems that few women actually use magic in their relationships, but the idea that they *could* is a powerful discursive element of the dating scene. In the past, women have been subjected to unilateral decisions about relationships through repudiation, single motherhood, and forced virginity testing. Curses invert these fears and allow women to make unilateral decisions about their love lives and potential for marriage. That said, the majority of stories that I gathered were ones where a woman was caught in the act or implicated by an ex-boyfriend. In these cases, reputation is still harmed, which may complicate future relationships.

Conclusion

The implications of *sihr* influence the landscape of both the dating culture in Fez and the transnational reputation and treatment of Moroccan women. Stories of impotence, seizures, and the inability to marry are publicized on radio advice shows, in newspapers, and on Facebook, often casting women as villainous witches without considering context and preexisting power dynamics. In Saudi Arabia—home to migrant laborers from Morocco, Sudan, and Sub-Saharan Africa—rumors of *sihr* have prompted the creation of an anti-witchcraft unit within the Committee for the Promotion of Virtue and the Prevention of Vice (Perlmutter 2013). The majority of women arrested by this unit are migrant laborers accused of practicing "black magic" on their Saudi employers. Global stereotypes of Moroccan women as prostitutes also feed into these accusations (El-Feki 2013, 207). Some Saudi women, feeling threatened by the idea of a hypersexual Moroccan woman in the home, would rather accuse them of witchcraft than believe in their husbands' potential for infidelity. Rumors about witchcraft quickly turn into threats that jeopardize the already precarious position of transnational migrant laborers.

Grappling with stories of local cases of *sihr*, Moroccan men are hypervigilant around suspect female partners, especially if they have had sexual intercourse or if they are considering a breakup. Curses—or the possibility of being cursed—become a site of vulnerability for men, which can conversely become a site of asserting power and control for women. Entering a premarital relationship, even today, remains risky for a Moroccan woman whose parents often expect a traditional path to marriage with as few challenges to her reputation as possible. Historically, this has been very precarious, even within marriage—it was only in the past few decades that men lost the right to unilaterally repudiate their wives. By believing in and utilizing *siḥr*, a force primarily harnessed by and for women, young women can assert—or at least, feel that they are asserting—control over their relationships and therefore, their futures. Curses are ultimately a means to achieving stability in a system where a rumor whispered into the wrong ear can still eliminate the potential for an engagement.

ACKNOWLEDGMENTS

I would like to thank Georgetown University's School of Foreign Service for awarding me the summer research grant that made this work possible. I would also like to thank my advisor, Dr. Fida Adely, for her advice, guidance, and inspiration throughout the research and thesis process. I also appreciate the efforts of Meriem Aderdor in her unending efforts to make introductions and spread the call for participants in Fez.

NOTES

1. I am using magic to mean the process of using objects and intention to bring about a desired change, whether positive or negative, in one's own situation or that of another. See Shanafelt (2004) for a discussion on the use of the terms *magic* and *supernatural* in anthropological writings.
2. See Newcomb (2017) and Inhorn (2007) for more detailed descriptions of IVF and its impact on relationships and romance in the Middle East and North Africa.
3. Quotation marks added to signify the negative connotations of the word *witchcraft*, particularly in the West where it is often either conflated with Satanism or reduced to its Hollywood stereotype.
4. See Perlmutter (2013) for a synopsis of the differences between licit and illicit magic in Islam as well as the politics around how these types of magic are viewed, solicited, and penalized.

REFERENCES

Bakass, Fatima, Michèle Ferrand, and Roger Depledge. 2013. "Sexual Debut in Rabat: New 'Arrangements' between the Sexes." *Population* (English Edition) 68, no. 1: 37–59.

Chafai, Habiba. 2017. "Contextualising Street Sexual Harassment in Morocco: A Discrim-inatory Sociocultural Representation of Women." *Journal of North African Studies* 22, no. 5: 821–40.

Chtatou, Mohamed. 2016. "'Moroccan Islam' Is Couched in Sufism." *Arab Weekly*, January 4, 2016. https://thearabweekly.com/moroccan-islam-couched-sufism.

———. 2017. "Timeless Beliefs in Saints and Spirits in Morocco." *Morocco World News*, January 19, 2017.

Daley, Colleen. 2012. "The Search for the Shawafa." *Arabesques* (blog), May 30, 2012. http://zineb-returns.blogspot.com/2012/05/search-for-shawafa.html.

Davis, Douglas A., and Susan Schaefer Davis. 1995. "Possessed by Love: Gender and Romance in Morocco." In *Romantic Passion: A Universal Experience?*, edited by William Jankowiak, 219–38. New York: Columbia University Press.

Dialmy, Abdessamad. 2002. "Premarital Female Sexuality in Morocco." *Al-Raida* 20, no. 99: 75–84.

Dockery, Wesley, and Meriem Marghich. 2018. "Saudi Arabia: Critics Slam Human Traf-ficking of Moroccan 'Maids for Sale.'" Deutsche Welle, February 28, 2018. https://www.dw.com/en/saudi-arabia-critics-slam-human-trafficking-of-moroccan-maids-for-sale/a-42760030.

El Feki, Shereen. 2013. *Sex and the Citadel: Intimate Life in a Changing Arab World*. New York: Pantheon Books, 2013.

Inhorn, Marcia C. 2007. "Loving Your Infertile Muslim Spouse: Notes on the Globaliza-tion of IVF and Its Romantic Commitments in Sunni Egypt and Shi'ite Lebanon." In *Love and Globalization: Transformations of Intimacy in the Contemporary World*, edited by Mark B. Padilla, Jennifer S. Hirsch, Miguel Munoz-Laboy, Robert Sember, and Richard G. Parker, 139–60. Nashville, TN: Vanderbilt University Press.

Kapchan, Deborah. 1996. *Gender on the Market: Moroccan Women and the Revoicing of Tradi-tion*. Philadelphia: University of Pennsylvania Press.

Menin, Laura. 2015. "The Impasse of Modernity: Personal Agency, Divine Destiny, and the Unpredictability of Intimate Relationships in Morocco." *Journal of the Royal Anthropo-logical Institute* 21, no. 4: 892–910.

Mernissi, Fatima. 1987. *Beyond the Veil: Male-Female Dynamics in Modern Muslim Society*, rev. ed. Bloomington: Indiana University Press.

Newcomb, Rachel. 2004. "Disorganised Shantytowns, Disorderly Fundamentalists: The 'Other' Sense of Fassi Rumours." *Journal of North African Studies* 9, no. 4: 91–109.

———. *Everyday Life in Global Morocco*. Bloomington: Indiana University Press, 2017.

Pais, Jose Machado. 2011. "Mothers, Whores and Spells: Tradition and Change in Portu-guese Sexuality." *Ethnography* 12, no. 4: 445–65.

Perlmutter, Dawn. 2013. "The Politics of Muslim Magic." *Middle East Quarterly* 20, no. 2: 73–80.

Pew Forum on Religion and Public Life. 2012. "Other Beliefs and Practices." In *The World's Muslim: Unity and Diversity*, 67–82. Washington, DC: Pew Research Center.

Rhanem, Karima. 2012. "Witchcraft in Morocco: A Day with Shawafa." Morocco World News, May 6, 2012. https://www.moroccoworldnews.com/2012/05/38333/witchcraft-in-morocco-a-day-with-shawafa.

Sachdev, Ailsa. 2014. "Love and Witchcraft in Morocco." *The Riveter*, September 19, 2014. https://www.therivetermagazine.com/love-and-witchcraft-in-morocco.

Serajuddin, Umar, and Paolo Verme. 2012. *"Who Is Deprived? Who Feels Deprived?: Labor Deprivation, Youth and Gender in Morocco."* Policy Research Working Paper, no. 6090. Washington, DC: World Bank.

Shanafelt, Robert. 2004. "Magic, Miracle, and Marvels in Anthropology." *Ethnos* 69, no. 3: 317–40.

Singerman, Diane. 2007. "The Economic Imperatives of Marriage: Emerging Practices and Identities among Youth in the Middle East." Working Paper. The Middle East Youth Initiative. Dubai: Wolfensohn Center for Development: Dubai School of Government.

Wilson, Anika. 2012. "Of Love Potions and Witch Baskets: Domesticity, Mobility, and Occult Rumors in Malawi." *Western Folklore* 71, no. 2 (Spring): 149–73.

PART II

ENGAGED AND MARRIED

CHAPTER 6

God under the Bedsheets

Pleasure, Porn, and Piety
among Iranian Revolutionary Women

YOUNES SARAMIFAR

"You should know I have a good relationship with my body," Majideh said in a hushed tone. She fixed her *chador* (a black cloak worn over other attire) before anyone could see a few strands of hair slipping out of her scarf. I looked at her inquisitively and waited for further explanation but her eyes were fixed on the patterns of the tablecloth.

I was surprised by her shy demeanor. She usually kept a straight face and firm expression, looking into my eyes while speaking with a voice that was always expressive and clear. I had brought up questions about women's bodily experiences since our first interview and she had answered my questions without shyness. Majideh was one of the twenty-three women whom I interviewed and conversed with about sexuality, sexual conduct, and the struggles of *becoming* a Muslim woman according to expectations of conservative circles of Islamic societies. My research project aimed to investigate how young Iranian women inhabit their bodies, craft subjectivities, and negotiate their sexual desires within the everyday framework of religion. I talked to the young revolutionary women who expressed firm allegiances to Islamic values, and particularly to the values of Shi'i Islam. They passionately believed in martyrdom, the return of the Messiah, and the guardianship of the state by a jurist, and they observed religious ordinances strictly. Islamic practices and rituals were the highest priorities in their everyday lives and the *chador*, which enveloped their bodies from head to toe, was their choice of garb for Islamic modesty. While in public, they remained constantly vigilant to ensure that the shape of their bodies and their hair were not seen by unrelated males.

To study embodiment among young revolutionary Shi'a women, I investigated how everyday religion and Islamic ordinances are experienced by women in compliance rather than subversion. What does it mean to comply with Islamic ordinances as women and how does the willingness to comply shape the corporeal experiences of young women? These questions emerged during my project, entitled *God under the Bedsheets*, in which I investigated sexuality and sexual conduct in the intimate lives of Shi'a combatants who had volunteered to fight against ISIS (Islamic State of Iraq and Syria).

The project sought to explore whether there was any link between combat behaviors and the sexual lives of those who had volunteered to fight in the name of a religious cause. To that end, I interviewed the wives and fiancées of the combatants from Iraq, Iran, Lebanon, and Afghanistan. However, I focus only on Iranian women in this chapter. They were well aware of my research on the militancy and writings about Shi'a militant networks since my years in Lebanon. My interlocutors respected my "scientific interests" and stressed that they accepted my invitation to participate in the research because they wanted the world to know that they are not closed minded and accordingly shared their stories. Additionally, my gatekeepers—interlocutors' male partners or well-established Iranian academics—assured them of my "scientific interests." Therefore, they agreed to the interviews and audio recording under the condition of anonymity, which was verbally affirmed in the audio recording. There were some women who initially saw anonymization as unnecessary and stated that "the world should know religious women also enjoy their bodies and we just don't pray," as one interlocutor noted. However, I have changed all names and any information that may allow others to deduce the identity of my interlocutors.

I never opened my interviews with questions directed toward body and sexual conducts. I would start with inquiries about religion, rituals, jurisprudence, and political commitments in relation to choosing a husband. Such inquiries would take two sessions, each exceeding two hours. I would establish trust and emotional safety in these initial sessions, aided by my previous training in psychoanalysis, Islamic jurisprudence, and a robust familiarity with the emotional textures of dedicated Shiʻa believers. Additionally, I would mention during interviews my partner and her European mindset toward religion to make interlocutors aware of my own relationship and sexual orientation, and I shared with them my own stories as much as they shared theirs. Revealing to them that I was an engaged man whom they presumed to be pious allowed us to converse as if we belonged to the same political-religious community and further consolidated their sense of emotional safety in our conversations.

Some academic peers (mostly white, Euro-American women) find it difficult to accept it is possible for a male researcher to interview and converse with such interlocutors about their corporeal, sexual experiences. These respected peers operate through a gender-duality mindset and impose that mindset on Middle Eastern women. To address such doubts, since apparently a locally situated male anthropologist is not able enough (read with sarcasm and also see Deeb and Winegar 2015; Çankaya and Mepschen 2019), I trained a female Iranian research assistant from a similar religious and political background to conduct further interviews with other interlocutors and we compared our collected "data." This research assistant was previously my interlocutor and absorbed my interview techniques quickly. Interestingly, we were able to obtain similar information despite our different gender identities. However, interlocutors shared accounts of sexual assaults and abuse more often with her than with me.

The question of body, sexual habits, attitudes, and what goes on in the bedroom could not be separated from how a Shiʻa Muslim woman *becomes* a sexual being while remaining observant of Islamic regulations. My interlocutors constantly took detours to discuss the times before their marriages and outside the bedroom in order to explain what, why, and how certain encounters happened in the bedrooms. Their intimate lives were produced through lifelong journeys and the accumulation of lived experiences such as parental relationships, puberty, political commitments, the process of choosing their husbands, how they recognized their bodies within Islamic ordinances, and finally how they inhabited their bodies, all of which contributed to a broader picture of how God crawled under their bedsheets.

Finding Porn in Iran in the Internet Era

Majideh was the first woman who brought up pornography explicitly during these interviews. Her comments encouraged me to add pornography and accordingly masturbation to the list of questions toward which I guided my interlocutors. The case study of Shiʿa women in Iran and their encounters with porn is a particularly interesting one because access to pornography is not easy due to Internet censorship in Iran. Accessing cyber content that the government deems inappropriate is a challenge that all Iranians have to deal with in their everyday lives. Almost all Iranians access the Internet through virtual private networks (VPNs) by purchasing hourly access from local contacts who deal in VPN access. This form of accessing the Internet is a socially accepted legal transgression because Internet censorship in Iran targets cyber content through keywords rather than content. For instance, all content linked to the keywords *sex* or names of sexual organs are blocked, which makes searching for academic articles by medical students a challenging task. A user can google and find the content, but when the user then clicks on the link to view the content, they are redirected to a page with government-approved content. Therefore, finding porn—*film e super* or *film e mostahjan*, as some Iranians call it— was not a simple click away as it might be in Lebanon, Iraq, Afghanistan, or Pakistan. The Iranian state is so concerned about sexually explicit content that the state often employs unusual technological tactics to hinder Iranians' access to porn. In 2017, these tactics were so effective that users as far away as India, Russia, and Indonesia also lost access to pornographic content along with Iranian Internet users (Griffin 2017).

Iranian women of my stories faced both considerable cost and some risk when accessing porn. First, they had to buy VPN access more often, because searching for porn would increase their Internet traffic, especially for those not familiar with English-language and porn-streaming services. Repeated VPN purchases would raise the curiosity of their husbands, children, and the VPN sellers, who often work as informers for the state intelligence services. Also, buying a VPN with a longer subscription would be beyond the usual budgets of many. The Internet is expensive in Iran, where people already struggle with back-breaking inflation due to the unilateral sanctions imposed by the US and compliance with those sanctions by European Union–based businesses. Watching porn for Iranians is not easy, not because of the religious and ideological beliefs of users as outsider observers might imagine based on a simplistic understanding of Iranian religiosity, but because access to porn requires complex preparation, some technological and linguistic sophistication, and strategic decision-making.

In this chapter, I share some of my interlocutors' encounters with porn to critique naïve and biased scholarship that portrays Muslim women's agency either as a limited operation of autonomy or a subversive reaction against imposing structures. I also depart from scholarship that portrays women as resorting to Islam in order to create some kind of critical distance from their own background and society (see Afshar 1985; Afkhami and Friedl 1994; Moallem 2005; Afary 2009; Sharifi 2018). I go against the grain of popular approaches that have focused on women, gender, and sexuality by assuming religion and governance by religion as constraints. Instead, I ask how religion becomes the platform of negotiation for Muslim women and I trace their ways of crafting cosmologies via corporeal experiences. I also depart from the approach of Saba Mahmood, who critiqued feminist anthropologists for framing the agency of Muslim women in terms of the extent to which they are "free from relations of subordination" (2006). Like Mahmood, I elaborate on *agency in compliance*, but unlike Mahmood I explore how compliance is integrated into the cosmologies of Muslim women. This is not through Islamic ordinances but instead through the ways that while engaging with something completely un-Islamic—pornography—they fashion compliance with Islam and commitment to Shi'i political Islam. As a male Iranian Shi'i anthropologist, my attempt perhaps puts me at odds with the approaches of some of my white feminist anthropologist colleagues, but to quote the late Sohrab Sepehri, an Iranian poet, "eyes must be washed, the ways of seeing must be changed, the word must be washed . . . the word must be rain itself" (Sepehri 2013). Here, some context about Iran and Iranian revolutionary women is needed to set the context for elaborating a fresh approach toward understanding religious experiences, embodiment, and agency in authoritarian and conservative settings.

Becoming a Revolutionary Woman in Iran

The 1979 Revolution was a decisive moment for Iran and Iranians. Muhammad Reza Pahlavi, the last monarch, was deposed when many Iranians took to the streets and demanded change. They shouted "*isteqlal, azadi, jomhuri islami*" (independence, freedom, Islamic Republic) to demand a new direction for their country. The protests and demands for regime change brought together two opposing political views against the monarchy: leftist intellectuals inspired by Marxist and socialist frameworks and the Muslim clergy inspired by Shiʻi ideology. The establishment of the Islamic Republic of Iran as the result of the revolution signaled the clear failure of leftist political and ideological agendas in Iran. The Republic declared Shiʻi Twelver Islam as its religion and it expected that all Iranians subscribe to it; other religious practices and minorities had to respect and obey the general rulings of the dominant religion imposed by the state (Abrahamian 1982). Shiʻa Islamic ordinances infused the new constitution and Shiʻi Islamic canon determined the law of the land.

Certain codes of conduct were imposed, including mandatory wearing of hijab (modest women's head covering worn in public) and gender segregation in schools, and alcohol (consumption, production, and distribution), sex work, intimate interactions with unrelated members of the opposite sex, and various genres of music were among many other things that became illegal in the new Islamic Republic. Disciplinary forces and morality police were established to surveil the population for any transgression from Islamic ordinances. Based on politically motivated interpretations of Islamic history, the principle of *vilāyat-i faqīh* (the guardianship of the learned jurist) was added into the constitution, assigning a member of the clergy to the highest office of the land. The learned jurist who would occupy the office of Supreme Leader holds both representational symbolic capacity *and* political judicial power over all branches of the government. The Islamic Revolution not only made the Islamic canon and the clerical authority pervasive in Iran, it also brought a new sense of generation and generationality in Iran. In the way of the Revolution, different generations can often be distinguished according to their commitment to *vilāyat-i faqīh*.

The state, and Iranians by extension, measure population groupings and demographic developments in terms of their generational distance from the Revolution. For instance, my father, who was born in early 1960s, is the first generation of the Revolution because its earliest political mobilizing began in the 1960s. Those born in 1980s were named the second generation, and so on. Each generation is marked by certain political features that emerged as part of the political climate of the era. For instance, my generation, those born in the 1980s, is known as *nasle sukhte* (the "burnt generation") because our childhood was dominated by the Iran-Iraq war

(1980–1988), and the Islamic Republic had yet to find a coherent narrative to absorb the new generation. Therefore, the generation that could not align its sociocultural and political identity with the Islamic Republic was deemed "burned" and untrustworthy. This became especially apparent for the state when the burnt generation elected Muhammad Khatami, a reformist cleric with explicit liberal inclinations toward the interpretation of Islam, to the presidential office (1997–2005). The electoral success of Khatami placed the burnt generation, who were mostly first-time voters in 1997, in opposition to Ayatollah Khamenei, the ruling jurist, who supported a right-leaning conservative candidate. The burnt generation explicitly demonstrated their lack of political commitment to revolutionary values and the guardianship of the learned jurist.

However, the generation that was born in the 1990s and 2000s showed still different political interests, and groups of highly committed revolutionary youth emerged from the era of Khatami. The newly emerged generations were disenchanted with the reformist and relaxed approach toward Islamic regulations such as hijab, gender segregation, and somewhat freer sexual interactions between genders. Highly politically committed new generations emerged that were deeply invested in the political values advocated by *vilāyat-i faqīh* because they believed their political commitment to the learned jurist would guarantee a true Islamic society.

The political commitments of the 1990s generation, considered the third generation of the Revolution, became tangible in their voting patterns and their vibrant presence in Shi'i transnational militancy across the region. In 2005, they voted for the presidential candidate supported by Ali Khamenei and supported every political decision taken by his office. This generation had not experienced the era of the Iran-Iraq war, but consumed the war era via narratives and stories orchestrated by the state. This generation romanticized the war era as the golden era of brotherhood, revolution, martyrdom, and grace and thus aspired to follow the revolutionary path to attain the same salvation that the martyrs of the Iran-Iraq war achieved. I call this generation that of the revolutionary youth and focused on them during my research, in contrast with most research conducted on post-revolution Iran, which has focused on the secular, somewhat liberal earlier generation that pitted itself in opposition to the Islamic Republic. This current scholarship is mostly based in larger metropolises such as Tehran or Shiraz (see Mahdavi 2009; Siamdoust 2017). In contrast, the revolutionary youth of my encounters hail from regions like Isfahan, Mashhad,

Hamedan, Azerbaijan, and Kerman, where income levels are lower than in more prosperous cities and cultural-religious traditions differ from those in Tehran, the capital.

The women of the third generation of the Revolution are now in their twenties, which means they are sexually capable adults who are mostly married, engaged, or about to be married, or they are in the process of meeting their future husbands. Those of the third generation whose stories I share were married or officially engaged to someone. They had either sexual experience with their husbands as their first sexual partner or they had experienced some form of sexual intimacy without vaginal penetration or complete nudity with their fiancés. What was most striking about their narratives about sexuality and sexual experience was the degree to which their sexual conduct was informed by their political commitments. For instance, Asmā, twenty-five years old and married for almost a year, hailed from a religious and traditional family in the outskirts of Isfahan. She disliked oral sex but she continued to perform fellatio on her husband. I asked why she continued to perform it if she disliked it, not expecting an answer, but she surprised me by replying, "Think about it: my man leaves his job, sacrifices his vacation time to volunteer and fight in Iraq. The pleasure of such a man should come before my own likes and dislikes. We all serve a larger cause differently." Asmā exemplified a revolutionary woman in Iran who conceptualized her devotion to religion and to her political commitments through the body and sexuality.

She would often pray that she and her husband would achieve martyrdom, she reported, because martyrdom was the path to realizing the true of mission of the Islamic Revolution. I stress her commitment to martyrdom in order to highlight the political dimensions of religiosity among the third generation. For such members of the third generation, martyrdom is the ultimate sacrifice, which orients them toward a particular understanding of their allegiance to the state and accordingly how to foresee life in its social and cosmological sense. Asmā did not dream of children, buying a house, having a car, or obtaining other worldly comforts; she wished to determine the meaning of her own life and her marital life by the manner that her biotic life could be ended. Therefore, her sexual conduct was integral to her political commitment and she adjusted her practices according to the desires of the man whom she deemed worthy of co-committing to martyrdom with.

Parvaneh, who was recently married at the age of twenty-nine, made her choice of husband after meeting and talking to more than fifty eligible bachelors. Fifty different young men had visited Parvaneh's family in the span of a year to ask for her hand and talk to her. My eyes were wide when I heard the number, and I repeated, "Fifty young men during one year? And if you have spent three hours, at least, talking to each of them, then it means 150 hours just to assess who can be your potential partner? Aren't you the picky one?"[1] Parvaneh clarified, "The man of my dreams, the man who will stand beside me to fight against injustice, was not among them. I waited for my Che Guevara and I finally found him." Her husband was an officer of the Iranian Revolutionary Guard, and his valor was exemplary amongst the combatants who had fought against ISIS in Iraq. Asmā and Parvaneh had relatively moderate conceptualizations of the relationship between their commitment to religion and patriarchal authority in the home. Other women whom I encountered during my research explicitly stated that their husbands represented the authority of Khamenei in the house and thus their compliance with husbandly demands was given not to their husbands but to what their husbands represented.

It is productive to analyze the ideas and political commitments of the third generation in relation to ethico-political structures explored by Janet Afary in her book *Sexual Politics in Modern Iran* (2009). She explores the role of women in the formative years and the first decade of the Islamic Revolution and argues that women of the first generation "seem to gain a new sense of purpose and identity as a result of joining the Islamist movement and adopting its ethico-political structure" (257). The revolutionary youth of the third generation among whom I conducted my research also craft their subjectivities in *relation to* (not according to) that structure; however, it is far less linear and causal than Afary portrays for earlier generations. Afary states that "allegiance to a highly authoritarian and patriarchal movement that advocated women's subordination to men nonetheless allowed them to gain a measure of *personal* power . . . and to live more gratifying *personal* lives" (257; emphasis added). Afary reduces the political commitment of revolutionary women to an individual gain generalized among them. In the process, she overlooks how this "gratification" is forged through negotiations that do not confirm patriarchy and Islam; rather, that gratification produces a mode of freedom that falls beyond Western assumptions about modes of subjectivity. Further, she separates the personal from the political, as if any political gain is located in some public wilderness and revolutionary sphere and has no relation with the personal except through a utilitarian gratification for a revolutionary individual. In contrast, Asmā and Parvaneh are good examples of how the personal and the political are intertwined through what *appears* to be submission for Afary and her epigones (see Charrad 2011; Kashani-Sabet 2011), but which in fact is a far more intricate compliance and agentive expression of piety.

The postwar generations have enjoyed the privileges of economic prosperity, an information boom due to Internet access, and global connectivity, in contrast with the earlier generations that had highly limited and lesser-informed views of the world outside of Iran. The state has actively organized an ideological-informational machinery to compete with global flows of information by feeding the political curiosity of these generations through its preferred scripts and narratives. The ideological-informational machinery narrates the past, such as the history of revolution, resistance, and the war era, to shape their perceptions of the future (Saramifar 2019). Additionally, the state had to tackle new challenges in the postwar era such as reconstruction of the country and feeding the fast-growing population of what was one of the youngest countries in the region in the 1990s and early 2000s. Therefore, the ideological-informational machinery took sex education and family planning into consideration along with everything else.

Unlike earlier generations, the 1990s generation became familiar with ideas of contraception and HIV and other sexually transmitted infections (STIs) because of the challenges of population growth and the threats of human immunodeficiency virus (HIV) and other STIs. The state was thus forced to focus on issues of sexual and reproductive health. The threat of and growth of awareness about STIs highlighted the role of the body in the everyday lives of these generations (Simbar, Tehrani, and Hashemi 2005). Courses in family planning and sexual health were introduced into the curricula of high schools and universities, but these classes were mainly organized for female students. The course contents remained highly constrained by religious and sociocultural mores and codes of decency according to Islamic traditions (Mehryar, Ahmad-Nia, and Kazemipour 2007). Motherhood, childbearing, fertility, and pregnancy became the socially acceptable labels for curricular content through which school pupils and college students learned about sexuality and sexual interactions. The regime of biopolitics administered by the Islamic Republic and its ideological-informational machinery were not equipped with a language to discuss intimacy and sex outside of traditional forums and beyond the limits of urban environments (Tremayne 2006).

Traditional religious forums such as mosque gatherings, sermons by female preachers, and workshops on Islamic ordinance organized by

women theologians compensated for the inefficiencies and inarticula-
tion of the Islamic Republic. Consequently, discourses on sexuality, intimacy, sexual conduct, and affairs of body more generally were once again
framed through the Islamic canon. They were reproduced by the patriarchal core that shapes the Islamic canon and permitted fewer possibilities for women to become the agents of their own bodies. Almost all my
interlocutors learned about menstruation through their encounters with
Islamic texts. They would be gifted or indirectly made aware of a *resalih*,
a textual treatise which compiles all the ordinances of a learned jurist, by
their parents. The young women who would unexpectedly face bodily
changes were referred to the chapters that discussed the rituals of ablu-
tion and bodily hygiene for a Muslim woman during menstruation. In
another words, religious texts prescribing rituals for how to "act" Islamic
and inhabit a Muslim female body made these revolutionary young women
to become aware of their bodies and the changes that they experienced.
Of course, a *resalih* is not an all-encompassing means of knowledge about
a subject, and informal modes of knowledge exchange introduced new
ideas outside of the religious canon and modes of authoritative knowledge. These informal modes for the 1990s generation include peer groups,
familial networks (such as older female cousins, younger aunts, and sometimes grandmothers), social media, and books. My research revealed that
peer groups and social media have the highest priority in these modes of
informal, nonauthoritative knowledge exchange, and these often introduced the possibilities of encounters with pornography, or what I will here
call "pornographic encounters." The pornographic encounters described
by my research participants highlight the intricacies of compliance, the
so-called measure of personal power, and the forging of alternative modes
of becoming a Muslim woman.

Pornographic Encounters

I return to Majideh, expanding upon the sentence I used to introduce
this chapter, and explain how her "good relationship with [her] body"
introduced porn into our conversations. Majideh, twenty-seven years
old, came from a religious family who always voted for the right-leaning
conservative candidates. Her father was a retired brigadier of the Revolutionary Guard, her younger brother was a deeply committed revolutionary man, and her challenging mother's idea of Islam had become

a barrier between her and her children. Majideh found her mother emotionally detached and blamed her for not making her aware of bodily the daunting trajectory of becoming a woman. She had been engaged twelve times and had met nearly ninety-five eligible bachelors, but none were the man she sought after. She explained, "Talking to men, spending time in a room alone with them and imagining a beautiful future, the scent of their bodies and all that gentle roughness frustrated me. I used to get weird after each meeting. I would get impatient and short tempered for no reason. It would affect my study and my concentration to pray and I could not sense the presence of the divine for a while." Initially Majideh was unaware that her meetings with young men had awakened her sexual desires and unable to acknowledge how arousal affected her concentration and self-composure. Finally, she had shared her confusion with a classmate who was married and was more experienced about the complexities of sexual desire.

Majideh looked at me and I could see she blushed visibly, despite her dark complexion. She recalled, "My friend laughed at me and said you are just feeling horny and making such a big deal about it." Majideh did not recognize the term *hashari* (horny) because she had been brought up in a very "polite" family. She googled the term and found some unexpected Instagram pages. Instagram is the only social media platform that is not filtered in Iran; therefore, all content is accessible on this social media platform. Majideh discovered porn on Instagram and this was the beginning of how she had begun to establish "a good relationship with [her] body," as she put it. Porn became an outlet through which she could channel her sexual desires, masturbate, and "get over it." In the process, she gained a new sense of control over her body. She calmly explained, "My body and I became friends later than others, but watching porn lets me find my center. I recognize my bodily needs so that I can serve my ideals better." Majideh reconciled herself with the "sinful" acts by thinking about the larger goals in her life rather "being stuck with small things." She stressed that she used porn like a tool, in the same way that one would eat to not die of hunger.

Majideh elaborated on how she had found porn and what use of porn had in her life, but she stopped talking about it when I asked about the pleasures of watching porn. She looked straight at me and I felt her anger when she said, "Were you listening to me at all? This is just a matter of satisfaction. Just chemicals in my body. I find porn to be a better bargain than polluting my body in an *unholy* sexual relationship. Please, understand I am not seduced by what is *in* porn, but it allows me to take charge

of my unruly mind." Porn, watching porn, and masturbation were accommodated beside every other religious ritual in her life because she saw this
as a way she could preserve her virtue and remain a good Muslim woman
by holding onto her virginity. Majideh found no contradiction between
porn and living in accordance with the religious framework she ascribed
to; on the contrary, she used porn as the instrument to comply. Her compliance falls in tandem with the political commitments that expect "virtue" and "dedication" from Iranian Muslim women who should preserve
their bodies in service of a divine calling. This mode of compliance is not
obedience or submission to gain anything, because revolutionary women
like Majideh often felt alone and isolated in Iranian society despite the ruling Islamic Republic. She was scorned for her *chador*, her political commitment to the Islamic Republic, and seeing martyrdom as the highest form
of grace. She crafted her subjectivity within an ambiguous terrain where
self, self-maintenance, and finding one's boundaries are not as straightforward as Afary (2009) suggests.

In this ambiguous terrain, becoming a revolutionary Muslim woman is
linked to a corporeal position vis-à-vis Islam and the state; however, there
are a multitude of other relationships that contribute to this link. Body
and the tingling sexual desires that seek release shape the link and corporeal positioning; they actively do so both by compliance and by refusal to
submit. The body in compliance refuses to be subsumed but rather con-
sumes the state in compliance. For instance, Arezu divorced her husband
after less than a year of marriage because "he did not have the backbone
to enlist for deployment, among other reasons." Arezu, thirty-one years
old and brought up in a wealthy family in Hamedan, studied clinical psychology and enjoyed experimenting with her "mental conditions," as she
put it. She explained this while smiling, raising one eyebrow, and biting
the tip of her finger. "Porn made me pray better because I have a curious
mind. I used to watch Iranian TV series and found myself excited by the
tension that I could read between the man and woman in the story. Can
you imagine one would get stimulated by the TV of the Islamic Republic?" She stressed this because all the women are appropriately covered
and any suggestion of innuendo is avoided in content broadcast in Iran.
Television characters observe hijab strictly, wear loose attire, and exhibit
absolutely no physical contact between men and women.

Arezu's excitement combined with her curiosity provoked her to ask
what comes after the tension. She was aware of sexual intimacy and what

happens in the bedroom, but she wanted to see the depiction of sexual activity. Her teacher, a licensed sex therapist, suggested some female-friendly porn. Arezu continued with excitement, "It was beautiful. The TV made sense now and I could smile and tell myself, 'I know what comes next,' without feeling stupid and cheated by what was shown in TV." I gently asked what happened to the excitement and she jumped slightly as if suddenly remembering that I was sitting there. She shrugged, "Nothing! The excitement and lust become prayers."

Arezu would find herself sexually stimulated but she would turn the stimulation into prayers, unloading her lust through tears and worship. She found porn could distract her mind from the sexual tension depicted in the TV, but also it provoked sexual arousal, which she tackled through devotion and prayer. She added:

> I was happiest last time during the commemoration of martyrs. The porn that I had watched earlier came to my mind again and again and I could not brush it away. I felt frustrated and guilty. But then, I looked around me and I saw all the young revolutionary women attired in black *chador* and standing strong next to me. I realized I am not alone in my struggles and suddenly I felt that I am part of something large.

Arezu located *herself* within the larger collective of revolutionary women, not through submission to a larger ideology but rather via a body that felt the warmth of lust that was aroused by porn. Porn supplied her imagination with the images that the Islamic Republic deemed inappropriate for her eyes but which Arezu's curiosity decided otherwise. However, her curiosity and sexual arousal did not push her to transgress, and she fit watching porn into her mode of compliance. Porn encouraged her prayers. She gained new insights into how bodies "look" on the screen when they engage sexually, but her struggles with the stimulation that came about through what she watched delivered her to something larger. She arrived at the revolutionary assemblage from a most unexpected route.

Pornographic encounters don't always appear in the manner of an informative awakening that some revolutionary women would absorb into their Islamic cosmologies. Nazgul was an interesting case who found religion through pornography. She was a thirty-four-year-old architect with a successful practice and a revolutionary passion that led her to rebuild historical mosques in impoverished provinces. She would dedicate three months every year to rebuilding martyrs' burial grounds and mosques across Iran. She hailed from a family in which her father always teased her about not having a boyfriend, while her mother is a practicing devout Muslim with no interest in political Islam. Nazgul married a younger man who had lost his right arm while deployed overseas to fight against ISIS in Syria and she described her marital life as experiencing bliss. She turned shy when she explained how she rediscovers herself anew every time she lays besides her husband and added, "I discover myself anew because I discovered my body and religion in a manner that no one else did." I was skeptical, assuming that there was nothing new that I could hear after listening to many encounters with porn and learning unusual details of the sex lives of young revolutionary women. She then surprised me by declaring, "I learned religion because of porn."

Nazgul enjoyed reading about Islamic mysticism and practiced the usual rituals until a few years prior to our interview, but she avoided any aspect of Islam that implied politics. She avoided boyfriends and marriage proposals in order to finish her studies successfully, but she had one particular pleasure that filled her empty hours. "I liked playing with my nipples and enjoyed the sensation," she said before becoming quiet. I held my composure and asked, "So, you did not mind pleasuring yourself?" And she immediately said, "No, I mean yes . . . I enjoyed it but I did not know that it was masturbation and sinful." Nazgul's areola became overly sensitive due to excessive manipulation and she began to search for a suitable brassiere online. She stumbled on a porn-streaming website where users shared their "sore nipple" experiences and Nazgul realized the erotic potentials of what she did. Nazgul explained calmly, "I was pleased for a while because there are others who enjoy the same thing and I am not a freak. I always thought there is something wrong with me that I feel so itchy on my breasts." Then, she firmly but quietly explained, "But I also learned from that porn that I was different. I took pleasure in my actions, but it was similar to the pleasure that one gets when a sore muscle is massaged or the simple pleasure of a cold autumn breeze on my face. It was a pleasant thing to do but it was nothing sexual for me." Nazgul was ashamed of her discovery and went to the *resalih* where she learned her indulgence was considered sinful. She said with pride, "I broke into tears; I realized how God has been patient with my ignorance. I took responsibility and began to learn." Taking responsibility for her action and seeking pleasure in a manner that she found unbecoming for a woman developed into a political commitment and finding her revolutionary passion. Nazgul looked at me with a stern expression and a mild frown and declared, "We are more than our pleasures and it is *unbecoming* to remain imprisoned within the desires of flesh. I want to leave a legacy and not just the vibration of my moans and sexual satisfactions. So, that is why porn led me to God."

Oh My God, This Is My Body

There was one consistent element in the pornographic encounters described by the Iranian revolutionary women I interviewed: they discovered their bodies during these encounters. They were aware of their bodies while they passed through puberty and became familiar with the Islamic ordinances and rituals through *resalih* or other resources. However, they resided in their bodies like a puppeteer. The body was a performative thing that would be treated accordingly to *be* a Muslim; however, finding pleasure and discovering how body and mind are merged entities delivered them to *becoming* a Muslim. Here, I distinguish between *being* and *becoming* a Muslim by highlighting how my interlocutors evolved through a dialogic negotiation and thinking *through* Islam, rather than just submitting to the demands of religion.

Finding pleasure and discovering the jolt of orgasmic satisfaction informed them about their bodies. Therefore, they re-imagined their Islamic cosmologies differently via pleasure and especially sexual pleasures. However, they did not describe this pleasure as transgressive; rather, they described how it opened the path to compliance. Afary asserts that "Khomeini [the religious leader of Islamic revolution] tapped into the discontent with modernity and its technologies of the body and succeeded in setting the ideological, organizational, and political agenda for the revolution" (2009, 262). She frames the Islamic Revolution as a singular idea that conveys no meaning beyond that which the religious-political authorities convey. This neglects and underestimates how Muslim women during and after the revolution crafted and manifested their womanhood in a larger assemblage that exceeded the Revolution, Islam, and religious leadership altogether.

Afary's approach has the remnants of modernist views that separate the personal from the political and overlook *how* the personal becomes political through bodies; however, the body that has remained unknown to a woman is constantly connected to politics outside the home. The Islamic Republic militarizes these bodies, and official Islamic discourses shape and sometimes hinder the platforms of awareness for women who are committed to the Republic. They may not develop sexual autonomy due to the state's interference, but they should not be targeted with analytical bias and political prejudice. The stories of these women explain how God is accessed through an agentive mode of engagement with body and pleasure, a mode of access that may appear in compliance with the larger patriarchal order but is actually transgressive of the canon and official state politics. Pious bodies and the corporeal pleasure of pious women enlighten how God is accessed through crafting Islamic cosmologies that emerge from ambiguities rather than from clarity of theology, doctrine, canon, and jurisprudence. These cosmologies explain how a woman becomes Muslim and embodies what seems to be "Islam" through a trajectory in which she is an agent of her compliance. Any further query should probe the individuation and intertwinement of the personal and the political within compliance and becoming pious.

NOTES

1. I gradually learned fifty is the baseline. Any girl who does not exceed that number is not considered a popular choice. However, religious and revolutionary families often tried to break these shallow ideas by checking the potential groom out during a short phone conversation with his family to see if the families align politically, then the family would check if their daughter is ready to marry anyone at all. They try to accept fewer candidates in their homes and invite only those who match their political and religious worldviews.

REFERENCES

Abrahamian, Ervand. 1983. *Iran: Between Two Revolutions*. Princeton, NJ: Princeton University Press, 1982. Citations refer to 2nd printing, with corrections.

Afary, Janet. 2009. *Sexual Politics in Modern Iran*. Cambridge, UK: Cambridge University Press.

Afkhami, Mahnaz, and Erika Friedl. 1994. *In the Eye of the Storm: Women in Post-Revolutionary Iran*. New York: Syracuse University Press.

Afshar, Haleh. 1985. "Women, State and Ideology in Iran." *Third World Quarterly* 7, no. 2 (Spring): 256–78.

Çankaya, Sinan, and Paul Mepschen. 2019. "Facing Racism: Discomfort, Innocence and the Liberal Peripheralisation of Race in the Netherlands." *Social Anthropology* 27, no. 4 (August): 626–40.

Charrad, Mounira. 2011 "Gender in the Middle East: Islam, State, Agency." *Annual Review of Anthropology* 37, no. 2 (March): 417–37.

Deeb, Lara, and Jessica Winegar. 2015. *Anthropology's Politics: Disciplining the Middle East.* Stanford, CA: Stanford University Press.

Griffin, Andrew. 2017. "Porn Blocks in Iran Break the Internet Across the World." *Independent*, January 09, 2017. https://www.independent.co.uk/life-style/gadgets-and-tech/news/porn-blocks-iran-internet-down-russia-hong-kong-adult-websites-sites-censorship-a7517621.html.

Kashani-Sabet, Firoozeh. 2011. *Conceiving Citizens: Women and the Politics of Motherhood in Iran.* New York: Oxford University Press.

Mahdavi, Pardis. 2009. *Passionate Uprisings: Iran's Sexual Revolution.* Stanford, CA: Stanford University Press.

Mahmood, Saba. 2006. "Feminist Theory, Agency, and the Liberatory Subject: Some Reflections on the Islamic Revival in Egypt." *Finnish Society for the Study of Religion* 42, no. 1 (April): 31–71.

Mehryar, Amir H., Shirin Ahmad-Nia, and Shahla Kazemipour. 2007 "Reproductive Health in Iran: Pragmatic Achievements, Unmet Needs, and Ethical Challenges in a Theocratic System." *Studies in Family Planning* 38, no. 4 (February): 352–61.

Moallem, Minoo. 2005. *Between Warrior Brother and Veiled Sister: Islamic Fundamentalism and the Politics of Patriarchy in Iran.* Berkeley: University of California Press.

Saramifar, Younes. 2019. "Emotions of Felt Memories: Looking for Interplay of Emotions and Histories in Iranian Political Consciousness since Iran–Iraq War (1980–1988)." *Anthropology of Consciousness* 30, no. 2 (September): 132–51.

Sepehri, Sohrab. 2013. *A Selection of Poems from The Eight Books.* Translated by Bahiyeh Afnan Shahid. Bloomington, IN: Balboa Press.

Sharifi, Nafiseh. 2018. *Female Bodies and Sexuality in Iran and the Search for Defiance.* Cham: Springer International Publishing.

Siamdoust, Nahid. 2017. *Soundtrack of the Revolution: The Politics of Music in Iran.* Stanford, CA: Stanford University Press.

Simbar, Masoumeh, Fahimeh Tehrani, and Zahra Hashemi. 2005. "Reproductive Health Knowledge, Attitudes and Practices of Iranian College Students." *Eastern Mediterranean Health Journal* 11, no. 5–6 (September): 888–97.

Tremayne, Soraya. 2006 "And Never the Twain Shall Meet: Reproductive Health Policies in the Islamic Republic of Iran." In *Reproductive Agency, Medicine, and the State: Cultural Transformations in Childbearing,* edited by Maya Unnithan-Kumar, 181–202. New York: Berghahn.

CHAPTER 7

The Gendered Relationship between Sex and Marriage in Egypt

Interrogating Secret Marriages among Urban Youth in Cairo and Minya

RANIA SALEM

In Egypt, the Arab region's most populous country, a number of commentators have argued in scholarly and media accounts that the institution of marriage is in a state of crisis, and that *'urfi* (customary) marriages among young people are one manifestation of this crisis (Abaza 2001, 20; Fawzī 2000; Hasso 2011; Salem 2016, 231). 'Urfi marriages are established by an informal contract drawn up by heterosexual Muslim couples in the presence of either two male witnesses or one male and two female witnesses (Ibn Mahmud 2004, 70; 'Umrān 2001, 14). Four features of 'urfi marriages are worth noting. First, many of these marital unions are secret: the couples involved hold no public celebration, they do not cohabit, and their families remain ignorant of the nuptials. Second, the marriage contracts are not registered with the state; in conventional marriages, state registration is carried out by a marriage registrar (*ma'zoun*) after having officiated and overseen the drafting of the marriage contract. Third, 'urfi marriages may go unregistered, but they can be recognized by the courts after the fact (Bernard-Maugiron 2010, 17). Egyptian courts only began recognizing 'urfi marriages in 2000 with the passage of a new Personal Status Law. However, proving the existence of an 'urfi marriage is complicated, because if one party denies the union, the courts will only consider a claim if a marriage document is produced (Bernard-Maugiron 2010, 17). In addition, the law allows 'urfi wives to petition for a judicial divorce, but several limitations on their entitlements remain. Following divorce from an 'urfi marriage, women do not enjoy any rights to financial maintenance from former husbands, but if paternity is proven, the father must pay child support. However, proving paternity is difficult since DNA testing is not compulsory (Bernard-Maugiron 2010, 9). Fourth, 'urfi marriages are considered by many experts in Islamic jurisprudence to establish valid unions in the eyes of God (al-Ashqar 2000, 129; Hasso 2011, 9; Husayn 1999, 96; Sonneveld 2012, 57). The permissibility of 'urfi unions in Islam hinges on a number of criteria. Some argue that 'urfi marriages are not valid unions because they lack public announcement of the marriage (ishhar) and the consent of the bride's male guardian (wali). This latter criterion is required only for underage brides, according to some schools of Islamic thought (al-Daryūwīsh 2005, 81; Hasso 2011, 6; Ibn Mahmud 2004, 88; Sonneveld 2012, 57; 'Umrān 2001, 23). Still, 'urfi unions provide a modicum of legitimacy to "pre-marital" or "extra-marital" sexual activity, otherwise considered taboo (El Feki 2013, 45, 131; Wynn 2016, 547; Zuhur 2003, 31). 'Urfi marriages, however, remain stigmatized (Singerman and Ibrahim 2003, 83; Zuhur 2003, 31).

Little is known about the genealogy of 'urfi marriage in Egypt, but many believe such marriages are more common today compared to the past (Abaza 2001, 20; Abdalla 2015, 44; El Feki 2013, 44; Hasso 2011, 83; Ibn Mahmūd 2004, 89; Singerman 2007, 31). Public discussion of this phenomenon first emerged in the late 1960s, when it was associated with women who entered into unregistered 'urfi marriages in order to avoid losing the state benefits they were entitled to as war widows who had not remarried (Hasso 2011, 81). Since the late 1990s, 'urfi marriages have come to be associated in the public imagination with urban university students (Abdalla 2015, 44; Hasso 2011, 85; Ibn Mahmūd 2004, 4; Karkabi 2011, 85), who are thought to enter into such marriages either because they cannot afford conventional marriages or because they hold sexual values that are more permissive than those of the broader society.

Most existing empirical accounts of 'urfi marriage rely primarily on the analysis of public discourse or public attitudes toward 'urfi unions (Eum 2005; Fawzi 2000; Hasso 2011; Shahrani 2010) or on the analysis of second-hand reports of the circumstances underlying 'urfi unions (for notable exceptions, see Abdalla 2015; Abdallah and Yousef 2004; El Feki 2013; Karkabi 2011; Sonneveld 2012; Walby 2010; and Wynn 2016). In contrast, this study relies on forty semi-structured interviews with young hetero-sexual Muslim women and men who were involved in secret 'urfi unions in the cities of Cairo and Minya. The focus of this study is on "secret" 'urfi unions, that is unions in which knowledge of the marital union was restricted to the bride and groom and a limited and carefully selected cir-cle of friends, relatives, or neighbors. A female interviewer, Amal Refaat (AR), conducted all semi-structured interviews after having been trained to use an interview guide designed by the author, Rania Salem (RS). AR recruited respondents using snowball sampling methods and she conducted digitally recorded interviews from May to September 2012. The average duration of the interviews was sixty-seven minutes. A transcriber, Zeinab Ali (ZA), transcribed the interviews in Arabic and RS carried out spot checks of the interviews and transcripts and used the MAXQDA software package to manage the data during the analysis phase. Prior to fieldwork, the author (RS) submitted an ethics protocol to the Institutional Review Board at Princeton University and obtained ethical clearance. All names used here are pseudonyms, and RS modified details of respondents' lives to mask their identities.

The total study sample of forty respondents included nine women and eleven men from Cairo, and eleven women and nine men from Minya. Respondents' ages ranged from eighteen to thirty-five, with an average age of twenty-seven. The respondent with the lowest educational attain-ment had completed fourth grade and the respondent with the highest educational attainment had completed a five-year university degree. The majority (twenty-three respondents) had attended a post-secondary educa-tional institution. Four respondents (three women and one man—the latter was performing paid employment alongside his studies) were currently in the school system. Thirteen respondents were not currently working for pay (twelve of these were women). At the time of interview, twenty-six respondents were currently in 'urfi marriages and twelve had previously been in 'urfi marriages. Two women reported that their 'urfi husbands had disappeared and their current marital status was unknown. The longest 'urfi marriage reported lasted eight years (the couple was still married 'urfi at the time of interview) and the shortest lasted three weeks (the couple had divorced and the male respondent was married conventionally to someone else at the time of interview).

In this chapter, I examine the meanings young Egyptians ascribe to 'urfi marriage to illuminate normative attitudes toward the relationship between sex and marriage. I interrogate three claims in the literature on 'urfi marriage: that 'urfi marriages are a response to economic constraints, that 'urfi marriages are a result of permissive sexual values, and that 'urfi marriages are a substitute for conventional marriage. I argue based on my qualitative interviews that while a majority of respondents resorted to 'urfi marriages after encountering material barriers to conventional marriage, as the existing literature predicts, others entered 'urfi unions to avoid state interference in their intimate lives. My findings also suggest that young Egyptians involved in 'urfi marriages continue to value conventional marriage. They view conventional marriage as the ideal setting for sexual intimacy, contrary to arguments that hold that 'urfi unions are evidence that youths' values differ markedly from those of mainstream society. My findings show that men, but more often women, characterized 'urfi unions as inferior to conventional marriages, suggesting that they are not a substitute for conventional marriage, as some scholars contend, but rather that 'urfi unions are a substitute for sex outside of marriage. I close by offering new insights into the gendered nature of attitudes toward 'urfi marriage in the Egyptian context. I demonstrate that some men depicted their 'urfi marriages as an act of defiance that would force the bride's family to accept a conventional marriage once the 'urfi marriage was revealed. In addition, many women understood their entry into an 'urfi union as signaling their love and commitment to the relationship, whereas some men saw women's entry into an 'urfi union as a sign that she is unfit for conventional marriage. Thus, the meanings attached to 'urfi marriages diverge according to gender, a fact that reflects the very different roles and risks associated with 'urfi marriages for women and for men.

'URFI MARRIAGE AS A RESPONSE TO ECONOMIC CONDITIONS

Existing treatments of 'urfi marriage contend that these marriages are a response to the prohibitively high costs of conventional unions. Most sources list the expensive nature of conventional marriage as the sole or most important motivation for 'urfi marriage (Abaza 2001, 20; Abdalla 2015, 44; Abdallah and Yousef 2004, 166; al-Ashqar 2000, 142; Eum 2005, 68; Fawzi 2000, 40; Hasso 2011, 9; Singerman 2007, 29; Sonneveld 2012, 561; Wynn 2016, 547; Zuhur 2003, 31). Estimates calculated using survey data on conventional marriages indicate that the average Egyptian groom requires three and a half years of saved wages to afford his share of marriage expenditures, while the average bride requires six months of saved wages (Salem 2016, 245). Conventional matrimonial outlays, which are agreed upon in negotiations between the groom's side and the bride's side, include spending on housing, furniture, appliances, housewares, celebrations, and clothing and jewelry for the bride (Salem 2018, 402; Singerman and Ibrahim 2003, 89). Because the couples involved in 'urfi unions do not set up a joint household and because their marriages are kept secret from their parents, they evade most of the costly outlays associated with conventional marriages.

My findings on young people's motivations for entering into 'urfi marriages indicate that the majority of respondents (twenty-five) did indeed resort to 'urfi marriages wholly or partially due to material barriers to conventional marriage. Still, most couples entering into 'urfi unions symbolically marked the occasions of their secret marriages with economic transactions—but these transactions fell within their limited means. Some respondents made use of a lawyer's services to draft their 'urfi marriage contracts, and in these cases the groom usually incurred this expense. Some of my respondents also reported that the groom and bride exchanged rings on the occasion of their 'urfi weddings. However, these were often made of silver or "Chinese gold" and represented a small fraction of what they would have paid if their marriages were publicly acknowledged.[1] Some couples reported that they also held a small celebration, but this typically consisted of an outing to a café with three or four friends. Finally, although some couples made other arrangements, many couples needed to rent a place to meet in private. In these cases a room with minimal furnishings was rented, usually by the groom. In comparison with the US$10,700 spent by the average Egyptian couple on conventional marriage (Salem 2015, 176), the expenditures described above are very modest.[2]

While economic constraints factored into the decisions of twenty-five of the forty cases of 'urfi marriage, other cases reported different motivations for entering into 'urfi unions. One reason was to avoid state interference in their intimate lives, as was the case in three different scenarios.

The first scenario occurred when married men sought to hide a second wife from their first wife. When a married man's second marriage is registered formally, the first wife is notified by the state, and she can use the fact of her husband's polygamy to petition for a judicial divorce. The second scenario occurred when female survivors of fathers or husbands who had died sought to retain a pension they would lose if they married formally. The official rationale for this policy is that the daughters or wives of pension-earning men deserve their pensions so long as they lack a male breadwinner. The third scenario occurred when divorced women wanted to remarry but keep custody of their children. Legally, the custody of children whose mothers remarry goes to the maternal grandmother. However, many divorced women were not aware of this and assumed that their children's fathers would be granted custody if they remarried conventionally.

While the avoidance of state interference motivated many parties to turn to 'urfi marriages, others resorted to 'urfi marriages because of parental disapproval of their choice of partner. A limited number of respondents entered into 'urfi unions to legitimize (and assuage their guilt over) a sexual encounter that had occurred within an existing romantic relationship. Finally, in a limited number of cases, 'urfi unions served as a cover for sex work. I illustrate how material barriers to conventional marriage motivated one 'urfi marriage in the first vignette presented in this chapter and then I detail alternative motivations for entering into 'urfi marriages with two other vignettes.

'Essam's Story

In 2012, 'Essam was a twenty-five-year-old Cairene who held a vocational secondary school degree.[3] He worked as a microbus driver and his monthly earnings ranged between US$160 and US$175. He and his neighbor Amany had been in love for about a year and a half, during which time 'Essam suggested that they have an 'urfi marriage when she refused to have an affair. But when she also objected to an 'urfi union, 'Essam then proposed to Amany's father, who rejected his proposal because of 'Essam's "middling financial circumstances." According to 'Essam, Amany's father "had very manipulative demands." He explained that her father wanted 'Essam to own rather than rent an apartment ('Essam estimated that this would cost him at least US$12,250), he wanted an expensive gold gift for the bride (this would cost about US$3,500), and he wanted the duration of the engagement to be short. After her father's rejection of 'Essam's proposal of conventional marriage, Amany agreed to marry in secret and they had been married 'urfi for two years.

'Essam and Amany's case represents an example of a couple who married 'urfi in order to bypass the burdensome costs associated with conventional unions insisted upon by parents. In the majority of cases like 'Essam's, parental opposition to conventional marriages centered on the limited financial means of the prospective groom. In the remaining cases, parents objected to a match for other reasons, such as conflict between the couple's families or the bride's status as previously married. Overcoming parental opposition to a marriage must be understood in the context of young Egyptians' low incomes and insecure employment, for many young men in particular simply cannot finance conventional marriage or support their new households without material assistance from their parents. Young women, many of whom do not work after completing their educations, are also reliant on their families for providing the matrimonial goods expected of them (Salem 2018, 408). Therefore, there are important economic disincentives for acting contrary to the wishes of one's parents.

Unlike 'Essam's case, where 'urfi marriage served to circumvent the family and its financial demands, in other cases, 'urfi marriage served to circumvent the state.

──────────────*Do'aa's Story*──────────────

Do'aa was a thirty-four-year-old divorcee from Minya who lived with her widowed mother, her younger brother, and her daughter from her previous (conventional) marriage. She held a university degree and did not work. She was in love with Mustafa, who was married conventionally to another woman whom he did not love, but with whom he had two children. They resorted to a secret marriage because Do'aa was concerned that if they married formally, she would lose her deceased father's pension, which she relied on, together with her ex-husband's child support payments, for her day-to-day expenses. She was also worried that a formal marriage would deprive her of custody of her daughter. By marrying secretly, Do'aa was able to maintain the limited entitlements accorded to her by the state.

For both Do'aa and Mustafa, this second marriage eluded detection by the state by remaining unregistered as an 'urfi marriage. Do'aa and Mustafa were unusual in that he was willing for his conventional wife to find out about his second marriage. In other cases, husbands were concerned about the separation from their children that might result if their 'urfi marriages were found out. There were a total of nine cases of polygamous marriages in the sample. In three cases, husbands could not antagonize their conventional wives because they were relatives and they worried that any marital problems would endanger their relationships with their families. In one of those cases, the husband relied on his family for his livelihood and he therefore could not afford to alienate his family with a marriage they would disapprove of.

Sahar's Story

Sahar was thirty-one, held a vocational secondary school degree, worked in the packaging department of a factory, and lived in Cairo. She entered into an 'urfi marriage with an elderly Saudi man when her family faced a financial crisis that threatened to lead to their eviction from their apartment. The marriage was arranged by a middle-woman (*simsara*) who specialized in procuring young women for Gulf Arabs who were in Egypt for the summer holidays. The Saudi paid about US$350 for Sahar's services, US$90 of which went to the middlewoman. The middlewoman drew up the 'urfi marriage contract in her office, which Sahar and the groom signed, with the middlewoman and the Saudi's friend as witnesses, thus making the contract invalid, since only one man and one woman had served as witnesses. Sahar and the Saudi groom then went to a furnished flat he had rented and consummated the marriage. Although Sahar had planned to remain with the Saudi groom in hopes of extracting more money from him, she escaped when later that night he became violent and abusive. Badly beat up, Sahar returned to the middlewoman's office, demanded her US$90 back, and ripped up the marriage contract. She then considered herself to be divorced. Later in the interview, Sahar speculated that the only reason the Saudi married her was to provide some protection in case they were caught by the vice police.

Sahar's narrative echoes that of other respondents, several of whom expressed concern about being apprehended by the police for engaging in what might be suspected to be illicit sexual activity. In Sahar's case, this fear was well founded because she was performing sex work under the cover of a 'urfi marriage contract, but for other respondents, fear of the police remained although the remunerative nature of their sexual liaisons was less clear cut (see for instance Usama's case below).

The cases I have discussed thus far provide a glimpse into the myriad factors that inform young Egyptians' decisions to enter into 'urfi unions. Material barriers to conventional marriage feature in many of the narratives, as expected based on the existing literature. However, in a considerable number of other cases, 'urfi marriage was motivated by parental objections to the young person's choice of partner, by men's desire to hide a second wife from a first wife, by women's effort to preserve pensions they would lose if they married conventionally, by women's desire to maintain custody of their children, or by the need to legitimize sex work.

'Urfi Marriage as a Result of Permissive Sexual Values

A second assertion found in the existing public discourse and scholarly work on 'urfi marriage is that such unions are merely a legal and religious cover for "premarital" or "extramarital" sex among young people, whose values differ markedly from that of previous generations or from mainstream society (al-Daryūwīsh 2005, 88; Fawzī 2000, 51; Hasso 2011, 87; Ḥusayn 1999, 94; Ibn Maḥmūd 2004, 89). Some scholars further attribute young people's permissive sexual values to deficient knowledge of religion or cultural mores (al-Daryūwīsh 2005, 89; Ḥusayn 1999, 94; Ibn Maḥmūd 2004, 89; ʿUmrān 2001, 73).

In contrast to the literature from Egypt, my findings suggest that the parties to ʿurfi unions almost universally aspire to enter into conventional marriages someday. When asked whether they would like to marry and have a home and family one day, almost all the respondents replied "of course." In spite of their present choice to marry secretly, most young Egyptians continue to value conventional marriage, which remains the ideal framework for sexual intimacy, a claim I return to in the section on ʿurfi marriage as a substitute for conventional marriage. The one case that presented an exception to this pattern of not aspiring to a conventional marriage someday bears mentioning because of the female respondent's unusual views and circumstances.

Ghada's Story

Ghada was a thirty-three-year-old graduate of a post-secondary technical institute from Cairo. As a teenager she was sent to live with her maternal grandfather who was ill and needed someone to care for him. In return, Ghada's grandfather left her his apartment and arranged for her to receive his pension payments after his death. She has since become estranged from her widowed mother and siblings; Ghada feels they resent the inheritance she received from her grandfather. After her grandfather died, Ghada began working as a social worker in a nearby school. There she met and became romantically involved with Mohammad, another employee at the school, who was married with three children. They eventually entered into an ʿurfi marriage. Ghada sold her grandfather's apartment and bought and furnished an apartment in a faraway suburb, where no one knew either of them. This anonymity was important because Mohammad feared that his wife would file for a divorce if she found out, and Ghada feared that her mother might report her marriage to the pension office if she found out.

Unlike the other respondents in this sample, Ghada had no wish to have children. Ghada did not hope to formalize her marriage someday, largely because of the absence of the desire to have children and because she was content to share her husband with another woman. In that respect, her aspirations were unique in this sample, where the remaining respondents all expressed a desire to marry conventionally in the future.[4]

The assertion that 'urfi marriage is concentrated among young people, and particularly urban university students raises the possibility that they constitute a subculture that rejects the sexual mores of mainstream Egyptian society. There was limited evidence of this in my data. Only two respondents described belonging to a community of peers in which 'urfi marriage was regarded as normative.

Usama's Story

Usama was a twenty-five-year-old Cairene with a degree from a postsecondary technical institute. He lived alone in a rental apartment, in a neighborhood far away from that of his parents and siblings. He managed a cabaret and was married 'urfi to two belly dancers, neither of whom knew about his relationship with the other. Usama explained that for him and for others in his professional milieu, sexual relations outside of marriage were commonplace and normal.

Usama was the only respondent in my sample who did not oppose sexual intimacy outside of wedlock. He described two very practical benefits of having an 'urfi marriage as opposed to a sexual relationship without marriage: the fact that his wives could avoid unwanted male attention in the environment of the cabaret by saying that they were married and the fact that he could present an 'urfi marriage contract to the police if he was stopped together with one of his wives.

Like Usama, twenty-one-year-old Shaimaa also associated with a social circle in which 'urfi marriages were seen as socially acceptable.

————————————*Shaimaa's Story*————————————

Shaimaa was from Minya and she attended university in the nearby governorate of Beni Suef, where she met and fell in love with her classmate Waleed. Waleed proposed marriage to Shaimaa's father, but he was rejected because of his difficult financial situation. After that, Shaimaa and Waleed were encouraged to marry 'urfi by the fact that four of her closest girlfriends at the university and many others were in 'urfi marriages. Shaimaa explained that among her university peers, 'urfi marriage was necessary to legitimize physical contact between men and women: "When [Waleed] would try to hold my hand in front of our friends and I would say no, he would say it's normal among our friends. I would say, 'no, those couples are married 'urfi and they're planning to marry formally [*rasmy*].' And he would always say, 'I don't want to do anything to upset God, and ['urfi marriage] is the solution, and I know that God willing you will be mine.'"

Like Usama, Shaimaa recognized that outside of a particular social milieu, 'urfi marriage was stigmatized as far from respectable and sexual activity within 'urfi marriage was seen as a serious taboo. Like Usama, Shaimaa kept her 'urfi relationships secret from her parents and siblings. Shaimaa's father had beaten her on several occasions when acquaintances reported that they had seen Shaimaa with Waleed in public, so it was clear to her that dire consequences would result if she was found out to be sexually active. Still, she hoped to wed Waleed openly someday, perhaps after he graduated and traveled abroad to make money. Usama also planned to marry someone outside of "the profession" of cabaret work conventionally someday with the blessings of his family.

The hard symbolic boundary between 'urfi and conventional marriage was reinforced by the extensive precautions all respondents reported taking to avoid being found out to be sexually active in an 'urfi union, including carefully hiding their 'urfi marriage contracts, deleting messages from their mobile phones, and using various contraceptive methods. Until they found partners with whom they would enter into conventional marriages (as in the case of Usama), or until they converted their 'urfi marriages into conventional marriages (as hoped by Shaimaa and Waleed), young people took wide-ranging measures to keep their 'urfi unions a secret.

'Urfi Marriage as a Substitute for Conventional Marriage

A third claim found in the literature is that 'urfi marriage is a substitute for conventional marriage. Singerman and Ibrahim (2001, 86) and Singerman (2007, 31) draw on economic theory to argue that when something becomes unattainable because of the costly outlays associated with it, substitutes will be found to replace it at a lower cost. Thus conventional marriage, and the taxing financial obligations that come with it, has as its substitute 'urfi marriage. However, my data indicate that young people, having eliminated the possibility of conventional marriage or having never considered conventional marriage in the first place, most often compared 'urfi marriage to the alternative of sex outside of marriage.

Consider the case of 'Essam, the microbus driver discussed above. Knowing that he would be turned away by Amany's father, before 'Essam proposed conventional marriage, he tried to persuade Amany to have sex, which he referred to with the euphemism "a relationship that would be illicit or sinful [haram]." Similarly, Ghada spoke of her inability to control her desire before her marriage to Mohammad: "I started becoming attached to [him], and I couldn't take it. . . . At first our relationship was normal. He used to ask after me and I was happy and excited that he was asking after me. After that I began to have impulses [*gharaez*] and feelings and other needs. These things were inside of me and I wanted this man especially, not just anyone. No, I wanted this man to practice my femininity with." Ghada's fear of committing adultery led her to take the initiative in suggesting an 'urfi marriage to Mohammad. In both these cases, sex outside of marriage was the initial course of action considered before the alternative of 'urfi marriage was conceived of.

Not only is there a hard distinction between 'urfi and conventional marriage, but most respondents characterized 'urfi unions as inferior to conventional marriages in a number of ways. For one, the majority of respondents labeled 'urfi marriages as either wrong, illegal, immoral, religiously proscribed, or a combination of these attributes. Consider the example of Mo'men, a Cairene who reported that some sexual contact had occurred between him and his 'urfi wife prior to their marriage. But Mo'men refused to "continue doing wrong" and he seemed to suggest that his secret marriage had cleared his conscience somewhat. However, in the same interview he was unequivocal in his conviction that 'urfi marriage was haram. He reasoned that 'urfi marriages create all sorts of social problems (such as children whose paternity is unknown, and women who are unable to prove that their sexual relationships were legitimate), and as a result God has forbidden it. Of his own marriage he said, "Yes, it's haram, and God forgive me, but at least it's there." Another respondent, Ahmad from Minya, described his 'urfi union by saying "it is a marriage *shar'an* but not *qanoonan*," that is, it was a marriage according to the shari'a, but not according to the laws of the Egyptian personal status code. Ahmad held this view in spite of the fact that he had his 'urfi marriage contract drawn up by a lawyer. Huda from Cairo characterized 'urfi marriage as wrong (*ghalat*) because she was doing something behind her family's back, although 'urfi marriage itself was religiously permissible (*halal*).

'Urfi marriages were regarded as inferior to conventional marriages for other reasons. Respondents contrasted the temporariness of secret unions with the stability and permanence of conventional unions. Men, but more often women, considered 'urfi marriage as coming with its own costs, even if it did represent sex on the cheap. In a society that views sex outside of conventional marriage as particularly taboo for women, the reputational and physical dangers of being found out cannot be overstated. Women in my sample spoke of the liability involved in losing their virginity (or as many put it, becoming a *madam* rather than a *bint*), and the need to resort to hymen repair surgery if they failed to convert their 'urfi marriages to conventional marriages. Beyond that, women face the prospect of being refused a divorce by their 'urfi husbands and having to either remain unmarried conventionally or to seek marital dissolution of their 'urfi unions through the courts. If they become pregnant, they run the risk of their children's paternity being denied (with all the difficulties that entails in terms of registering the "illegitimate" child and obtaining educational and health services for the child). 'Urfi unions therefore involved risks that were highly gendered.

'Urfi marriage may represent a means that deviates from those sanctioned by mainstream society to achieve the ends of a committed sexual partnership, but it is an imperfect substitute. The meanings associated with 'urfi unions include the belief in their immorality, their temporariness, and, for women in particular, their riskiness—all attributes that are not believed to apply to conventional marriages.

The Gendered Relationship between Sex and Marriage

This study provides evidence that both confirms and challenges claims that can be found in the existing literature. In addition, this study offers new insights into the gendered nature of the relationship between sex and marriage in the Egyptian context. Specifically, some couples who had encountered obstacles to a conventional marriage reported that their 'urfi marriages were an act of defiance that would force the bride's family to accept a conventional marriage once the 'urfi marriage was revealed.

─────────────────────'Emad's Story─────────────────────

'Emad was a twenty-three-year-old accounting student who was in love with Rasha. In his final year of his undergraduate studies in Minya, 'Emad visited Rasha's father to propose marriage to his daughter. 'Emad told her father that they were peers at the university and that his financial situation was good, but her father surprised him with his response. Her father said he does not have any girls for marriage now and that he considered students children who still take an allowance from their parents and therefore shouldn't marry now. 'Emad therefore returned to see Rasha's father after graduating and her father then revealed that there was a relative from his family that he wanted this daughter to marry. 'Emad was very humiliated and provoked by her father's response. When asked what motivated him to marry secretly, 'Emad said, "I mean, the situation became a matter of stubbornness [*'end*]. [Her father's relative] is no better than me and she loves me and so I couldn't let her slip through my fingers. . . . So the alternative solution [to marrying formally] was to present her father with a fait accompli [*amr waqe'*], and there was no other way [but 'urfi marriage]." 'Emad explained that once Rasha finished her studies, they planned to tell her mother (who was opposed to her marriage to the relative) that they were in an 'urfi marriage, and Rasha's mother would persuade Rasha's father to agree that they wed conventionally. If this did not work, 'Emad said that they would have to confront Rasha's father with the truth, even though 'Emad feared that her father would react violently and take his anger out on his daughter. However, his fear for his daughter's reputation and his knowledge that she could no longer wed anyone else conventionally would cause her father to come around eventually. 'Emad said that he wanted to have a big wedding that would treat his wife like she was a girl (*bint*) who was getting married for the first time.

'Emad portrayed himself as cornered into resorting to an 'urfi union in order to attain his ultimate goal, namely, a conventional marriage. Other respondents reported slightly different circumstances, but they still planned to present the bride's family with a fait accompli. For example, in some instances, the groom had not yet approached the bride's family, but he intended to publicize the 'urfi marriage if the bride's family pressured her to accept another suitor. In general, this strategy for converting an 'urfi marriage into a conventional marriage was most often articulated by men, who have less to lose from such a course of action.

In my sample, only three cases actually transitioned to conventional marriage after an 'urfi union, and all of them were from Minya.[5] In twenty-four-year-old university graduate Sarah's case, the 'urfi marriage was never revealed. At the time of interview, Sarah reported being formally engaged to marry a man whose secret marriage with her had preceded the formal engagement. Her husband had proposed conventional marriage and was rejected by her family because of his limited means and student status, but he was told to come back when he was ready, which he did after working in the Gulf. In two other cases, the 'urfi marriage was found out when the female partner became pregnant, thus forcing the hand of her parents, who wanted to avert a scandal. However, rebelling against parental control with a secret marriage only to reveal it at a later date came with disadvantages for the bride.

Marwa's Story

Marwa, a nineteen-year-old with a vocational secondary school degree, was formally engaged to Sayyed when they decided to enter into an 'urfi union. The couple reasoned that an 'urfi marriage would be useful if her mother acted on her opposition to the match. When

Marwa discovered that she was pregnant, she and Sayyed confronted their parents with the truth. They quickly threw a wedding party and the couple had been married conventionally and living in a room in Sayyed's parents' apartment for a year and a half at the time of interview. However, Marwa spoke bitterly about the fact that her mother (who was divorced from Marwa's father, who never found out about the 'urfi marriage) was forced to pay for Marwa's furniture and wedding expenses, which are customarily provided by the groom. Marwa also complained of her disempowerment vis-à-vis her in-laws, who regarded her with contempt for having been sexually active outside of a conventional marriage.

As Marwa's case illustrates, entering into an 'urfi marriage with the intention of later revealing it to force the hand of recalcitrant parents has material and relational downsides for the women involved. Marwa's mother bore the financial obligations of conventional marriage typically borne by the groom, and Marwa herself suffers a fraught relationship with her in-laws because of her transgressive 'urfi marriage. These factors may represent further reasons why men were more likely than women to mention this strategy for achieving a publicly recognized match. Regardless of whether or not the strategy of coercing the bride's disapproving family succeeds, the frequency with which respondents reported adopting this strategy suggests that 'urfi marriage is perceived to be a stepping stone to conventional marriage.

Another way the meanings of 'urfi marriage are gendered has to do with symbolic interpretations of what an agreement to enter into an 'urfi union signifies. Women understood it as signaling their love and commitment to the relationship.

Huda's Story

Huda, a thirty-year-old university graduate from Cairo, was in an 'urfi marriage until four years before our interview. Her husband never came to propose to her brothers (her parents are deceased) for a variety of reasons—first because he was in and out of work and could not afford conventional marriage, then because his younger sister was getting married and all the family resources were diverted to her, and then because his father was hospitalized. But when he suggested a secret marriage, Huda agreed because "he wanted to guarantee that I would be his, because he considered my refusal [of the 'urfi marriage] to mean that I was abandoning him because of his circumstances." Huda eventually realized that she was being strung along, and they divorced. She subsequently found out that her ex-husband was conventionally married with children. Huda herself had stopped getting marriage proposals because of her age, and she said that no one would agree to marry her if they knew about her past.

Huda interpreted her agreement to marry 'urfi as a sign that she would remain devoted to her partner throughout his difficult circumstances, and until he was able to marry her conventionally. In spite of her disappointment with her own situation, Huda was better off than Nadia, whose 'urfi husband refused to divorce her.

Nadia's Story

Nadia was a thirty-two-year-old university graduate, and she entered into an 'urfi marriage with Hossam, who was very hard hit by the January twenty-fifth uprising of 2011, which had caused him to lose all his savings and to fall into debt. Hossam suggested that they enter into an 'urfi union, and Nadia, sensitive to his feelings of insecurity and wanting to prove her love, submitted to his wishes. She explained, "He really needed me a lot more and he felt that I might leave him at any moment, and so I decided to show him that I would stand by him." However, after more than a year of 'urfi marriage and about a month prior to the interview, Nadia found out that Hossam's parents had nominated a bride for him and that he had agreed to move ahead with a formal engagement. When Nadia confronted him, Hossam said that he could not propose conventional marriage to her because his socially conservative parents would disapprove of the fact that they had gotten to know one another outside of a formal engagement. Yet he refused to divorce Nadia because he said that he still loved her. Nadia characterized Hossam's refusal to divorce her as a bind (*warta*) because this would leave her in limbo, unable to marry anyone else.

Like Huda, Nadia demonstrated her dedication to cash-strapped Hossam with a 'urfi union. While women saw 'urfi marriage as a way to reassure their partners of their commitment, some of the men saw a woman's willingness to enter into 'urfi marriage as a sign that she was unfit for conventional marriage.

————————————*Sa'eed's Story*————————————

Sa'eed, a twenty-six-year-old university graduate from Cairo, speculated that girls enter into 'urfi marriages either because they are weak or because they are deviant (*munhalleen*). In his own case, his ex-wife's willingness to marry him in secret was evidence of her dishonesty. If she could do such a thing behind her parents' back, he reasoned, how could he trust her with his home and children? Although his original plan was to conventionally marry his 'urfi wife once he could afford it, Sa'eed later divorced his 'urfi wife and became engaged to his cousin. He said, "When I got older and thought about the matter, I found that a girl who submits herself in that way and goes with a young man to an apartment could go with anyone and do anything. When it comes time to marry [conventionally], one looks for a girl from a [good] family. I mean, I'm going to marry my cousin, and she is very religiously observant and from a good home, and I can guarantee that because we were raised together since we were infants."

For Sa'eed, a woman who agreed to marry 'urfi was fundamentally lacking in morality and trustworthiness. Similarly, when we asked twenty-eight-year-old plumber Diaa from Cairo whether he would marry his 'urfi wife conventionally, he replied, "it never crossed my mind." When asked what it would take for him to marry her conventionally, he said, "if I know that she is walking on the straight and narrow path," later elaborating that he would need to ascertain that she had never done with other men what she did with him. For their part, women are not unaware of this attitude that interprets sex within 'urfi marriage as evidence that a woman is sexually promiscuous or unfaithful. For example, Shaimaa from Minya said, "A boy can be going with you and he pampers you and everything. Then he gets bored, and he feels like it came easily, and he'll say if she did it with me, she'll do it with other people too."

Conclusion

On a practical level, conventional marriage in Egypt is the gateway to residential independence and regular access to a sexual partner. On a symbolic level, conventional marriage is a marker of financial success, social adulthood (Singerman 2007, 7), and social respectability (El Feki 2013; Wynn 2018). As a type of conjugal union, secret 'urfi marriage affords sexual intimacy to young Egyptians but none of the positive social meanings, roles, or entitlements of conventional marriage. Those who enter into 'urfi unions knowingly break from socially acceptable sexual conduct and settle for a form of marriage that is regarded as inferior. They do so in large part because of the insurmountable material and social obstacles in the way of conventional marriage, and because of their own objections to sex outside of some kind of marital union, however questionable it may be.

This chapter has shown that the meanings associated with 'urfi marriages are gendered in important ways. Although both types of unions offer sexual expression, women in my sample considered 'urfi marriage to be inferior to conventional marriage more frequently than men did. This was likely because women recognized that they disproportionately bear the risks associated with having sex outside of conventional marriage. These risks include the fact that their 'urfi husbands might interpret their willingness to participate in an 'urfi marriage, which women consider to be a token of love, as indicating that they are unsuitable for conventional marriage.

It is worth noting here that women's vulnerability to the risks inherent to 'urfi marriages ironically stems, in large part, from their inability to secure the protection of the patriarchal family. Egyptian women in conventional marriages often use their male relatives to pressure or police their husbands, or they rely on their natal families to provide economic backing in the event of abuse or abandonment. Because of the secret nature of their marriages, women in 'urfi unions cannot avail themselves of these forms of support. Thus, patriarchy can be recast as a resource women can draw upon to mitigate the risks inherent to the unequal institution of marriage (Salem 2018, 417). The "pleasures of patriarchy," as some have put it, include the important privilege of having male kin who will defend women against the whims of their husbands, a privilege that women in secret unions lack access to.

ACKNOWLEDGMENTS

I would like to thank Amal Refaat for recruiting and interviewing respondents and Zeinab Ali for transcribing the audio recordings for this study. I am also grateful for Laila Murad's assistance in reviewing the Arabic literature on 'urfi marriage.

NOTES

1. "Chinese gold" refers to fake gold in colloquial Egyptian Arabic.
2. I have converted all Egyptian pound values to 2012 US dollars.
3. I use pseudonyms throughout and have masked or redacted other identifying information.
4. Ghada was one of the few respondents who insisted that her actions were morally sound. According to Ghada, marriage in Islam requires *ishhar*, public acknowledgment of the union, and she says that her neighbors know they are married. She pointed out that all the other conditions for a valid marriage contract in Islam were met by her 'urfi marriage. Ghada felt no guilt for not informing her family because they were not much of a family anyway and she reasoned that the secrecy of their marriage was merely a practical matter.
5. It may be that this strategy was more effective in the more socially conservative setting of Upper Egypt, but there were too few cases to make this more than a speculation.

REFERENCES

Abaza, Mona. 2001. "Perceptions of 'Urfi Marriage in the Egyptian Press." *International Institute for the Study of Islam in the Modern World (ISIM) Newsletter*, no. 7: 20–21.

Abdalla, Mustafa. 2015. "Challenged Masculinities: Sexuality, 'Urfi Marriage, and the State in Dahab, Egypt." In *Gender and Sexuality in Muslim Cultures*, edited by Gul Ozyegin, 37–54. New York: Routledge.

'Abdallah, Mo'taz Sayyed, and Jom'a Sayyed Yousef. 2004. *Al-Zawaj al-'Urfi: Waqi'ah wa Atharoh al-Nafsiyya wa al-Ijtima'iyyah*. Al-Qahira: Matbou'at Markaz al-Buhuth wa al-Dirasat al- Ijtima'iyyah, Kulliyat al-Adab, Jame'at al-Qahira.

al-Ashqar, Usāmah 'Umar Sulaymān. 2000. *Mustajaddāt fiqhīyah fī qaḍāyā al-zawāj wa-al-ṭalāq: Zawāj al-misyār, al-zawāj al-'urfī, al-faḥṣ al-ṭibbī, al-zawāj bi-nīyat al-ṭalāq*. 'Ammān: Dār al-Nafā'is.

al-Daryūwīsh, Aḥmad ibn Yūsuf ibn Aḥmad. 2005. *al-Zawāj al-'urfī: Ḥaqīqatuh, wa-aḥkāmuh, wa-āthāruh, wa-al-ankiḥah dhāta al-ṣilah bihi: Dirāsah fiqhīyah muqāranah*. al-Riyāḍ: Dār al-'Āṣimah lil-Nashr wa-al-Tawzī'.

Bernard-Maugiron, Nathalie. 2010. *Personal Status Laws in Egypt: FAQ*. Cairo: Deutsche Gesellschaft fur Technische Zusammenarbeit (GTZ).

El Feki, Shereen. 2013. *Sex and the Citadel: Intimate Life in a Changing Arab World*. Toronto: Doubleday Canada.

Eum, Ikran. 2005. "Urfi Marriage, an Egyptian Version of Cohabitation?" *Al-Raida* XXI–XXII 106-107: 64–69.

Fawzī, Mahmud. 2000. *al-Zawāj al-'urfī: al-Zawāj al-sirrī!* Madīnat al-Sādis min Uktubir: Nahḍat Miṣr.

Hasso, Frances. 2011. *Consuming Desires: Family Crisis and the State in the Middle East.* Stanford, CA: Stanford University Press.

Ḥusayn, Yāsir. 1999. *al-Zawāj al-sirrī fī Miṣr wa-al-Khalīj.* Cairo: al-Taḥaddī lil-Nashr wa-al-Iʻlām.

Ibn Maḥmūd, Jamal Ibn Mohamed. 2004. *al-Zawāj al-'urfī fī mīzān al-Islām.* Beirut: Dār al-Kutub al-'Ilmīyah.

Karkabi, Nadeem. 2011. "Couples in the Global Margins: Sexuality and Marriage between Egyptian Men and Western Women in South Sinai." *Anthropology of the Middle East* 6, no. 1: 79–97.

Salem, Rania. 2018. "Matrimonial Transactions and the Enactment of Class and Gender Difference among Egyptian Youth." *Qualitative Sociology* 41, no. 3: 399–421.

———. 2016. "Imagined Crises: Assessing Evidence of Delayed Marriage and Never-Marriage in Contemporary Egypt." In *Domestic Tensions, National Anxieties: Global Perspectives on Marriage Crisis,* edited by Kristin Celello and Hanan Kholoussy, 231–54. Oxford: Oxford University Press.

———. 2015. "Changes in the Institution of Marriage in Egypt from 1998 to 2012." In *The Egyptian Labor Market in an Era of Revolution,* edited by Ragui Assaad and Caroline Krafft, 162–81. Oxford: Oxford University Press.

Shahrani, Shahreena. 2010. *The Social (Re)Construction of 'Urfi Marriage.* MA Thesis, Ohio State University.

Singerman, Diane. 2007. *The Economic Imperatives of Marriage: Emerging Practices and Identities among Youth in the Middle East.* Middle East Youth Initiative Working Paper 6. Washington, DC: Middle East Youth Initiative, Brookings Institution.

Singerman, Diane, and Barbara Ibrahim. 2003. "The Costs of Marriage in Egypt: A Hidden Dimension in the New Arab Demography." *Cairo Papers in Social Science* 24, no. 1: 80–116.

Sonneveld, Nadia. 2012. "Rethinking the Difference between Formal and Informal Marriages in Egypt." In *Family Law in Islam: Divorce, Marriage and Women in the Muslim World,* edited by M. Voorhoeve, 53–77. London: I.B. Tauris.

'Umrān, Fāris Muḥammad. 2001. *al-Zawāj al-'urfī: Wa-ṣuwar ukhrá lil-zawāj ghayr al-rasmī.* Cairo: Majmūʻat al-Nīl al-'Arabīyah.

Walby, Joanne. 2010. "Extended Holiday in Hurghada: Russian Migrant Women and 'Urfi Marriage." *Surfacing* 3, no. 1: 39–70.

Wynn, L. L. 2018. *Love, Sex, and Desire in Modern Egypt: Navigating the Margins of Respectability.* Austin: University of Texas Press, 2018.

———. 2016. "'Like a Virgin': Hymenoplasty and Secret Marriage in Egypt." *Medical Anthropology* 35, no. 6: 547–59.

Zuhur, Sherifa. 2003. "Women and Empowerment in the Arab World." *Arab Studies Quarterly* 25, no. 4: 17–38.

CHAPTER 8

For Us, There Is No Love

Becoming "American" and the Politics of Intimacy

MORGEN A. CHALMIERS

She came in here at the age of seventeen, asking for infertility treatments. She'd been married at the mosque at fifteen—that's how they always do it—and she was trying to get pregnant. She's still a child! That's what we told her—your body just isn't mature yet. Then—can you imagine?!— she came back, threatening to call her insurance, threatening to sue us! The problem is that they want to live a Syrian life in America. (Mardina, healthcare professional)

This narrative arose during one of my conversations with Mardina, a healthcare professional who works regularly with the Syrian refugee community in Southern California. Mardina's account casts Syrian refugees' reproductive desires as "deviant" and evokes the particular moral abhorrence associated with childhood sexuality (Giddens 1992, 21), most recently seen in public health literature on the practice referred to as child marriage among the Syrian refugee diaspora (Bartels et al. 2018; Charles and Denman 2013; Mourtada, Schlecht, and DeJong 2017).

Sensationalized accounts of Syrian refugees' "backward" sexualities and "oppressive" culture abound in clinical and humanitarian settings. These hyperbolic narratives echo wider, transnational discourses that construct Muslim women as victims of patriarchy who must be taught—often by white European-American feminists—to exercise their right to freedom, equality, and individual autonomy. While Mardina's sentiments certainly reflect common perceptions of Syrian women among healthcare professionals, few others had expressed their views quite so vehemently as Mardina. What was at stake for Mardina—an Iraqi, Christian refugee herself—in her depiction of Syrian refugees as so drastically "Other" and, by implication, so dramatically different from the two of us? By disavowing her patient's stated desire to "live a Syrian life in America," Mardina, who had been living in the US for nearly ten years, establishes a distinction between herself and the recently arrived Syrian refugees. Within this brief anecdote, she portrays Syrian refugees as irrationally conforming to social norms informed by a religion that, she suggests, is traditional, patriarchal, and antithetical to the values of an American life. In doing so, she is, of course, expressing a viewpoint that she truly holds yet, at the same time, she also affirms her own status as a properly assimilated refugee. Her repulsion and incredulity—however genuine—represent an affective process of self-fashioning through which the refugee becomes legible as a proper liberal subject by embracing normative American values surrounding love, marriage, and reproduction.

The imperative to perform this role arises within a larger political climate of heightened xenophobia, specifically toward refugees, and perhaps more acutely, through the power dynamics that shaped her interactions with me: a white medical student and American citizen by birth. Our shared membership in the medical community did nothing to lessen and, in fact, exacerbated the inequalities of race, class, and immigration status that shaped our relationship. The historical legacies of racism and patriarchy remain present within medicine today and create a particular onus for women, people of color, and—especially—women of color like Mardina to prove that they too can become one of the "Boys in White" (Becker 2002) or, at the very least, can emulate the normative values and comportment that characterize white, heterosexual masculinity. Even as a woman, my whiteness and American accent automatically function as indices of my legitimacy within the medical field. In contrast, despite her seniority as a clinician, as a woman of color with a heavy accent, Mardina experiences a constant pressure to prove her competence and frequently encounters xenophobic, racist stereotypes that I will never face. Thus contextualized, her account must be interpreted not only in relation to the specific forms of Islamophobia that characterize contemporary political discourse but also in light of the overlapping imperatives to affirm her authority as a clinician and to perform her identity as a properly assimilated, Christian refugee.[1] She achieves both these goals by insistently espousing the quint-essential liberal values of freedom, autonomy, and equality.

Within the realm of love, intimacy, and sexuality, these Enlightenment values coalesce in what Giddens has termed the "pure relationship," char-acterized by two autonomous individuals consenting to remain in intimate relation with one another for as long as it serves their respective self-inter-ests (Giddens 1992, 49–64). Liberal ideals of freedom and gendered equality define the pure relationship in explicit contrast to the imagined premodern society in which individual choice is constrained by tradition and social convention. These binaries co-produce the Western Subject of Rights and Orientalized Subject of Culture—the civilized and the savage—and, in doing so, justify continued Euro-American imperialism in the Middle East (Povinelli 2006; Abu-Lughod 1998, 2002).

Since the colonial period, Arab Muslim women have remained a fetishized object of Orientalist fantasy, simultaneously sexualized, as in the Western imaginary of the harem, and patronized, as victims of an Indigenous patriarchy whose rights must be defended by a white, secu-lar savior. In the same vein, Muslim refugee intimacies, whether conju-gal, extramarital, normative, or nonconventional, are often imagined as potential sites of gendered oppression and thus perpetually defined as a problem to be solved (Espiritu 2014; Espiritu and Duong 2018) through humanitarian intervention.

I open this chapter by quoting Mardina because her words represent much more than one individual's opinion. Her accusation—"they want to live a Syrian life in America"—reflects a fundamental logic that under-girds the work of many organizations and individuals seeking to support resettled refugees. That is, while innocuous forms of cultural difference enrich the proverbial American melting pot and thus are allowed—even encouraged—to persist in the name of diversity, refugees' willingness to internalize, endorse, and assimilate to certain core American values is nec-essarily the rubric against which "successful resettlement" is defined and evaluated.[2] This chapter illustrates how these core values are intertwined with normative ideals of love and marriage practices and presents an eth-nographic example of one woman's attempts to navigate the imperatives she encounters to articulate her marital relationship in terms congruent with these core values.

This chapter explores the ways in which these hegemonic norms continue to inform evaluations of Syrian refugees' deservingness and success after resettlement. I focus specifically on the experiences of a married couple, whom I call Rima and Khalil, that I came to know over twelve months of ethnographic fieldwork with Syrian refugees in Southern California. This account illustrates how refugee encounters with disciplinary institutions, specifically the clinic, are frequently structured by the demand that they affirm their deservingness as properly assimilated sexual subjects by performing love in ways that reflect liberal ideals of autonomy in intimate relationship.

At the same time, my in-depth description of Rima's experience is certainly not a representation of any monolithic "Syrian" or "Muslim" attitude toward love and marriage. Following Narayan's call for feminists to problematize "static picture[s] of culture by insisting on a historical understanding of the contexts in which what are currently taken to be 'particular cultures' came to be seen and defined as such" (1998, 92), the chapter provides some elementary background on the larger structural and historical conditions that have in part, but certainly not exclusively, shaped Rima's values not only as a Muslim, Syrian woman but as an individual from a specific class background and particular region within Syria itself.

Context, Setting, and Positionality

"Have you ever had a miscarriage?" I looked over at Rima who, in turn, looked to her husband Khalil. "No," he responded in Arabic, "no, nothing ever like that." Rima nodded silently in agreement. The medical assistant had stopped typing and was watching curiously, clearly puzzled by the unlikely trio: Khalil, answering my questions attentively as I helped them fill out the intake forms, his wife Rima, whose pregnant belly was concealed by the loose folds of her black abaya, and me, a blonde university student who—at the age of twenty-nine—is frequently asked to present identification when buying movie tickets for an R-rated film. Five months later, when I knocked on the door of Rima's hospital room in the maternity ward, the nurse would insist that I was mistaken and must have misunderstood the room number.

The three of us sat alone in the waiting room at the prenatal clinic, where Rima had recently transferred her care. She had been frustrated by the long wait times at the local health center, but more than anything, she was offended and angry that the physician had asked her husband to leave the room during one of her appointments and requested that Rima come alone to future visits. Although I hadn't been present on that occasion, I could easily imagine why. My own initial reaction had been one of annoyance and even concern when Khalil consistently answered for Rima, listing her medications, obstetric history, even the date of her last menstrual period. No matter how emphatically I directed my gaze and my questions to Rima, she continued to look to her husband for confirmation. From the perspective of medical providers trained to look for signs of intimate partner violence, Khalil's behavior could be seen as overly controlling, even obsessive, and potentially indicative of domestic abuse.

The ethnographic anecdotes presented here recount the intersubjective processes of representation and interpretation through which communication takes place between doctors and patients, anthropologists and interlocutors, or even, I would argue, between any two individuals. My goal here is not to redeem the Muslim refugee subject by offering evidence of her agency within a marital relationship nor is it to provide an essentializing account of "Syrian" forms of love that aims to refute stereotypes about the patriarchal nature of Islam or Arab culture.[3]

Nevertheless, readers will notice an obvious contrast between the assumptions that Mardina and other providers made about Rima's relationship with Khalil and the interactions that I observed and describe here. I do not include these latter scenes for the purpose of providing counterexamples to the widespread stereotypes about Syrian women's intimate lives that characterize hegemonic discourses about Muslim refugees. Participating in such a debate would only reinforce the false, essentializing notion that there is some stable, culturally specific affective experience of love shared by Syrians (or, for that matter, Americans). Furthermore, to dignify assumptions rooted in American racism and Islamophobia by engaging them as valid arguments for debate would be to perpetuate the violence these structures enact. Instead, I seek to emulate and respect what I later identify as Rima's refusal (McGranahan 2016; Simpson 2007; Tuck and Yang 2014) to respond to the question of her agency within and beyond her marital relationship, a question that has remained central to scholarship and popular discourse on Muslim women for over a century (Bilge 2010; Chapman 2016; Glapka 2018).

Despite this disclaimer, I remain wary of the potential for the ethnographic anecdotes presented here to be read as redemptive assurances that Rima and Khalil's marriage reflects the ideals of mutual affection, respect, and autonomy that characterize the pure relationship. Nevertheless, I include detailed descriptions that portray the complexity of their relationship in order to avoid producing an account that reduces my interlocutors to one-dimensional subjects of Foucauldian governance and biomedical discipline. In doing so, I hope to harness the potential of ethnographic specificity (Abu-Lughod 2008) to both interrogate the processes through which hegemonic power structures enact violence against the individual and to illustrate the ways that individual is always more than the overdetermined, acted-upon object of power by attending to the contextual particularities of her subjectivity and lived experience.

"In through the Door and not through the Window"

I first met Rima in September 2018. She had heard about my research on reproductive health from a friend and had agreed to participate. Near the end of our first interview, when I asked if she hoped to become pregnant again, she responded with excitement: "Yes, I want to. I've been thinking about having my IUD [intrauterine device] removed." During our second meeting, I returned to the topic of contraception and she mentioned that she had visited the local health center and asked the clinician to remove the IUD in hopes that she might soon become pregnant.

In contrast to the shy, reserved behavior that I would later notice in clinical settings when she asked me to drive and accompany her to her prenatal appointments, at home Rima was bubbly and laughed often. However, when we met several months later for a third interview, she appeared especially cheerful and greeted me with a beaming smile, clearly excited to share the happy news: a test from the 99-cent store had revealed that she was pregnant. As we celebrated over coffee and sweets, I asked how her husband felt about the pregnancy. "He was very happy," she replied. "He bought me the [pregnancy] test. He's really excited because he's the main one that wanted it." I was taken aback by this new information but reluctant to offend Rima by pointing out what seemed, at least to me, to be the contradictions between this more recent narrative and her original assertion that the decision to pursue pregnancy had been her own.

I wondered if the shift from her initial representations of the pregnancy as her idea to her current assertion that it was mainly her husband who wanted another child was reflective of a mode of relationality described by Suad Joseph (2005) in which desires are not necessarily understood as emanating from the individual psyche but rather are co-constructed within intimate relationships. While liberal moral frameworks idealize—even fetishize—the pure relationship (Giddens 1992, 49–65) between two autonomous individuals, Joseph (2005) has illustrated how other ways of intimate relationality are more highly valued within many social worlds across the Middle East. Desire, she argues, arises within and is intersubjectively shaped by the relational context and, in turn, by the social, cultural, and religious ideologies that structure it.

This form of intimacy is quite distinct from the pure relationship, which remains deeply informed by the liberal logic of the contract (Giddens 1992, 184–203). Within the pure relationship, each individual identifies her own needs, requests her partner's support in meeting them, and evaluates the "health" or value of the relationship through the partner's ability to meet these needs over time, as is clearly evident in the prolific body of contemporary American self-help literature. In contrast, Joseph's ethnography demonstrates how, at her field site in Lebanon, an individual comes to recognize her own desires "as they [are] reflected, mirrored, or offered in the statements and actions of others" (2005, 86). Within this model, to love someone is not only to want what she wants but to attend to the relationship in such a way that overt requests or expressions of desire are unnecessary. A loving partner doesn't need to ask what the other wants—they come to know each other's desires (Ali 2002, 82) through thoughtful practices of care and, crucially, do not identify these desires as belonging exclusively to one party but experience them as mutual. Love is not a spontaneous affective state that unexpectedly overcomes the rational individual but rather an attentional practice that must be continually and thoughtfully cultivated.

Of course, as Joseph (2005) points out, her characterization of relational desire reflects an ideal toward which her interlocutors aspire and does not imply that these ideals are necessarily or consistently achieved. Like the pure relationship described by Giddens, relational desire functions as a model against which intimate relationships are evaluated. To identify Rima's seemingly contradictory accounts of who had desired the pregnancy as reflecting the norms of relational intimacy is not to negate the possibility that she could also have felt pressured to pursue pregnancy.

In my field notes following our interview, I described feeling conflicted about the significance of her statement. I worried that she had been trying to begin a discussion about feeling pressured to become pregnant and, in my attempts to avoid interpreting her statement through my own ethnocentric framework, I had inadvertently refused to listen.

Several months later, Rima and I were driving back from another prenatal appointment. She indulged my persistent questions as we drove, listening to Fares Karam. We had to pause the music frequently to answer her husband's phone calls. He was at home preparing lunch for us and their four children and video-called Rima at least every ten minutes to ask her about the best way to cook the relatively simple meal. It seemed to me that, as much as he may have needed cooking advice, he also missed her and was impatiently awaiting our arrival.

As we drove, Rima laughed at her nosy anthropologist friend as I continued to pester her about her perceptions of the clinical care she had received. She was largely unimpressed with American doctors, whom she felt relied on numerous, seemingly unnecessary tests compared to physicians back in Syria, where she had carried four pregnancies to term without complication. Overall, however, she was generally happy with the care she was receiving, other than the inconvenience caused by the frequent checkups, blood draws, urinalyses, and ultrasound scans that she was required to complete to ensure her access to the greater level of respect "compliant" patients are typically afforded.

Rima was highly cognizant of the ways the gendered norms that inform her social, religious, and cultural practices have been politicized within transnational discourses about Muslim women. She recalled her previous visits to the local health center and once again expressed her annoyance with the physician who had asked her husband to leave the room. I asked her what she thought had motivated the request and she was quick to reply. "Racism," she stated matter-of-factly, "a type of racism against women who wear the hijab."

Later in the pregnancy, due to scheduling difficulties, her final ultrasound appointment was arranged at a clinic nearly forty miles away. A local social service organization had booked a car to take her to the clinic, where I would meet her and drive her home, stopping at Target on the way to shop for baby clothes and for pajamas for Rima to wear after the delivery. Khalil had called ahead to ensure a female driver would be available the morning of the appointment. Nevertheless, the car that arrived was driven by a male. Although Khalil was expected at the local grocery store where he worked stacking produce, he skipped his shift and drove Rima to the appointment himself so that she wouldn't be alone in the car with another man.

We had become close over the hours we spent together throughout her pregnancy and I was less nervous about offending Rima with questions related to sensitive topics. Driving back from the ultrasound, I asked her if she would have felt comfortable riding alone with a male driver. She seemed confused by the question and replied matter of factly, "My husband doesn't like it." I tried to ask again, insistently distinguishing between her husband's preferences and her own, "No, but if he didn't mind, if he wasn't opposed to it, would it make *you* uncomfortable?" She continued texting and repeated, "Khalil doesn't like it." I rephrased the question again, "But what about you? What do you think about it?" Perplexed by my failure to comprehend her response, she elaborated, "I don't like it because my husband doesn't like it." She was clearly uninterested in and, perhaps, unwilling to entertain the hypothetical scenario I had proposed.

Throughout our conversations, she resisted what I have now come to see as my attempts to understand her relationship with Khalil through interpretive frameworks founded upon the primacy of the autonomous individual. During one of my first visits to her home, I asked how she had met her husband. She laughed and remarked, "that's the first time a *mar'a ajnabia*"—a term directly translated as "a foreign woman" but used in the local context to refer to Americans—"has asked me that." She continued, "Us, we have customs and traditions. There is no love." She went on to describe the circumstances of her marriage to Khalil:

> His brother was in my seventh-grade class. He saw me and told his brother about me. After that, his family came to my house and asked my father about me. Over the next three months, he would visit me at home and we got to know each other. And that was the very normal way. Everyone in our area used to meet this way, through meetings between families. I think this is the best thing. The guy comes in through the door and not through the window. Everything under the frame of our religion and under God.

Liberal Modes of Intimacy and Their Alternatives

Her response is significant for several reasons. First, her reference to my position as an American woman alludes to the power differentials that structure our relationship. In emphasizing my identity as an American woman, she implicitly contextualizes our interactions in relation to transnational discursive tropes that construct Muslim women as victims who must be educated about their right to equality by white feminists. Immediately after, she goes on to contrast Syrians, who in her narrative have "customs and traditions," with an unidentified "Other." Though she doesn't make the comparison explicit, her initial comment seems to imply that this speculative Other represents, in fact, foreign (i.e., American) women like me.

Her statement that, in Syria, "there is no love" clearly refers to a specific type of premarital romantic or sexual intimacy rather than love as it is used more generally to describe feelings of affection toward friends and family. Yet her claim that Syrians have customs and traditions—not love—is explicit, unqualified, and unapologetic.

This claim takes on particular meanings when considered in the context of Syrian history and the recent struggle for revolution—the conflict that began in her hometown of Daraʻa and ultimately led to her displacement.[4] The state's historical attempts to transform women into particular types of gendered subjects take on a particular intensity in the postcolonial context, which has been characterized by a "deep crisis over how to find a path toward accepted forms of modernity and national identity" (Al-Ghazzi 2013, 598). These efforts arise out of a longer colonial history in which Muslim women's alleged subjugation was used as a justification for colonial rule.

The French and other colonial powers in the Middle East actively sought to reshape normative models of love, intimacy, and marriage through the promotion of the nuclear family (usra) over larger, extended kinship networks (ʻaʼla) (Hasso 2011; Fortier, Kreil, and Maffi 2016). Under colonial rule, dyadic forms of conjugal intimacy gained "unprecedented importance" and were defined in contrast to precolonial forms of love that viewed intimacy and dependence as characteristic not only of marital relations but, more importantly, of larger relations between extended family members (Fortier, Kreil, and Maffi 2018, 17). These ideals continue to inform love and marriage practices throughout the Middle East as illustrated by Allouche (2018) in her study of "inclusive intimacy" and Joseph (1994, 1997, 2010) in her description of "patriarchal connectivity."

As Povinelli (2006) suggests, colonial and contemporary imperial powers have historically distinguished between modern, egalitarian forms of intimate relations and alternative marriage practices that do not prioritize conjugal intimacy or romantic love between partners, emphasizing instead the function of ties cemented by marriage within larger webs of kinship networks. This binary constructs kinship obligations that fall outside the nuclear family as constraints upon individual freedom and autonomy—barriers to the reflexive project of self-discovery and self-actualization that liberalism mandates (Povinelli 2006, 4). The liberal model of love imagines the relationship as a contract (Giddens 1992, 182–203) that, by definition, requires that the individuals involved possess a certain degree of autonomy, an autonomy that is in direct tension with familial obligation. Claims made upon the individual through kinship are thus antithetical to Enlightenment ideals of self-determination, freedom, and autonomy (Povinelli 2006, 226–85). This logic informed colonial policies designed to educate women about their autonomy, for example in campaigns that "empowered" them to adopt biomedical methods of contraception independently of their husbands' or in-laws' desires for more children. These interventions were met with fierce resistance from the women, for whom the liberal model of the free individual did not resonate with and, in fact, directly contradicted the modes of relationality they experienced and valued (Ali 2002, 118).

Following decolonization, commitment to women's equality served as a central discourse through which the Syrian regime internationally asserted its claims to legitimacy.[5] In practice, this meant that "Syrian women had to be prised out of backwardness" so that they could properly represent the state's modernity and, to an extent, secularism (Rabo 2004, 169). At times of extreme political tension, such as the period following the 1982 Hama massacre, when the army indiscriminately massacred residents to dissuade rebels' efforts to organize opposition to the Syrian state, women's bodies were often the physical sites at which the ideological conflict between secular modernity and "traditional" religiosity was manifest. Following this brutal violence against Hama, women across Syria donned the hijab and abaya in "silent protest" and "clear political demonstration against the state and the Ba'ath party" (Rabo 2004, 166–67). Newly veiled women continued to enter public spaces where the secular policies of the Ba'athist state had forbidden the display of religious symbols, including the hijab. These incursions sparked additional state violence against women themselves, who on more than one occasion were attacked and forcibly unveiled in public by officials and regime supporters (Rabo 2004, 165).

The onus historically placed on Syrian women by the Alawite regime to embody the nation-state's modern values of secularism and equality is quite different from the imperative Rima experiences to enact particular forms of gendered subjecthood as a resettled refugee in Southern California. Nonetheless, striking parallels between these two discourses are evident in the ways that Islam is stigmatized as "traditional" and juxtaposed with proper, modern modes of performing gender.[6] Both invoke the same disciplinary logic that compels Rima to represent herself as a properly gendered subject citizen by embodying contextually specific, normative ideals of modern womanhood.

Within this context, I see her assertion that, in her social world, "there is no love" as a refusal to comply with the demand that she justify her marital relationship in terms consistent with the values of secular modernity. She refuses to defend her marriage through the vocabularies of gendered subjecthood that have been imposed upon her historically by the Syrian state and, more recently, by resettlement agencies and other NGOs that aggressively encourage her assimilation to hegemonic "American" values. Instead, she juxtaposes marriage practices stigmatized as "traditional" with dating in America, where a romantic partner sneaks in "through the window" rather than the door to the family home.

As Espiritu (2001) suggests in her appropriately titled article "We Don't Sleep Around like White Girls Do," racialized immigrant communities contest their subordination to dominant groups through assertions of moral superiority. Rima similarly lays claim to a certain moral authority by emphasizing her own relationship as religiously sanctioned and evolving within a larger web of relations between families. In doing so, she challenges the claim—pervasive in American culture, primetime television shows, and popular music—that intimate, companionate love is the highest ideal toward which the individual should aspire.

Rima's rejection of these normative values is precisely what Mardina condemns in the opening anecdote. In fact, Mardina's culminating, most damning accusation is that Syrian refugees have failed to assimilate by stubbornly holding on to differences that are incompatible with American ideals of secularism and individual autonomy. Instead, she suggests, they insist on living "a Syrian life in America" and refuse to perform their cultural differences in ways that can be accommodated within the framework of liberal multiculturalism.

The discourse of liberal multiculturalism claims to celebrate difference while simultaneously insisting on its superficiality. Liberal multiculturalism

teaches us to value diversity by demonstrating its triviality, by revealing that underneath the outer trappings of religious, linguistic, and cultural differences we are all the same, at least in the ways that really matter (Povinelli 2006; Hage 2012). The violence of this discourse becomes
apparent in the imperative experienced by individuals marked as culturally "Other" to prove that they, too, are like the dominant group. Underlying the happy (Ahmed 2010) unifying slogan of "same, same, but different" (Kostecki-Shaw 2011) is the logic of "even though." It is through
such logic that refugees ultimately are made legible as (potential, future)
Americans: "even though they're refugees, they're just like you and me."
These "even-though" narratives subtly reinforce hegemonic power structures by privileging the dominant group as the normative referent against
which all others are measured. It is this assumption Rima rejects in her
refusal to express any individual preference regarding the male driver and
her refusal to tell the story of her marriage through the apologist framework of "even though." I have come to understand this silence as an act
of self-protection from the scrutiny of the Western gaze (Mohanty 1988)
under which she can only ever appear as a victim of Islamic patriarchy or
as the narrator of an "even-though" parable affirming that her marriage is
like "our" marriage and her love is like "our" love. These are the only two
scripts available to her within the paradigm of liberal multiculturalism.

Conclusion

According to Mardina, refugees refuse assimilation into the happy (Ahmed
2010) narrative of liberal multiculturalism by rejecting American ideals
of individuality, autonomy, and gender equality. For Mardina and many
others who work with the Syrian community, this refusal evokes a particular moral outrage that I have attempted to characterize and historicize
here. Nguyen (2012) demonstrates how US policy and rhetoric relating to
refugee resettlement reflect Maussian theorizations of the gift as always
accompanied by debt. Refugees, Nguyen argues, become indebted to the
nation that offered them the gift of freedom in the form of resettlement.
This debt is, in turn, repaid through demonstrations of gratitude (2012,
25–30)—what Ahmed (2010) describes as embracing the "happy objects"
of the nation. Conversely, to reject the opportunity to self-actualize as an
autonomous individual is to reject America's gift of freedom. In refusing
to accept the happy objects of liberal love, freedom, equality, and individ-

ual autonomy, the refugee betrays her lack of gratitude and thus reveals herself as undeserving of American generosity.

ACKNOWLEDGMENTS

I am thankful for the support of my advisor Thomas Csordas throughout the development of my dissertation project. I am also especially grateful for the feedback and suggestions generously provided by participants in the University of California Critical Refugee Studies Collective's summer 2019 writing workshop and for the Critical Refugee Studies Collective's generous support for this research through a graduate student grant. In particular, I thank Ly Thuy Nguyen, Tory Brykalski, and Christiane Assefa, as well as Y'n Lê Espiritu, whose thoughtful critiques were formative in the preparation of this chapter. Most of all, I am grateful to Rawnaq Behnam, whose assistance and contributions were essential to all aspects of this project, and to all the Syrian families who invited me into their homes and lives and generously shared the privilege of their friendship with me.

NOTES

1. Other forms of Islamophobia that evolved over centuries of religious tension between Chaldeans like Mardina and Muslims within her native country of Iraq are unfortunately beyond the scope of my focus here but are undoubtedly of equal importance in shaping the narrative I recount in the introduction.

2. Hage (2012) offers a nuanced analysis of multiculturalism as a disciplinary discourse while Ong (2003) provides an in-depth ethnography of the subtle ways Cambodian refugees experience the imperative to assimilate in institutional settings and everyday interactions.

3. See Mahmood's (2011) critique of Boddy (1989).

4. While an adequate historicization of the conflict is not possible within a single chapter, it is essential to understand some of the most basic ideological tensions that have long characterized the Syrian state's relationship with the larger population and specifically with communities like Rima's that are relatively more religious, rural, and socioeconomically marginalized than the governing urban elites. For a more detailed discussion, see Thompson (2000).

5. In Syria, a religious minority, the Alawites, gained power through the denunciation of wealthy landowners belonging to the Sunni Muslim religious majority. Power remained in the hands of a class of Indigenous elites, many of whom had been educated in Europe and had learned to establish their own authority by drawing upon the binary of the modern, educated subject in contrast to rural and poor populations, dismissed as religiously zealous, ignorant, and illiterate. While the disenfranchised rural poor at first embraced—

or at least did not actively oppose—the Ba'athist regime and its efforts to undermine the landed elites, as the avowedly secular regime became more emboldened in its attempts to regulate religious life, it was met with widespread resistance. The authoritarian, socialist state consistently struggled to maintain a balance between the image of secular modernity it projected internationally and the population's resistance to policies that sought to regulate marriage practices, gender norms, and religious commitment (Joubin 2013; Rabo 2004; Sparre 2008; Ventura 2018; Wedeen 2015).

6. I use quotations here to emphasize the ways Islam was represented as "traditional" in state rhetoric to denigrate the religion as backward and outdated when, in fact, the new religious practices that became widespread during the Islamic Revival departed significantly from historical forms of religiosity.

REFERENCES

Abu-Lughod, Lila. 1998. *Remaking Women: Feminism and Modernity in the Middle East.* Princeton, NJ: Princeton University Press.

———. 2002. "Do Muslim Women Really Need Saving? Anthropological Reflections on Cultural Relativism and Its Others." *American Anthropologist* 104, no. 3: 783–90.

———. 2008. *Writing Women's Worlds: Bedouin Stories.* Berkeley: University of California Press.

Ahmed, Sara. 2010. *The Promise of Happiness.* Durham, NC: Duke University Press.

Al-Ghazzi, Omar. 2013. "Nation as Neighborhood: How Bab al-Hara Dramatized Syrian Identity." *Media, Culture and Society* 35, no. 5: 586–601.

Ali, Kamran Asdar. 2002. *Planning the Family in Egypt: New Bodies, New Selves.* Modern Middle Eastern Series, no. 21. Austin: University of Texas Press.

Allouche, Sabiha. 2019. "Love, Lebanese Style: Towards an Either/and Analytical Framework of Kinship." *Journal of Middle East Women's Studies* 15, no. 2: 157–78.

Bartels, Susan Andrea, Saja Michael, Sophie Roupetz, Stephanie Garbern, Lama Kilzar, Harveen Bergquist, Nour Bakhache, Colleen Davison, and Annie Bunting. 2018. "Making Sense of Child, Early and Forced Marriage among Syrian Refugee Girls: A Mixed Methods Study in Lebanon." *BMJ Global Health* 3, no. 1: e000509. http://dx.doi.org/10.1136/bmjgh-2017-000509.

Becker, Howard S., Blanche Geer, Everett C. Hughs, and Anselm L. Strauss. 1961. *Boys in White: Student Culture in Medical School.* Chicago, IL: University of Chicago Press.

Bilge, Sirma. 2010. "Beyond Subordination vs. Resistance: An Intersectional Approach to the Agency of Veiled Muslim Women." *Journal of Intercultural Studies* 31, no. 1: 9–28.

Boddy, Janice. 1989. *Wombs and Alien Spirits: Women, Men, and the Zar Cult in Northern Sudan.* Madison: University of Wisconsin Press.

Chapman, Madeleine. 2016. "Feminist Dilemmas and the Agency of Veiled Muslim Women: Analysing Identities and Social Representations." *European Journal of Women's Studies* 23, no. 3: 237–50.

Charles, Lorraine, and Kate Denman. 2013. "Syrian and Palestinian Syrian Refugees in Lebanon: The Plight of Women and Children." *Journal of International Women's Studies*

14, no. 5: 96–111.

Espiritu, Yến Lê. 2001. "'We Don't Sleep Around like White Girls Do': Family, Culture, and Gender in Filipina American Lives." *Signs: Journal of Women in Culture and Society* 26, no. 2: 415–40.

———. 2014. *Body Counts: The Vietnam War and Militarized Refugees.* Berkeley: University of California Press.

Espiritu, Yến Lê, and Lan Duong. 2018. "Feminist Refugee Epistemology: Reading Displacement in Vietnamese and Syrian Refugee Art." *Signs: Journal of Women in Culture and Society* 43, no. 3: 587–615.

Fortier, Corinne, Aymon Kreil, and Irene Maffi. 2016. "The Trouble of Love in the Arab World: Romance, Marriage, and the Shaping of Intimate Lives." *Arab Studies Journal* 24, no. 2: 96–101.

Fortier, Corinne, Aymon Kreil, and Irene Maffi. 2018. Introduction to *Reinventing Love?: Gender, Intimacy, and Romance in the Arab World,* edited by Corinne Fortier, Aymon Kreil, and Irene Maffi, 9–32. Bern: Peter Lang.

Giddens, Anthony. 1992. *The Transformation of Intimacy: Sexuality, Love and Intimacy in Modern Societies.* Cambridge, MA: Polity Press.

Glapka, Ewa. 2018. "Veiled or Veiling? Turning Back the Gaze on the Western Feminist: Understanding Hijab from the Socio-Culturally Located Positions of Knowing." *Women's Studies International Forum* 71, no. 11: 103–13.

Hage, Ghassan. 2012. *White Nation: Fantasies of White Supremacy in a Multicultural Society.* New York: Routledge.

Hasso, Frances S. 2011. "Desiring Arabs." *Journal of the History of Sexuality* 20, no. 3: 652–56.

Joseph, Suad. 1994. "Brother/Sister Relationships: Connectivity, Love, and Power in the Reproduction of Patriarchy in Lebanon." *American Ethnologist* 21, no. 1: 50–73.

———. 1997. "The Public/Private—The Imagined Boundary in the Imagined Nation/State/Community: The Lebanese Case." *Feminist Review* 57, no. 1: 73–92.

———. 2005. "Learning Desire: Relational Pedagogies and the Desiring Female Subject in Lebanon." *Journal of Middle East Women's Studies* 1, no. 1: 79–109.

———. 2010. "Gender and Citizenship in the Arab World." *Al-Raida Journal,* no. 129-130: 8–18. https://doi.org/10.32380/alrj.v0i0.50.

Joubin, Rebecca. 2013. *The Politics of Love: Sexuality, Gender, and Marriage in Syrian Television Drama.* Plymouth, UK: Lexington Books.

Kostecki-Shaw, Jenny Sue. 2011. *Same, Same but Different.* New York: Henry Holt.

Mahmood, Saba. 2011. *Politics of Piety: The Islamic Revival and the Feminist Subject.* Princeton, NJ: Princeton University Press.

McGranahan, Carole. 2016. "Theorizing Refusal: An Introduction." *Cultural Anthropology* 31, no. 3: 319–25.

Mohanty, Chandra Talpade. 1988. "Under Western Eyes: Feminist Scholarship and Colonial Discourses." *Feminist Review* 30, no. 1: 61–88.

Mourtada, Rima, Jennifer Schlecht, and Jocelyn DeJong. 2017. "A Qualitative Study Exploring Child Marriage Practices among Syrian Conflict-Affected Populations in Lebanon." *Conflict and Health* 11, no. 1: 53–65.

Narayan, Uma. 1998. "Essence of Culture and a Sense of History: A Feminist Critique of Cultural Essentialism." *Hypatia* 13, no. 2: 86–106.

Nguyen, Mimi Thi. 2012. *The Gift of Freedom: War, Debt, and Other Refugee Passages.* Durham, NC: Duke University Press.

Ong, Aihwa. 2003. *Buddha Is Hiding: Refugees, Citizenship, the New America.* Berkeley: University of California Press.

Povinelli, Elizabeth A. 2006. *The Empire of Love: Toward a Theory of Intimacy, Genealogy, and Carnality.* Durham, NC: Duke University Press.

Rabbo, Anika. 1996. "Gender, State, and Civil Society in Jordan and Syria." In *Civil Society: Challenging Western Models,* edited by Chris Hann and Elizabeth Dunn, 155–57. London: Routledge.

Simpson, Audra. 2007. "On Ethnographic Refusal: Indigeneity, 'Voice' and Colonial Citizenship." *Junctures: The Journal for Thematic Dialogue* 12, no. 9: 67–80. https://www.junctures.org/index.php/junctures/article/view/66.

Sparre, Sara Lei. 2008. "Educated Women in Syria: Servants of the State, or Nurturers of the Family?" *Critique: Critical Middle Eastern Studies* 17, no. 1: 3–20.

Thompson, Elizabeth. 2002. *Colonial Citizens: Republican Rights, Paternal Privilege, and Gender in French Syria and Lebanon.* New York: Columbia University Press.

Tuck, Eve, and K. Wayne Yang. 2014. "Unbecoming Claims: Pedagogies of Refusal in Qualitative Research." *Qualitative Inquiry* 20, no. 6: 811–18.

Ventura, Lorella. 2018. "'Thank God We Are in Syria!': Modernization, Interfaith Relations and Women's Rights in Syria before the 'Arab Spring' (2000–2010)." *Islam and Christian-Muslim Relations* 29, no. 3: 349–69.

Wedeen, Lisa. 2015. *Ambiguities of Domination: Politics, Rhetoric, and Symbols in Contemporary Syria.* Chicago: University of Chicago Press.

CHAPTER 9

The Wives of the Heroes, Smuggled Sperm, and Reproductive Technologies

Palestinian Women Building Families on Their Own

LAURA FERRERO

The heterogeneous array of technologies encompassed under the rubric of assisted reproductive technologies (ARTs) are now available in many countries of the Middle East and North Africa (MENA). Since the world's first "test-tube" baby was born via in vitro fertilization (IVF) in 1978, many anthropologists have written about the effects of such technologies on concepts like kinship, motherhood, procreation, and gender (see, for example, Inhorn and Birenbaum-Carmeli 2008; Franklin 2013). Assisted reproductive technologies are innovative ways of achieving reproduction and one of their most distinctive characteristics is the separation between sexual acts and reproduction itself. Retrieving sperm and eggs from bodies, fertilizing the egg and transferring the embryo back to the woman's uterus (as in IVF), or injecting spermatozoa directly into oocytes (as in intracytoplasmic sperm injection or ICSI) fragments a reproductive event into several phases that need medical supervision and ultimately substitutes sexual intercourse with medical techniques. The consequent marginalization of sexual activity artificializes—and at the same time denaturalizes—reproduction, something historically imagined as strongly dependent on nature and biology (Strathern 1992).

Assisted reproductive technologies have a two-fold effect on family formation. On the one hand, ARTs allow married heterosexual couples who suffer infertility to overcome their "biological limits" and achieve procreation, thus supporting traditional kinship structures and the cultural value of having biological offspring. On the other hand, thanks to gamete donation and surrogacy, ARTs open up new spaces of technological possibilities where new families and new forms of "nonbiological" parenthood can emerge. Those new forms of parenthood have been investigated in the Global North more than elsewhere, because it is mainly in Europe and the Americas that same-sex couples and single men or women have accessed ARTs to start a process of procreation (Franklin and Ragonè 1998; Thompson 2001, 2005).

In the MENA region, there are a number of countries with permissive laws regarding ARTs. Iran, a Shiʻi Muslim country, allows third-party reproductive assistance through gamete donation (Abbasi-Shavazi et al. 2008; Tremayne 2009; Inhorn and Tremayne 2012). Lebanon, where Shiʻa Muslims comprise a large part of the population, is subject to Iranian influence and heterologous procreation is practiced (Inhorn 2006a; Clarke 2009). In Israel, the religious emphasis on procreation is strategically used as a tool in the demographic conflict (Kanaaneh 2002), creating one of the most "aggressive and proactive ART regimes in the world" (Inhorn and Birenbaum-Carmeli 2008, 184). Indeed, almost all the existing technologies are not only available and accessible to single women and same-sex couples in Israel (Kahn 2000; Haelyon 2006; Prainsack 2007; Birenbaum-Carmeli and Carmeli 2009), but some of them are also state subsidized (Kahn 2000; Birenbaum-Carmeli 2004, 902; Vertommen 2017, 215).

Sunni Islam dominates most of the rest of the MENA region. Those countries, too, are witnessing a rapid expansion of ARTs. One of the reasons behind the proliferation of reproduction technologies in the MENA region is that marriage is highly valued and one of its expected outcomes is having children. The Muslim world can be described as "pronatalist," and nearly all interpretations of Islam support the use of science, medicine, and biotechnology to find solutions that alleviate human suffering (Inhorn and Tremayne 2012, 2). Since a member of al-Azhar University issued the first fatwa (religious opinion, pl. fatwas) on reproductive health technologies in 1980, many other fatwas on reproductive health have appeared. These religious opinions have affected both the availability and the use of reproductive technologies by infertile couples, because both physicians and infertile couples are concerned about the halal/haram (licit/illicit) divide. In the Sunni world, there is a widespread agreement that IVF is permissible, but it should respect some conditions (*shurut*): the couple should be married, the wife should not be virgin, and use of third-party gametes (sperm or egg) is not allowed. As result of these *shurut*, gamete donation and surrogacy are not available in many Sunni-majority Muslim countries (Zuhur 1992; Inhorn 2003, 2006b; Rispler-Chaim 2020).

Although Sunni Islam has more rigid rules about ARTs, the availability of biomedical technologies is generating new Islamic bioethical discourses and local moral responses, as ARTs are used in novel and "unexpected ways" (Inhorn and Tremayne 2016). In this chapter, I investigate a way the combination of marriage by proxy and assisted reproduction shapes Palestinian families that are—at least for a number of years—one-parent families.[1] Indeed, in the case of wives of prisoners, marriage by proxy and assisted reproduction allow women to create families by themselves and reflects one of those unexpected ways ARTs can be used in a Sunni context.

Sperm Smugglers

At the end of July 2019, there were 5,150 Palestinian security detainees and prisoners being held in Israel Prison Service (IPS) facilities. According to the websites of B'Tselem (the Israeli Information Center for Human Rights in the Occupied Palestinian Territories) and Addameer (a Palestinian nongovernmental, civil institution that works to support Palestinian political prisoners held in Israeli and Palestinian prisons), this included around 38 women and 210 minors. In the early 2000s a Palestinian man was undergoing treatment at a fertility clinic because he and his wife could not conceive when he was arrested. Since his sperm sample was already frozen, his wife underwent the procedure and successfully got pregnant after his imprisonment. The man circulated the idea of smuggling sperm out of the prison and one man in particular, Ammar al-Zaban from the village of Silwad, was inspired.[2]

It took several years but in August 2012, Ammar's wife, Dalal Al-Zaban, gave birth to the first Palestinian child born as a result of sperm smuggled out of an Israeli prison. This phenomenon is referred to in Palestine as *tahrīb al nuṭaf*. Ammar is currently serving a life sentence in Israeli prison, and his baby is widely called *safir al hurreya* (the ambassador of freedom). This expression reveals that in the Palestinian case, the depiction of ART as a "hope technology" (Franklin 1997, 192) can overlap with the depiction of ART as a "freedom technology."

Following Dalal's example, many other wives of prisoners got pregnant; since 2012 more than fifty children have been conceived with Palestinian men's sperm smuggled out of Israeli prisons. This phenomenon has occurred across a wide range of social groups, and conceiving with smuggled sperm has been used by women from cities, villages, and refugee camps as well as by educated, uneducated, working, and unemployed women with husbands involved in both secular and religious parties.

From October 2015 through January 2016, I met and interviewed thirteen of these women. I obtained their numbers through the hospital that carried out the inseminations, contacted them, and visited them at their homes (some of them only once, others several times). I conducted unstructured interviews in Palestinian Arabic. In addition, I visited the hospital, spoke with the doctors, and interviewed the media director of the Razan Centre, the facility that carried out most of the inseminations. Razan Centre has three branches, but the first and main one is located in Nablus. It is not the only hospital that can provide reproductive services, but it is the only facility that provides all medical treatments to prisoners' wives free of charge (the average cost of treatment is around US$3000). When he welcomed me in the laboratory, Dr. Zyad Abu Khairazan—the nephew of Dr. Salem Abu Khairazan, who is known as the inventor of this practice—explained that they undertake ICSI treatment when it comes to the wives of prisoners. He was proud to show me the equipment in the laboratory that he said "is very modern; it is second in the world only after equipment available in Israel." Intracytoplasmic sperm injection is a variant of IVF designed to overcome male infertility problems. "As long as one viable spermatozoon can be retrieved from a man's body . . . this spermatozoon can be injected into an oocyte under a high-powered microscope, effectively forcing fertilization to occur" (Inhorn 2012, xvi).[3] Even if the prisoners are biologically fertile, they are affected by "political infertility" (Berk 2014). Bringing the sperm from the jail to the hospital is so difficult, dangerous, and uncertain that the seminal fluid has come to be considered unique and precious, and this is why ICSI treatment is preferred to standard IVF, which has less chance of ending in a pregnancy (Ferrero 2022).

Many elements shape the ontological choreography (Thompson 2005) that make this phenomenon possible. The high respect given to political prisoners (Hamdan 2019, 534–39), regardless of their political affiliation, and their wives (referred to in Palestinian Arabic as *fāqidat*, women who have been deprived of something or someone) provides the backdrop for the practice. When combined with a religious pronunciation that states that the practice is *halal* and widespread societal pronatalism and linked to the fact that childlessness implies difficulties in achieving old-age security because of the lack of strong social safety nets (Inhorn 2000) and a state that cannot offer a welfare system (Taraki 2006), the phenomenon becomes a legitimate avenue for family formation. The fact that a fertility clinic chose to provide an expensive treatment free of charge to the *fāqidat* shows how much the technologies are culturally and socially embedded: they are accepted by professionals and potential recipients only when perceived as reasonable in the context of existing social relations, cultural norms, and knowledge systems (Webster 2002).

The practice of giving birth to prisoners' offspring can be conceived as a threat to Israel, as a political act, and an embodied form of resistance (Vertommen 2017). However, the most common theme that emerges in the women's narratives is their desire for motherhood and the satisfaction of fulfilling a socio-cultural obligation in which procreation is the natural consequence of marriage (Ferrero 2022). In this chapter, I concentrate on three cases. In addition to giving birth while their husbands were in jail, these are stories of women who also became engaged or married by proxy while the men were already in prison. These stories shed light on a new phenomenon: not only the enlargement but also the creation of a family during the husband's captivity and physical absence. This is a clear example of what the history of anthropological research has already documented: both fertility and reproduction are subjected to social control and cultural and religious norms that are not independent from political situations and power hierarchies. The anthropological literature dealing with ARTs describe what these phenomena reveal about social institutions such as marriage, parenthood, and childbirth. In line with this orientation, I present the voices of those three women who, during their interviews, told me how they came to marry an incarcerated man and choose

to have a child with him. I argue that the political situation creates obstacles to family formation but also generates a social discourse that allows a
new practice that establishes kinship through strategic use of biomedicine.
I conclude by analyzing the impact of the sex/reproduction division on
these women's bodies.

————————————*Amina's Story*————————————

Amina is a kind woman with long, black hair. She is thirty years old.
I met her in her parents' house in Jenin, a northern city in the West
Bank of Palestine. She comes from a big family; she has six sisters and
three brothers. All of them are already married; only Amina and a
divorced sister are living with their parents. Amina got married when
she was sixteen years old in a traditional marriage, that is, a marriage
organized with the involvement of the intended spouses' families. She
left school before reaching secondary school and married soon after.
Describing how she met her husband, Amina said,

We didn't know each other. Someone of my husband's family noticed me,
his mother and his sister came to visit me and they liked me. The next time
they came back with him and soon after we read the *fatiha* (the first sura
of the Qur`an) and [signed] the marriage contract. We had a traditional
marriage and I moved to their place. . . . At that time, he had already been
imprisoned and as soon as he was released his mom said, "We want him to
be engaged." They were in a hurry because he was wanted by Israel again.

Twenty days after the marriage, Amina's husband was arrested
while he was working in Israel. This happened during the second
Intifada; the economic situation in the Occupied Palestinian Territories was very difficult, so he used to enter Israel illegally to work.
One year later he was released and soon after Amina gave birth to
their first daughter. When the baby was one year old the army came
and took him again.

My husband was not involved in the *muqawwama* [resistance]. But a friend
of his was and when his friend *istashhad* [was martyred, killed by the Israeli

army], my husband suffered a lot. He chose to take revenge, killing a set-
tler. It was in 2004. The army knew it and they came. It was two o'clock in
the night and we were sleeping. At the beginning they gave him a life sentence but thanks to our lawyer they reduced the penalty and he's now serving twenty-seven years.

Amina lived for the next seven years with her mother-in-law, visiting her husband only once because she did not have permission to
enter Israel.

When my mother-in-law went to visit him, she used to complain about me
and tell him false stories about me. Those were very hard times. It was like
we were in two different prisons: my husband in the Israeli one and me in
my mother-in-law's house. Everything was forbidden to me. I gave up and
I came back to my family. When I came back, he divorced me . . . through
the Palestine Red Crescent Society (PRCS) . . . to whom he gave a proxy.[4]

Amina and her ex-husband had no communication for about five
years. However, when his mother died, he got in touch with Amina
and explained to her that the divorce was a means to end the problems
while his mother was still alive. He asked her to marry him again and
she was happy to say yes.

The second marriage happened by proxy through the PRCS. My husband
gave the PRCS a right of proxy for his brother. The PRCS called me and
told me, "Amina, the papers for the *rugu'* [the second marriage, literally the
coming back] are ready." I was very happy. We had a new marriage contract in the court and we had a big party. I wore a white wedding dress, I
fixed my hair, I had a new ring, new *mahr* [bridewealth]. We arranged everything as if it was the first marriage, including the *ishhar* [announcement],
to ensure everybody knew that we were together again. It was important
to me, because we were already thinking of having a second child through
insemination. My father went to the *mufti* in Jenin and he told him that a
fatwa already declared that the practice is halal.[5] Since my case was different
because I had already gone through a divorce, we also spoke to the *mufti* of
Nablus, who confirmed that we could do it since we had already been married and we had had sexual intercourse before.

Infertility—and the consequent recourse to medical treatment to overcome the problem—is often shrouded in secrecy (Inhorn 1996; 2012, 80–81; Inhorn and Birenbaum-Carmeli 2008, 181; Demircioğlu Göknar 2015). The same is true in Palestine when IVF or ICSI is a solution for infertility. However, when it comes to wives of political prisoners, the treatment has to be public. First, this a way of avoiding social criticism and gossip in a generally conservative society. Second, a fatwa issued in 2013 by Dār al-Iftaʿ al-Filastiniyya stated that information about the treatment must be spread via local television or "by any means between the people."[6] In addition to the already existing fatwas, it is common for someone who is planning to undertake the practice to request a new one, specific for her own case, if it presents aspects that differentiate it from the previous cases.

————————————*Mariam's Story*————————————

Mariam is part of the El-Ghani family, from a village close to Tulkarem. She is forty years old and she has one daughter from her first husband and two small twins, Omar and Adil, from her second husband. Mariam comes from a big family: she has thirteen brothers, two of whom were martyred during the second Intifada. One of them was killed because he was responsible for the murder of a soldier.

I didn't complete my studies because I got married when I was just sixteen. He was older than me, he was thirty and he was not a good man. When I married, I discovered that he didn't pray and he had no moral values. He used to beat me. I was young, I didn't have any experience and he had no patience. I came back to my father and I told him *khalas* [enough, stop], I wanted to get rid of him. I gave up my dowry and we divorced.

Mariam's second husband, Ibrahim, is from a refugee camp close to Tulkarem. He used to go her village to meet his friends and comrades. He saw Mariam and got to know her story from one of her brothers.

It is not easy for a divorced woman to marry a bachelor but he knew it was not my fault. He asked so many people in the village and they knew that I married when I was too young and I divorced because my husband was not good. . . . When we got engaged, I was aware that he was wanted [by the Israeli Army]. I have to admit that at the beginning I doubted. My family didn't like the idea, but in the end I made my decision. I was living by myself and at the end of the day, I am still living alone but I thought that was the best solution. I didn't want to miss this opportunity. What God decided for us, that is the right thing.

Mariam and Ibrahim read the *fatiha* and signed the contract on the same day. They were in a hurry and wanted to be married before the Israeli Army took him.

They were apart after the engagement and Mariam did not know where Ibrahim was hiding himself. He visited her home periodically, but the rest of the time there was no communication. She remembers the noise of the helicopters that were looking for him. When he was captured, he was sentenced to twenty-three years in prison; thirteen of those had passed by the time I interviewed Mariam. Although they had never celebrated with a wedding, the signed marriage contract meant they were married from a legal and religious perspective. For this reason, she was able to apply for permission to visit him in prison; those visits began five years after he was first imprisoned.

We got to know each other more during those visits. The first visit was unforgettable. I was at the same time very happy and very sad because I could not hug my husband and I had to talk with a telephone through a glass. The first time as I saw him I broke down in tears, but he was optimistic. He told me, "Don't worry. Soon we will be happy." . . . When Ibrahim proposed insemination to me, I was afraid of the opinions and voices in the village and [that] my parents [wouldn't] support me . . . I did a *du'a al-istikhara* [a prayer to guide decision-making] and I understood that it was my path."

Mariam also expressed a fear that many women have:

Can you imagine what could have happened if he came out without children and I was over forty? He could have thought to take a second wife, but now that I gave him two sons, it won't happen. . . . I am happy. I built a new house, I moved into it, I did the insemination, and I gave birth to two sons. All [of it] happened without my husband, but everything in an Islam-ically lawful way.

Mariam's words shed light on some of the reasons women choose this practice to conceive. It is already well documented that people seek assis-tance with reproduction for many reasons, including wanting to be sure they have tried everything, satisfying the demands of in-laws, and not wanting to be seen to be complacent in the face of adversity (Franklin 1997). Other researchers have argued that people pursue IVF as a means of strengthening their conjugal relations (Sandelowski 1991, 1993; Ragonè 1994). For Mariam, there was the desire to give offspring to her husband, both to satisfy his desire for fatherhood (Ferrero 2022) and to avoid the risk of divorce after his release.

In Mariam's case there was no doubt about the religious permissibility of the practice; even though she had never had sexual intercourse with her second husband Ibrahim, she had been married previously so she was not a virgin when she undertook the treatment. Souad's experience was more complicated.

—————————————————————*Souad's Story*—————————————————————

Souad is thirty-eight and lives by herself in a modern flat in Ramallah. She holds a degree in architecture; she studied in Germany and she works for the United Nations Relief and Works Agency (UNRWA). Her family is from the north of Palestine but she has lived in Ramal-lah for many years, sharing a flat with other girls before living on her own.

Souad met Khaled in 2000. They got to know each other slowly, usually meeting during cultural or political meetings, and eventually started to think about becoming officially engaged.

Khaled was wanted. For three years the army looked for him without know-ing where he was. Also me, I didn't know where he was. There was no communication, no telephone calls. . . . I didn't know anything until Israel announced the arrest in December 2004. Until then I didn't know anything, but I was sure he had not been captured or killed, because I would have known it from the news.

Souad was not permitted to visit him because they were not married.

During the two years between imprisonment and final sentencing I used to go to the court and see Khaled at a distance. Talking with gestures we decided to make an official engagement. . . . Then he received his sentence: fifteen and a half years. My family started to doubt our engagement. They were afraid. His brother was serving a life sentence, got released during an exchange of prisoners, and then martyred himself. They were afraid to go through the same story again.

Souad and her family sought a fatwa for her situation. She admits that they are not very religious and for this reason they asked for the opinion of an imam whom they already knew, who had connections with the Popular Front for the Liberation of Palestine, the leftist party to which her husband belonged. Souad celebrated an engagement and a wedding party in 2006. "The imam suggested we organize a [wedding celebration], a real one with a white dress, the gold, and the guests . . . so I did it and during the ceremony I made the announcement. I announced that we wanted to do insemination."

As in Amina's case, the celebration held in the absence of the groom was primarily designed to announce their formal union to the community. However, Souad's case is quite different from the others presented here, because her marriage with Khaled was her first marriage and, since they married by proxy, she was assumed to be a virgin. The Razan Centre rejected Mariam's request for treatment, because they rely only on fatwas issued by Dār al-Iftaʿ al-Filastiniyya, which had stated that insemination of a virgin was not permissible. Souad turned to another private center that agreed to inseminate her, but unfortunately that insemination did not result in a pregnancy. She returned to Razan Centre, where they then agreed to accept her as a patient, because during the first insemination process she had undergone gynecological visits and medical procedures that resulted in the doctors at Razan Centre no longer considering her be a virgin. Souad was very motivated to achieve insemination. "I am already forty . . . after the age of forty the chances to get pregnant decrease. Furthermore, the prison is not a safe environment, maybe Khaled will also have health issues. . . . At the beginning he had many doubts . . . he was afraid of being judged because we were engaged, not married . . . what would have people said?"

Souad's experience is similar to that of other women in their mid- to late thirties who immediately seek assisted reproduction rather than attempting pregnancy through sex, in order to increase the chance of a pregnancy (Daly and Bewley 2013). Of course, in Palestine this is even more urgent if the husband is in jail, because the prison term can be longer than the "fertile life" of the woman.

Conclusion

Although reproductive technologies allow infertile couples to conceive, they have transformed how fertility, infertility, and fecundity are understood (Franklin 2013, 748). In the Palestinian context, ARTs offer the possibility of reproduction to the *fāqidat*, women biologically fertile but made "politically infertile" by their husbands' long prison terms. These couples are condemned to prolonged physical distance and sexual abstinence, because conjugal visits are not allowed to those Israel classifies as "political prisoners" (Baker and Matar 2011, vii).

The separation between sex and reproduction comes here in a situation in which the couple is already physically apart, and the community considers the resulting pregnancy not as something "unnatural" but as a strategy that allows the "natural" continuation of a family life in a context of deep deprivation of rights. Obstacles created by the political situation are overcome thanks to strategic solutions that are possible and make sense only in that specific context.

The cases presented in this chapter are characterized by marriage by proxy. This creates a situation in which the pregnancy is not only not the result of sexual intercourse between wife and husband but also in which potentially *that* woman and *that* man have never had sex together and, in the case of life sentences, never will. In those cases the concerns of the couples and their families focus more on the women's bodies than on the couple. Since marriages by proxy could potentially involve virgins, the sexuality of women attracts particular attention. Many societies in the MENA region are concerned with the virginity of women before marriage (Moghadam 2004), something that is not only important to her respectability as an individual but also widely considered a reflection of the respectability of her whole family.

The question of whether virgins should to be allowed to have children by artificial insemination also provoked public furor in Britain at the time of the Human Fertilisation and Embryology Act of 1990, which among other things allowed single women to access ARTs. In March 1991 it was disclosed that a twenty-year-old woman who had never before had sex was undergoing artificial insemination at a Birmingham clinic. Soon it emerged that she was not the only one, and these "virgin births" were at the center of a controversy. The idea of women wishing to have children without the "normal" sexual relations with men that produce them challenged not only the ideal of biological fatherhood but also that of the nuclear family itself and the sexual union that British society assumed to be the basis upon which conjugal relations and families are built. In Britain, the furor over "virgin births" was not only about changing concepts of paternity but also about the absence of sex in procreation (Shore et al. 1992), a debate that resonates with the cases investigated in this chapter in many ways.

This chapter shows that the combination of marriage by proxy with a prisoner and insemination with sperm smuggled out of the prison is a potential way through which new kinds of families are being constituted in Palestine. Even if *tahrīb al nutaf* is generally accepted and respected within the society, the three cases presented here were particularly sensitive because the couples married when the men were already in prison, a detail that publicly revealed the absence of sexual intercourse between them. The three cases offered different ways to create a family with a prisoner using ARTs: Amina remarried her previous husband; Mariam married a bachelor after having divorced her first husband; and Souad married for the first time a bachelor who was already in prison, meaning that society assumed she was a virgin. Importantly, Souad's presumed virginity required her to obtain a fatwa opinion and she requested one from an imam who was not part of the Dār al-Iftaʿ al-Filastiniyya, the official fatwa-pronouncing institution. Indeed, this imam's fatwa was at odds with those offered by the official fatwa-pronouncing institution, but nevertheless valid. The differences between these three case studies illustrate a range of ways that the interaction between marriage by proxy and ARTs are making possible the creation and enlargement of a family in the absence of a man in the Palestinian context.

ACKNOWLEDGMENTS

An Erasmus Mundus grant supported this research. I thank Professor Omar Ayed, who welcomed me at Nablus University, and Dr. Zyad Abu Khairazan and Mohammed Qablan of the Razan Centre for help in accessing the hospital and contacting the women. I also thank Tamara Taher for the help in transcribing and translating the material I collected.

NOTES

1. It should be noted that insemination has been undertaken by prisoners condemned to lengthy or life sentences.
2. I have maintained the real names of this family because this case is well known. I used pseudonyms or anonymized all other women's names in this chapter.
3. For a detailed explanation of ICSI's origin and diffusion in the Middle East, see Inhorn 2012.
4. In Israel and the Occupied Palestinian Territories, the Palestine Red Crescent Society visits detainees and helps maintain contact between detainees and their families.
5. A *mufti* is an Islamic jurist qualified to issue a nonbinding religious opinion. In Palestine *muftis* are part of the Dār al-Iftaʾ al-Filastiniyya, a government body established as a center for Islamic legal research. It offers Muslims religious guidance and education through the issuing of fatwas.
6. The *mufti* of Nablus gave me a copy of this fatwa.

REFERENCES

Abbasi-Shavazi, Mohammad Jalal, Marcia C. Inhorn, Hajiieh Bibi Razeghi Nasrabad, and Ghasem Toloo. 2008. "The 'Iranian ART Revolution': Infertility, Assisted Reproductive Technology, and Third-party Donation in the Islamic Republic of Iran." *Journal of Middle East Women's Studies* 4, no. 2: 1–28.

Baker, Abeer, and Anat Matar. *Threat: Palestinian Political Prisoners in Israel.* London: Pluto Press, 2011.

Berk, Elizabeth. 2014. *Political Infertility: Treatment as Resistance in Israel/Palestine.* Master's thesis, Washington University.

Birenbaum-Carmeli, Daphna. 2004. "'Cheaper than a Newcomer': On the Social Production of IVF Policy in Israel." *Sociology of Health and Illness* 26, no. 7: 897–924.

Birenbaum-Carmeli, Daphna, and Yoram S. Carmeli, eds. 2009. *Kin, Gene, Community:*

Reproductive Technology among Jewish Israelis. New York: Berghahn.

Clarke, Morgan. 2009. *Islam and New Kinship: Reproductive Technology, Anthropology and the Shari'ah in Lebanon.* New York: Berghahn.

Daly, Irenee, and Susan Bewley. 2013. "Reproductive Ageing and Conflicting Clocks: King Midas' Touch." *Reproductive Biomedicine Online* 27, no. 6: 722–32.

Demircioğlu Göknar, Merve. 2015. *Achieving Procreation: Childlessness and IVF in Turkey.* New York: Berghahn Books.

Ferrero, Laura. 2022. "Sperm-Smugglers: Manhood, Fatherhood and Political Struggle in Palestine." In *Arab Masculinities: Anthropological Reconceptions,* edited by Konstantina Isidoros and Marcia C. Inhorn, 211–28. Bloomington: Indiana University Press.

Franklin, Sarah. 1997. *Embodied Progress: A Cultural Account of Reproduction.* London: Routledge.

———. 2013. "Conception through a Looking Glass: The Paradox of IVF." *Reproductive Bio-Medicine Online* 27, no. 6: 747–55.

Franklin, Sarah, and Helena Ragonè, eds. 1998. *Reproducing Reproduction: Kinship, Power, and Technological Innovation.* Philadelphia: University of Pennsylvania Press.

Haelyon, Hilla. 2006. "'Longing for a Child': Perceptions of Motherhood among Israeli-Jewish Women Undergoing In Vitro Fertilization (IVF) Treatments." *Nashim: A Journal of Jewish Women's Studies and Gender Issues* 12, no. 10: 177–203.

Hamdan, Mohammed. 2019. "'Every Sperm Is Sacred': Palestinian Prisoners, Smuggled Semen, and Derrida's Prophecy." *International Journal of Middle East Studies* 51, no. 4: 525–45.

Inhorn, Marcia C. 1996. *Infertility and Patriarchy: The Cultural Politics of Gender and Family Life in Egypt.* Philadelphia: University of Pennsylvania Press.

———. 2000. "Missing Motherhood: Infertility, Technology, and Poverty in Egyptian Women's Lives." In *Ideologies and Technologies of Motherhood,* edited by Helena Ragonè and France W. Twine, 139–68. New York: Routledge.

———. 2003. *Local Babies, Global Science: Gender, Religion, and In Vitro Fertilization in Egypt.* New York: Routledge.

———. 2006a. "Making Muslim Babies: IVF and Gamete Donation in Sunni versus Shi'a Islam." *Culture, Medicine and Psychiatry* 30, no. 4: 427–50.

———. 2006b. "'He Won't Be My Son': Middle Eastern Muslim Men's Discourses of Adoption and Gamete Donation." *Medical Anthropology Quarterly* 20, no. 1: 94–120.

———. 2012. *The New Arab Man: Emergent Masculinities, Technologies, and Islam in the Middle East.* Princeton, NJ: Princeton University Press, 2012.

Inhorn, Marcia C., and Daphna Birenbaum-Carmeli. 2008. "Assisted Reproductive Technologies and Culture Change." *Annual Review of Anthropology* 37, no. 1: 177–96.

Inhorn, Marcia C., and Soraya Tremayne, eds. 2012. *Islam and Assisted Reproductive Technologies.* New York: Berghahn Books.

Inhorn, Marcia C., and Soraya Tremayne. 2016. "Islam, Assisted Reproduction, and the Bioethical Aftermath." *Journal of Religion and Health* 55, no. 2: 422–30.

Kahn, Susan M. *Reproducing Jews: A Cultural Account of Assisted Conception in Israel.* 2000. Durham, NC: Duke University Press.

Kanaaneh, Rhoda Ann. 2002. *Birthing the Nation: Strategies of Palestinian Women in Israel.* Berkeley: University of California Press.

Moghadam, Valentine. 2004. "Patriarchy in Transition: Women and the Changing Family in the Middle East." *Journal of Comparative Family Studies* 35, no. 2: 137–62.

Prainsack, Barbara. 2007. "Research Populations: Biobanks in Israel." *New Genetic and Society* 26, no. 1: 85–103.

Ragonè, Helena. 1994. *Surrogate Motherhood: Conception in the Heart.* Boulder, CO: Westview Press.

Rispler-Chaim, Vardit. 2020. "Ethical Aspects Concerning Sperm Smuggled by Muslim Palestinian 'Security Prisoners' out of Israeli Prisons." *Ethics, Medicine and Public Health* 14: 1–7.

Sandelowski, Margarete. 1991. "Compelled to Try: The Never-Enough Quality of Reproductive Technology." *Medical Anthropology Quarterly* 5, no. 1: 29–47.

———. 1993. *With Child in Mind: Studies of the Personal Encounter with Infertility.* Philadelphia: University of Pennsylvania Press.

Shore, Cris, R. G. Abrahams, Jane F. Collier, Carol Delaney, Robin Fox, Ronald Frankenberg, Helen S. Lambert, Marit Melhuus, David M. Schneider, Verena Stolcke, and Sybil Wolfram. 1992. "Virgin Births and Sterile Debates: Anthropology and the New Reproductive Technologies." *Current Anthropology* 33, no. 3: 295–314.

Strathern, Marilyn. 1992. *Reproducing the Future: Anthropology, Kinship and the New Reproductive Technologies.* New York: Routledge.

Taraki, Lisa. 2006. *Living Palestine: Family Survival, Resistance, and Mobility under Occupation.* New York: Syracuse University Press.

Thompson, Charis. 2001. "Strategic Naturalizing: Kinship in an Infertility Clinic." In *Relative Values: Reconfiguring Kinship Studies,* edited by Sarah Franklin and Susan McKinnon, 175–202. Durham, NC: Duke University Press.

———. 2005. *Making Parents: The Ontological Choreography of Reproductive Technologies.* Cambridge, MA: MIT Press, 2005.

Tremayne, Soraya. 2009. "Law, Ethics and Donor Technologies in Shia Iran." In *Assisting Reproduction, Testing Genes: Global Encounters with New Biotechnologies,* edited by Daphna Birenbaum-Carmeli and Marcia C. Inhorn, 144–63. New York: Berghahn Books.

Vertommen, Sigrid. 2017. "Babies from Behind Bars: Stratified Assisted Reproduction in Palestine/Israel." In *Assisted Reproduction across Borders: Feminist Perspectives on Normalizations, Disruptions and Transmissions,* edited by Merete Lie and Nina Lykke, 207–18. New York: Routledge.

Webster, Andrew. 2002. "Innovative Health Technologies and the Social: Redefining Health, Medicine and the Body." *Current Sociology* 50, no. 3: 443–57.

Zuhur, Sherifa. 1992. "Of Milk-Mothers and Sacred Bonds: Islam, Patriarchy, and New Reproductive Technologies." *Creighton Law Review* 25, no. 5: 1725–38.

PART III

IT'S COMPLICATED

CHAPTER 10

Blurred Lines between Transactional Sex and Paramarital Relationships in Egypt

L. L. WYNN

Yasmeen's Story

Yasmeen is the single mother of two young teens.[1] She divorced her daughters' father when her daughters were young and moved back in with her parents, where several siblings and cousins also lived. The multigeneration family crowded the two-bedroom apartment on the outskirts of Alexandria. Yasmeen has held a number of temporary jobs in the informal economy to support herself and her family, but she struggles to find regular work. She is a strikingly beautiful woman in her early thirties who is clever and witty, but she is illiterate, which limits her job options.

Even before her divorce, she had started to spend time with men who would give her money and gifts of perfume, jewelry, food, clothing, and toys for her daughters. These men with whom she had sexual relations gave her material gifts and cash, but they did not pay fixed amounts for particular sexual acts; rather, they gave her presents according to her daughters' needs and her desires for luxury items, like nice clothes and jewelry. They took her out to restaurants and dance clubs, and they bought her food and drinks.

Sometimes, though, she had encounters that were more straight-forwardly transactional. Her cousin explained it to me this way:

Look, the thing about Yasmeen is that she always wants to get married. She wants to live a clean life. She wants a man to marry her, take care of her, spend on her and on her daughters, on the house, you know? But there aren't many men like that around. Who's going to spend on her and on her two daughters and on the house? Everyone is constrained by their own limited means. So she was forced to meet guys, go with them, sleep with them, so they would give her money, give her presents, buy her clothes. One day, before the 'Eid holidays, she said, "I slept with seven guys in one day so I could get enough money for my daughters for the holidays." I said, "Isn't seven an awful lot?" She said, "I don't even feel anything anymore." Yeah. She feels nothing.

Sometimes, to bring in money to support the household, Yasmeen would contract sexual relationships through an agency that arranged 'urfi (customary) marriages between Egyptian women and Arab men visiting Egypt on holiday or business. The man would pay to marry her for several days or weeks and the procuress, Soumeyya, would arrange for an informal marriage contract to be witnessed in her offices. The marriage contract provided a veneer of religious acceptability to the sexual relationship and also protected the couple against the vice police. Here's how Yasmeen described one of these marriages:

There was a Lebanese guy; he was sixty-three years old. We got married in the marriage office. I was just going to marry 'urfi for two or three days, and then I would take three or four thousand [Egyptian] pounds. If I stayed with him for two weeks, he would pay six thousand. The office would take three and I take three. So I married him. He slept with me one time. Then the next time he came, so that he wouldn't sleep with me, you know what I told him? I pricked my finger with a needle and put some blood on a handkerchief and I told him, "Look, I got my period." It was enough for me to spend one day with him. Three thousand pounds and I have to spend weeks with him? No. Just one day.

Yasmeen chuckled over her own cleverness, as did her cousin who was listening to the tale. We were sitting in her living room in her apartment. Yasmeen's curvaceous figure was clad in a taupe velour tracksuit and her long black hair had been straightened. The scent of tobacco hung in the air. Yasmeen had been peeling an orange, and as she continued her story (which I was recording on a phone held between us), she offered me the fruit, conscious of her obligations as a hostess to feed guests.

He said, "Okay, go on home and when you finish your period, come back." I told him okay. He gave me some chocolates, some packages of potato chips for the home, some clothes for the girls, and he gave me one hundred dollars. I took my bags and I left. The next day I found him calling me and he says, "I want to marry you in the name of the prophet. Take permission from your father." Then he said, "I don't want you to work." I was working as a hairdresser in those days and I used to earn 500 a week.[2] And he said, "After I travel [back to Lebanon], I'll send you money the next month so you can buy an apartment." And he was buying a car; he had paid half the price and said that when he traveled he would pay the other half. He said, "I'll write you the contract in your name, the car ownership documents. When I'm here, I'll drive the car; when I'm abroad, you'll drive the car." We agreed. He came and he met my father and he gave me 10,000, and he gave everyone in my family 500 pounds each. And then he traveled. The first week, he sent me 500 dollars.

But then things went awry. Yasmeen had told a friend, Hiba, about her good fortune in finding a wealthy husband who would support her and her family.

I told her everything about Ahmed, just like I told you now. She took his number from my phone. It seems she called him, and she sent him a friend request on Facebook, and so on. Two days later, he had blocked me on every platform! I couldn't find out a thing about him.

Yasmeen was convinced that Hiba had stolen her new (and future) husband. She never saw or heard from Ahmed again, even though technically she was married to him, as they had signed a marriage contract and he had never, to her knowledge, divorced her. That didn't stop her from continuing to marry Arab foreigners through the marriage office. But she also sometimes married Egyptian men and stayed with them for varying lengths of time—days, weeks, months. She couldn't count how many times she had been married.

Most recently, Yasmeen had been married for several months to an Egyptian man, Yousef. Yousef was down on his luck. He told Yasmeen that he owned a car and a shop that sold and repaired mobile phones, but he had recently lost a lot of money. She entered into an 'urfi marriage with him and told him that she was going to "stand by him" during the hard times. He moved in with her extended family. She had another job at the time that brought in a steady salary. But then one day she went to the beach with Yousef and a group of friends and while Yousef was in the water, his friend told her that her husband was lying about everything; the cell phone shop he claimed to own actually belonged to his brother.

He was lying to me! He is such a scammer. He lives on women. How? He meets you, he makes you love him, he makes you feel that he's so pitiable [ghalban], this and that, and in the end it turns out he's a liar. I married him. I gave him everything. Food, drink, cigarettes, sleep—twenty-four hours a day he wants to sleep with me!

Then she found out that not only had he lied about his circumstances, he was also married to another woman named Nour. Yasmeen tracked down Nour and told her about Yousef's duplicity and persuaded her to ask Yousef for a divorce. Once Yasmeen was Yousef's only wife, she remonstrated with him for the deception.

I asked him, why did you lie to me? I live with you through the bad times before the good. But at least be honest with me. If you are working as a garbage collector and I love you and I want you, I'll help you out. I won't care about the garbage. But in a relationship and in a marriage there has to be trust. We can't make a life together with lies. . . . He reassured me; he promised he'd never lie again.

Money and Intimacy

I begin this chapter with an extended account of some of Yasmeen's many romantic and sexual encounters to illustrate the complexity of the relationship between money and intimacy. In Egypt (as in many other places), intimate and romantic relationships occur at the intersection between affect, practical considerations and material interests, and local cultural norms that structure people's ideas about the legitimacy of particular kinds of intimate relationships. These cultural norms, broadly speaking, legitimize sex within marriage and stigmatize it outside of marriage, but they are profoundly gendered, tolerating extramarital sex for men but condemning it in women. Yet, as Yasmeen's account shows, women nevertheless do engage in sexual intimacy outside of both registered and customary marriage and thus must put much energy into managing their reputations and the various dangers—both social and legal—associated with extramarital sex in Egypt. Yasmeen manages these sometimes by engaging in transactional sex within the protective framework of (unregistered) marriage. Yet she also marries without pecuniary reward and even liaisons that begin as transactional shade into potentially more permanent relationships characterized by more complex reciprocity.

Yasmeen is one of my contacts whom I have known for most of the more than two decades that I have conducted ethnographic research in Egypt. Much of this research has focused on the topics of intimacy and money (Wynn 2018, chapters 5–6). My research participants included not only men and women who engaged in transactional sex, but also those who were in more conventional relationships. In this chapter, however, I focus particularly on two key informants: Yasmeen and Maryam, two poor women with very different experiences of transactional sex and philosophies about love and lucre. I situate their experiences within broader Egyptian sociocultural discourses—both mainstream and marginal—around the relationship between intimacy and money.

Egyptian cultural norms around intimacy and kinship intersect with material interest by shaping Egyptians' ideas about, for example, how much money a couple needs to marry, or under what circumstances a man or woman should provide material support or gifts to a romantic partner. But affect—people's individual feelings of love and desire for a romantic partner—also intervenes to further complicate things. As we can see from Yasmeen's story, her affection for Yousef along with her cultural sense of the importance of "standing by" her partner combined to override other cultural norms that dictate that a man should be the one to support a woman financially. That this principle of "standing by" a partner through thick and thin is a cultural ideal was demonstrated to me when research participants mentioned it again and again in interviews, regardless of their social class or personal experiences.

As Yasmeen's story shows, intimate connections are complex and categories such as "transactional sex," "sex worker," "girlfriend," and even "wife" are far blurrier in practice than the labels might suggest (Groes-Green 2013, 105). Historically, social science research on sex work has often sought to create categories across variables such as the price they charge and how public or private their places of business; their orientation toward sex work as long-term career or temporary business opportunity; the intimacy and extent of the relationship between sex worker and client (one-off transactional sex versus more complex constructions of intimacy, such as a "girlfriend experience," a regular customer, or a more or less exclusive "kept woman"); forms of payment and reciprocity (money versus gifts); degrees of stigma or prestige associated with sex work (distinguishing, for example, between streetwalkers, high-price escorts, and courtesans, and between illegal and legal sex work); and reasons for engaging in sex work (drawing distinctions between those who need money to survive and those who do it because they want luxury items such as new model phones, clothing, and jewelry) (Brennan 2004; Day 2007; Hunter 2002; Kotiswaran 2011; Padilla 2007; Ratliff 1999; Weitzer 2009).

At the same time that this literature often seeks to neatly categorize the interactions between intimacy and money, authors also frequently point out that the reality of people's lives exists on a continuum (Brennan 2004; Carrier-Moisan 2017; Fassin, Le Marcis, and Lethata 2008; Groes-Green 2013; Padilla 2007; Williams 2013; Wynn 2018). In Egypt, there are practical difficulties in deciding what counts as sex work, in a context where all intimate relationships are characterized by material exchanges. A widespread cultural ideal dictates that men should pay for excursions, food, drink, and small gifts for women with whom they are intimately involved, whether the woman is a wife, fiancée, girlfriend, or a new date. Upon marriage, husbands give their new wives gifts and cash, including precious jewelry (ranging from silver to gold and diamonds, depending on means) and cash transfers that are written into the marriage contract (see the essays in Quraishi and Vogel 2009 for a discussion of how monetary concerns are differently written into Islamic marriage contracts across multiple geographical and cultural settings). Even transactional sex is rarely enacted as a straightforward transfer of cash for specific services; Yasmeen's story shows that she took different sums from different partners according to her circumstances (and their means) at the time, that she received a mix of gifts and cash, and that she was almost always open to turning temporary relationships into permanent ones.

As Viviana Zelizer (2005) has argued in her historical review of the links between money and intimacy in the United States, these are closely linked in culturally dictated norms of reciprocity, yet the links are simultaneously denied, as evidenced in pop culture where love and money are frequently portrayed as diametrically opposed (as in the Beatles' song "Can't Buy Me Love"). Not so in Egypt, where cultural norms openly associate money with intimacy. For most Egyptians, the exchange of money is not what makes sexual intimacy legitimate or not. Legitimate sexuality is determined based on whether a couple is married or not, and regardless of whether a relationship is legalized with marriage or not, there is a strong expectation that monetary and gift exchanges between a couple are markers of love, rather than its contamination.

Further complicating any simple classification of transactional sex in Egypt is 'urfi marriage, which can be easily entered into and then dissolved as such marriages are not registered with the state. 'Urfi marriage gives sexual intimacy a legal and moral cover, even as it creates gendered inequities (Abaza 2001; Kholoussy 2010; Salem 2015, 2016; Wynn 2016). Such marriages are, as Yasmeen's story shows, used in sex work formally transacted through a procurer, but they are also entered into by couples in love who lack the financial means or parental support to marry officially and publicly (see Salem, this volume).

In this chapter, I present ethnographic material from long-term fieldwork in Egypt on intimate relationships to ask: is the categorization of people as sex workers, or as types of sex workers, useful in this context?

Do these classifications reflect people's phenomenological experience of the economy of intimacy? In other words, looking at intimacy and economic exchange from the perspective of Egyptians participating in it, are labels like "sex work" meaningful? And from a more etic perspective, do categories help us better understand people's intimate lives and the intersection of sex and money, or do they obscure the real-life complexity of people's lives?

Methods and Research Ethics

This analysis is grounded in ethnographic research periodically conducted in Cairo and Alexandria, Egypt, over a twenty-three-year period, from 1997 through 2020. Much of this research has explored cultural configurations of intimacy, including the relationship between money and intimacy. Research participants and ethnographic interlocutors included men and women representing a range of social classes and age groups, from the very poor to the very wealthy, and from their teens to their sixties. My research participants also included men and women who sometimes engage in transactional sex but who did not define themselves as sex workers.

I recruited participants through social networks I have been building in Cairo and Alexandria for over two decades, starting from my PhD research on tourism at the turn of the millennium (which was ethically reviewed by Princeton University Department of Anthropology) and continuing to more recent research on sexual and reproductive health (which was approved by Macquarie University's Human Research Ethics Committee). I have multiple independent social networks with little to no overlap between them, because the people in those networks work in different professions and come from widely disparate class backgrounds. In simple technical terms, my participant recruitment strategies entailed snowball sampling using multiple starting points, but that description also obscures more complex ways of knowing people, of recruiting research participants, and the mix of friendship and instrumentality (on both sides) that characterizes my relationship with my long-term informants.

In addition to the broader, longitudinal ethnographic research, which helps to situate what people say in the context of their life histories, the fieldwork that informed this research consisted partly of formal, open-ended interviews. In fourteen formal interviews, I asked people from a wide range of backgrounds their opinion about intimacy and sexuality. I asked what they considered to be normal practices in Egyptian society. In addition to questions meant to elicit cultural ideals, I also invited participants to share specific stories of people they knew to give context to their opinions about what was normal and to illustrate how people (frequently) deviated from the norm and what the social consequences were for doing so.

Questions about general beliefs and practices allow people to make their own decisions about how much personal information they wish to share with me. Some participants talked at length while sharing nearly nothing about their personal lives, while others shared intimate secrets with me, and I had careful conversations with them about what identifying information to change in order to protect their identities when writing their stories. With participants' verbal consent, I audio-recorded the formal interviews presented in this chapter and then transcribed and translated them myself. At the request of participants, I did not record two interviews and instead took detailed notes. The names in this chapter are all pseudonyms chosen by research participants themselves.

In the following section, I focus on just two research participants. I continue telling Yasmeen's story and then I present Maryam's account and describe how intimacy and money figure into her life. Both are poor women who have quite different experiences of transactional sex; one is from Alexandria while the other is from Cairo. I have chosen to focus on these two key informants in order to address the research questions framing this chapter with ethnographic detail and depth. Following Yasmeen's and Maryam's stories, I analyze these case studies to ask how these women themselves understand the relationship between money and intimacy.

————————————*Yasmeen, Continued*————————————

All of the exchanges of money and gifts that characterized Yasmeen's relationships with the men she dated fit within local norms of gender relationships. Yasmeen expected any man she was dating to pay for food and drinks, unless there were extenuating circumstances. This wasn't a matter of sex work; most women had the same expectations. In any relationship—whether casual dating, courtship, engagement, or marriage—she expected the man to give her gifts and some degree of financial support. The extent of that support would increase with the formality of the relationship. Yasmeen enjoyed men, flirting, and sex, and she enjoyed that tantalizing interplay at the beginning of a relationship when you are attracted to someone and they are attracted to you and you don't know how exactly the relationship will develop. She also hoped that eventually she would find a man who would marry her conventionally and provide for her financially.

Thus, even though Ahmed (the Lebanese man she 'urfi married from the marriage agency) was twice her age, she was still thrilled about the possibility of a long-term, "official" (in her words) marriage with him. After Ahmed ghosted her, she twice married men from the Arab Gulf through the same agency, but the second time, the Saudi man she married beat her after having sex with her. Furious, Yasmeen returned to the agency and demanded that Soumeyya give her the cut she had taken from that man. Soumeyya did so. Yasmeen hasn't married anyone through that broker since then, not because of the physical assault but because she believed that Gulf men always cheated Egyptian women in these exchanges.

A [Gulf] Arab would say, "I'll pay 1,000 riyals [US$270] to her for me to sleep with me." And then he goes and exchanges his money and then he gives her only 1,000 Egyptian pounds [US$63] to sleep with him. He promises so much and doesn't come through.

Nowadays Yasmeen mainly dates Egyptian men. Some pay her to spend an evening with them. Sometimes her mother accompanies her to a man's apartment and sits in the outside room to lend their visit respectability while the man takes Yasmeen into the bedroom and has sex with her for money. "Yasmeen's mother is just like a pimp," her cousin told me with a chuckle. And sometimes Yasmeen sleeps with a man just for pleasure, with no financial reward in mind.

In 2019, she fell in love with Yousef. When she first married him, she thought he was just down on his luck. She was willing to support the household with her own income. After she discovered he had lied about his financial means, she still remained married to him, even persuading him to divorce another wife. Then Yasmeen's mother

got very sick and she had to borrow a large sum from a family friend
to pay for her care. The lender came over to their house. Yasmeen
welcomed him in to the living room where the whole extended
family was gathered to read the Qur'an and pray for her mother's
health. Yasmeen asked Yousef to act like a proper host and greet the
lender and to go buy some food and drink to serve their guests, but
he refused. He sprawled in his boxer shorts lazily and ordered her to
bring dinner to him in their bedroom. Disgusted, she yelled at him
to get up and greet the guests. He got mad and started hitting her.

As Yasmeen described it, her mother, "fierce as a lion protecting her cubs," rose from her sickbed and attacked Yousef. All the
women in the household ganged up on him (much to the shock of
the visiting lender) and physically expelled him from the house. Yasmeen recounted shouting (again, much to the shock of her visitor),
"Get out of here, you parasite! I spent on you and you want to eat
and drink and sleep and shit and pee and fuck for free? You son of a
bitch!" After that episode, she divorced him. Reflecting on the experience, Yasmeen said,

A woman needs a man who will stand by her, to pat her on the back when
she needs it. She wants hugs and comfort. But he was a liar. And because
I have a white heart, I believed him. But he was living his life with lots of
women, marrying all the time, and even now after we've been divorced for
a while, I keep hearing that he's married. Still lying to women. And by the
way, he sucks at sex. He leaves the woman wanting. He gets close to women
so that he can take advantage of them. I supported him. I used to make him
molokhiya [jute], chicken, rice, eggplant stew, stuffed vegetables, zucchini,
bell pepper, stuffed grape leaves. He didn't even buy his own cigarettes! I
got so sick of him.

After I finished recording Yasmeen's formal interview, I spent
several hours chatting with her extended family, where our conversations ranged widely. We discussed my children back in Australia
and the circumstances of all of Yasmeen's relatives and our mutual
acquaintances, and we reviewed each other's Instagram accounts
admiringly. In the midst of this sprawling socializing, various permanent and temporary household members circulated through the

living room. Tamara, who had slept over after a late night out with Yasmeen, wandered out from the bedroom, last-night's makeup still thick on her cheeks and her false eyelashes half falling off. Yasmeen's sister had a fever; the household mobilized to make her hot tea and tuck a blanket around her. Yasmeen's fifteen-year-old daughter shared the story of how she met her current beau, and her recently widowed grandmother told me a complicated story of the ups and downs of her own love life. Other friends and relatives stopped by the house, telephoned, or videochatted with us via WhatsApp. Some of these agreed to participate in short formal interviews with me. We ordered takeout *koshary* (an Egyptian dish of noodles, rice, lentils, and fried onions) for lunch, and later, Yasmeen used sugar paste to wax the hair off my arms, a service she has performed for me every time I have visited her over a decade.

Before I left, I discretely pressed Yasmeen (as the financial head of the household) to accept a wad of Egyptian pounds to the sum of around US$65, urging her to use it for household expenses. She had not only coordinated a half-dozen formal interviews for me, she had also fed us all. I calculated this sum to be a culturally appropriate form of reciprocity. Yasmeen's acceptance of the sum (after a polite ritual of refusal on her part and insistence on mine) signaled that my form of reciprocity was indeed appropriate.

When I left that evening, I could not fail to note the similarities between the way both Yasmeen's male clients and I gave her money for expenses in exchange for the services she provided us, all mediated through cultural idioms of hosting and generosity.

Maryam

Maryam was a friend of twenty years and when I visited Cairo, she came to pick me up from my hotel to take me downtown so we could talk and catch up. I climbed in the backseat of the car and Maryam sat in front next to the driver, her neighbor. As we drove, I tried to explain to her my latest anthropological research project. We decided to record an interview while we were in the car.

"I want to write about the relationship between money and

intimate relationships," I said. "You know, who pays for whom, and when, and why." Maryam commented, "Yeah, I've had to do that for money sometimes. When I need money, I do that work."

I was surprised that she had said this in front of a male neighbor. Every previous time I had talked to Maryam about sex and money, she had asserted that she had no interest in having sex for money. She liked men, and she liked sex, and she couldn't bear the idea of being paid to have sex with someone she didn't choose, though she would gladly take money from someone she loved. So telling me that she had taken up occasional sex work was new, and I wanted to hear more, but I decided to ask her to elaborate later, when her neighbor, Wael, was not present.

I continued to explain my research project. "There are a lot of people who have written about money and intimate relationships from the perspective of men who give money to women, so I thought I would do something a little less common and write about women who give money and gifts to men." I was interested in cases where women supported men financially because, although I had the impression that this was not uncommon, it also conflicted with cultural ideals of masculinity (Wynn 2022). I was curious about how the conflict between cultural ideal and reality was managed in people's narratives. But I soon realized that my grasp of the nuances of euphemism had failed me, and Maryam had understood my reference to "intimate relations," which I had hoped would convey both kinship and romantic relationships, as referring only to sex.

"Oh yeah," she agreed genially, "there's plenty of that around. Women who pay. But it's always older women, you know? Fifty, sixty years old. They don't have a husband so they pay a younger man. It's very common."

I explained my mistake in Arabic expression, but then said, "Actually, that would be an interesting topic to research. But how does this work?"

"What do you mean, how does it work?" Maryam said. "She pays him, and they have sex. It's business."

"Business," Wael echoed from the front seat. "I might, for example, have sex with you, but I don't love her." (I registered warily his switch between a hypothetical "you" and a hypothetical "her.")

"Business," he repeated. "I have intimate relations with you for one hundred dollars, two hundred dollars. Like that. You get it? And that's present everywhere."

I wondered how this worked in practice. How would a man looking for clients signal his availability? I asked Wael and Maryam, "How would a woman find a man who agrees to this?"

"I agree to that!" Wael interjected. We all laughed. Wael looked me in the eye and declared, "Just think, I earn 300 pounds [US$19] a day for driving. And I could earn maybe 500 pounds [US$31] for having sex." He held my gaze in the rearview mirror and repeated, "If there's any lady who wants it, I'm happy to help out."

I laughed nervously, suddenly acutely aware of the potential pitfalls of a middle-aged, female, foreign anthropologist asking an Egyptian man for his thoughts about having sex with older women for money.

After Wael had dropped us off and I was alone with Maryam, I asked her what had changed in her willingness to exchange sex for money.

Look, Lisa, when I didn't have any money, I started doing this. I go to someone, an old guy. When I have absolutely no money left, I call him. He says come over. I go and sit with him for an hour or two. He doesn't do anything. He kisses me; he plays around. He tires me out physically, you understand? But he doesn't come. He can't. He can't get it up and he can't come, because he has diabetes. But he's happy to just play around with me. I give him the feeling that he is very strong, that he's not weak. So that he doesn't feel broken inside. And then he gives me what I want.

I asked her how much he pays her. "It depends on how much I need," she replied.

Say if one day I need 200 pounds [US$13], another day I need 300 [US$19] urgently, if there's something I need. There's no fixed amount. It depends on my circumstances. He says, "Come to me for a couple of hours, we sit together, we have relations together, and I'll give you money in your hand so that you don't need anything from anyone."

I asked her if she thought marriage was in their future, because I knew she had long sought formal marriage with someone who would father children with her. She replied with indignation.

What are you talking about, Lisa? He is already married. And he has grown children who have children. He's a grandfather! What in the world would I do with him, marrying a grandpa? And anyway, I don't want him. I don't desire him. I'm the type where I can't stand it for just anyone to touch me. Or if I have to do something against my will, I get really upset about it.

This was the only time Maryam ever told me about engaging in transactional sex. Most of the stories she told me about her relationships over the years were about how she had lost money in her relationships with men.

For example, for a long time she was on-and-off 'urfi married to a policeman named Waleed. He was handsome and she enjoyed having sex with him, but their relationship was tumultuous and not emotionally intimate. When Maryam wanted to borrow money to start a small business, Waleed arranged a usurious loan with a wealthy acquaintance. Maryam later discovered that Waleed had kept two thirds of the interest payments she had given him to repay the lender, while telling the lender that she hadn't yet made a payment.

When I found out, I called him and I said, "Why didn't you just tell me? Tell me you want money. I'll give you whatever you want. Why do you cheat me like this? If you needed money, I'd have given it to you without you even telling me you need it." We used to travel together, Lisa, and I would rent the apartment. I'd pay for everything. I'd pay for the food. He didn't pay for anything. He kept saying he didn't have money. I used to love him. I saw no one but him. It's hard when you love someone and he doesn't love you. He took so much money from me. He cheated me.

When I asked Maryam about the gendered cultural norms governing the relationship between intimacy and money, she was adamant that for a man to accept money from a woman signaled that he was taking advantage of her and didn't love her. She said, "It means he's not a good man, in my view." In contrast, for a woman to accept money from a man in a loving relationship was the normal order of things.

But then I reminded her about her ex-fiancé, Nabeel. I said, "Didn't you used to spend on Nabeel?" She agreed that she had. "And does that mean he didn't love you?" She shook her head no.

He used to say he loved me, and he really did love me. I'm sure of that. But his dad controlled him. His dad never gave him any money. He was stingy. So I used to help Nabeel out. If his son was sick, for example, I'd give him money for medicine or to go to the doctor. I'd give him money to pay the electricity bill, the water bill, the gas, the rent. I'd get him clothing. Yeah. Because I used to love him, understand? Listen, Lisa, when you love someone, you don't see anything else except him. When you find he's facing difficulties, you help him. Understand? So. You love him.

Maryam's love for Nabeel, and her certainty that he loved her back, trumped cultural norms dictating that a man should support the woman in his life rather than the reverse. But despite promising to marry her for years, he never did, and eventually Maryam decided their relationship had no future. Desperately sad about this, she broke things off with Nabeel.

Intimacy, Sex, Money, and Gifts

The romantic and the instrumental are inseparable (Rubenstein 2004), yet attempts to categorize sex work persist in positioning them as opposites. For Zelizer (2005), this assumption that positions intimacy and money as diametrically opposed and that doubts the legitimacy of relationships contaminated by lucre is what she calls the "hostile worlds" theory. Ethnographic material from Egypt illustrates that, in local emic terms, what delegitimizes a romantic relationship is not the infusion of money into it. A legitimate intimate relationship is one where one "stands by" her or his partner. Offering financial support is often one way to do that. A legitimate (or "clean," in the words of Yasmeen's cousin) intimate relationship is also one that occurs in the context of marriage, but as we have seen, the category of marriage in Egypt is a blurry one.

These are only two case studies of poor women in Alexandria and Cairo, and their circumstances and opinions are far from representative of the attitudes of all Egyptians toward sex and marriage. But their views on intimacy and money reflect wider Egyptian beliefs that intimacy and money are closely and appropriately linked.

Yasmeen engages in relationships that most outside observers would call sex work. It is not a career for her and I don't have the impression that she considers herself a sex worker, which is not a locally meaningful concept in Egypt. She sees sexual intimacy as one skill in her wide repertoire for surviving in a precarious economy, along with talking to a foreign anthropologist, dressing her friends' hair, and other small jobs she hustled in the informal sector. But she was also clear with me—not only in the formal interview but over the years I have known her—that she enjoyed men and liked not only sex but the seductive process of getting to know someone new. As Groes-Green observes, "women's choice to engage in cross-generational and transactional sex can also be part of an economic strategy within unequal playing fields," but that doesn't render them "powerless and vulnerable victims of economic inequalities and patriarchal privilege" (2013, 102).

In contrast with Yasmeen, Maryam only occasionally engages in transactional sex, which she describes as a performance of sexual intimacy and a kind of emotional labor, as she strives to make her partner feel as if he is not sexually weak. She describes it as work and does it only when desperate for money. But she also describes her elderly partner's reciprocity as part of an ongoing relationship, and his payments as a form of care that offers her respite from the stresses of her financially precarious situation.

As we see not only in Yasmeen's and Maryam's accounts but also the quotes from Wael (Maryam's neighbor and driver), transactional sex occurs in the context of economic precarity among the poor unemployed and working classes and an everyday struggle to make ends meet in the formal and informal economies. People derive income and other material goods through whatever services they can offer. This meant seizing opportunities to marry wealthy Arab men, make an impotent grandfather feel that he still had sexual prowess, flag one's availability for sex work to a visiting foreign anthropologist, and turn one's home into an interview center and beauty salon for a day to accommodate the same anthropologist. Yet, in almost every one of these cases, the exchange of money was mediated by cultural rituals, gifts, expressions of emotional intimacy, and social connectedness that ensured that these exchanges were not alienated commodities but rather embedded into social relations that had, at the very least, the possibility to endure over time.

Despite Maryam and Wael's claim that sex between an older woman and a man would be "business," both Yasmeen's and Maryam's stories of transactional sex describe social and emotional labor that blur the line between economic transaction and gift. Even the most overtly transactional of Yasmeen's sexual relationships, those brokered by a procuress who took half of the client payment, were also marriages and thus completely outside of any Egyptian legal definition of prostitution. Yet this does not make them completely socially legitimate. They incur stigma—the Egyptian press frequently condemns the moral vacuity of such "summer marriages," as they are often called, since they coincide with the summer Gulf tourism season (see Wynn 2007, chapters 4–5, for a more detailed account of Egyptian social commentary on temporary marriages between Egyptian women and Gulf Arab men). The money she received in these transactions also fit within local cultural norms around marriage, in which the groom provides a payment of money and jewelry to the bride so that she can set up house and adorn herself.

If we take a phenomenological approach to sex and money in Egypt, that is, if we seek to understand it from the perceptual and experiential horizon of the people whose lives we are trying to describe (Desjarlais and Throop 2011; Ram and Houston 2015), then what does "transactional sex" mean to my Egyptian informants? As the two case studies illustrate, money or material exchanges are not, from the perspective of the Egyptians I have done research with, what "contaminate" a relationship. That's not to say that the concept of "transactional sex" is locally meaningless. On the contrary, it is clear that people have clear ideas about certain contexts in which they consider sex or intimacy to be morally vacuous or abhorrent. But we must examine transactional sex in the context of the social relationships within which it occurs, not just in terms of an exchange of money.

Yasmeen, Maryam, and almost all of the other people who I interviewed, regardless of their social class and experience of or opinion about transactional sex, repeatedly spoke about one's obligation to "stand by" the person with whom one has an intimate relationship. An intimate relationship was illegitimate not when gifts or even bald cash were exchanged between parties—indeed, these economic and gift exchanges were actually important signifiers of the *legitimacy* of the relationships. A relationship was illegitimate when one party deceived, swindled, or lied to the other. A relationship failed when one party refused an ongoing social connection, as when the Lebanese man Yasmeen was to marry disappeared from her life and blocked her on social media, or when a man took financial support from a woman and didn't give back in some way. In this respect, my Egyptian research participants' perspectives on what makes an intimate relationship legitimate is in line with what Faier describes for unequal relationships between Filipina women and Japanese men: moral value is based on a sense of respect and each partner giving the other what both feel is owed to them, not material exchanges (2007, 156).

This is substantiated by both historical and contemporary Egyptian legal ways of understanding and criminalizing "prostitution." Police may arrest men and women for sexual congress outside of marriage, not for the exchange of money for sex. Thus hastily executed 'urfi marriage contracts protect against being raided by the vice police. Prosecutors consider they have a viable legal case against a woman for prostitution not because she has received money from a man but because she has been found in a private space with a man or men with whom she does not have an ongoing social relationship (see Fahmy 2002 and Tucker 1985 for historical accounts of prostitution in Egypt and Wynn 2018, 127–39 for a more detailed contemporary accounting of this). And, as we can see from Yasmeen's story in particular, it is clear that relatives play a key role in mediating transactional sex and in defining the legitimacy of sexual intimacies.

Scholars of transactional sex have long recognized the complex ways intimacy and money intersect and the fact that people's lives are lived on a continuum where it is, in reality, difficult to define sex work and draw bright lines between sex that is socially defined as legitimate or not (Brennan 2004; Carrier-Moisan 2017; Constable 2009; Padilla 2007). Almost always, though, definitions in the social science literature around what constitutes authentic sexual intimacy revolve around the circumstances under which money is or is not exchanged. Perhaps this reflects the biases of scholars' own cultural backgrounds in which money is imagined to contaminate love.

As Constable notes, "The conflation of intimate social relations with monetary value is criticized by those who imagine a more altruistic or authentic precapitalist past or who view the domestic sphere as a proper shelter from the harsh and impersonal world of market capitalism. Yet the question remains of how the commodification of intimate relations is understood and experienced by those involved in such relationships and processes" (2009, 54). As I have argued here, the exchange of money is irrelevant to local Egyptian understandings of what makes sexual intimacy legitimate or not. The continuum on which sexual intimacy shades from ideal and legitimate to socially condemned and illegal is determined based on whether a relationship occurs within the context of marriage and the degree to which partners are committed to each other in enduring ties of mutual support, which includes financial support. Money may not buy love, but its exchange reflects and measures love.

NOTES

1. I use pseudonyms throughout.
2. Yasmeen sometimes mentioned pounds, dollars, or riyals but often gave figures without specifying whether she was referring to the Egyptian or Lebanese pound, American or Australian dollars, or Saudi riyals. Over the course of the afternoon as we spoke, figures and specified currencies changed as Yasmeen narrated her stories, I suspect according to the kind of impression she wished to give me and other listeners in the room (consisting of her cousin, two daughters, her mother, and a friend). Stories about large sums that men paid to spend time with her awed and impressed her listeners, so she may have inflated some figures, or said dollars when the currency exchanged was actually Egyptian pounds (at the time, the US dollar was worth about 17 Egyptian pounds). She may also have been broadly hinting to me at appropriate sums that I should expect to pay to spend time with her. Around the time of this interview, with the Arab Spring in the recent past along with the catastrophic economic inflation and currency devaluation that it triggered, American dollars were still valuable and rare (as they were worth more on the black market than at official exchange rates) and so she may have sometimes said that men gave her dollars in order to hint that I should do so as well. Thus the figures and currencies she provides in the quotes I have excerpted from her interview may not be very accurate and should be regarded with some skepticism and also admiration for her narrative flair and businesswoman's instincts.

REFERENCES

Abaza, Mona. 2001. "Perceptions of 'Urfi Marriage in the Egyptian Press." *International Institute for the Study of Islam in the Modern World (ISIM) Newsletter* 7/01: 20–21.

Bernstein, Elizabeth. 2013. *Temporarily Yours: Intimacy, Authenticity, and the Commerce of Sex.* Chicago, London: University of Chicago Press.

Brennan, Denise. 2004. *What's Love Got to Do with It?: Transnational Desires and Sex Tourism in the Dominican Republic.* Durham, NC: Duke University Press.

———. 2017. "Fighting Human Trafficking Today: Moral Panics, Zombie Data, and the Seduction of Rescue." *Wake Forest Law Review* 52, no. 2: 477–96.

Carrier-Moisan, Marie-Eve. 2017. "'I Have to Feel Something': Gringo Love in the Sexual Economy of Tourism in Natal, Brazil." *Journal of Latin American and Caribbean Anthropology* 23, no. 1: 131–51.

Constable, Nicole. 2009. "The Commodification of Intimacy: Marriage, Sex, and Reproductive Labor." *Annual Review of Anthropology* 28: 49–64.

Day, Sophie. 2007. *On the Game: Women and Sex Work*. London: Pluto Press.

Desjarlais, Robert and C. Jason Throop. 2011. "Phenomenological Approaches in Anthropology." *Annual Review of Anthropology* 40: 87–102.

Fahmy, Khaled. 2002. "Prostitution in Egypt in the Nineteenth Century." In *Outside In: Marginality in the Modern Middle East*, edited by Eugene Rogan, 77–103. London: I. B. Tauris.

Faier, Lieba. 2007. "Filipina Migrants in Rural Japan and Their Professions of Love." *American Ethnologist* 34, no. 1: 148–62.

Fassin, Didier, Frédéric Le Marcis, and Todd Lethata. 2008. "Life and Times of Magda A:
Telling a Story of Violence in South Africa." *Current Anthropology* 49, no. 2: 225–46.

Groes-Green, Christian. 2013. "'To Put Men in a Bottle': Eroticism, Kinship, Female Power,
and Transactional Sex in Maputo, Mozambique." *American Ethnologist* 40, no. 1: 102–17.

Hunter, Mark. 2002. "The Materiality of Everyday Sex: Thinking Beyond 'Prostitution.'"
African Studies 61, no. 1: 99–120.

———. 2009. "Providing Love: Sex and Exchange in Twentieth-Century South Africa." In
Love in Africa, edited by Jennifer Cole and Lynn M. Thomas, 135–56. Chicago: University of Chicago Press.

Jeffreys, Elaine. 2004. "Feminist Prostitution Debates: Are There Any Sex Workers in
China?" In *Chinese Women: Living and Working*, edited by Anne E. McLaren, 83–107.
New York: Routledge Curzon.

Joseph, Suad. 1999. "Brother-Sister Relationships: Connectivity, Love, and Power in the
Reproduction of Patriarchy in Lebanon." In *Intimate Selving in Arab Families: Gender,
Self, and Identity*, edited by S. Joseph, 113–40. Syracuse, NY: Syracuse University Press.

Kholoussy, Hanan. 2010. *For Better, for Worse: The Marriage Crisis That Made Modern Egypt*.
Stanford, CA: Stanford University Press.

Kotiswaran, Prabha. 2011. *Dangerous Sex, Invisible Labor: Sex Work and the Law in India*.
Princeton, NJ: Princeton University Press.

Padilla, Mark B. 2007. "'Western Union Daddies' and Their Quest for Authenticity: An Ethnographic Study of the Dominican Gay Sex Tourism Industry." *Journal of Homosexuality*
53, no. 1–2: 241–75.

Quraishi, Asifa, and Frank Vogel, eds. 2009. *The Islamic Marriage Contract: Case Studies
in Islamic Family Law*. Cambridge, MA: Islamic Legal Studies Program, Harvard Law
School.

Ram, Kalpana, and Christopher Houston, eds. 2015. *Phenomenology in Anthropology: A
Sense of Perspective*. Bloomington: Indiana University Press.

Ratliff, Eric A. 1999. "Women as 'Sex Workers,' Men as 'Boyfriends': Shifting Identities in
Philippine Go-Go Bars and Their Significance in STD/AIDS Control." *Anthropology and
Medicine* 6, no. 1: 79–101.

Rubenstein, Steven L. 2004. "Fieldwork and the Erotic Economy on the Colonial Frontier."
Signs: Journal of Women in Culture and Society 29, no. 4: 1041–71.

Salem, Rania. 2015. "Changes in the Institution of Marriage in Egypt from 1998 to 2012." In
The Egyptian Labor Market in an Era of Revolution, edited by Ragui Assaad and Caroline

Krafft, 162–81. Oxford: Oxford University Press.

———. 2016. "Imagined Crises: Assessing Evidence of Delayed Marriage and Never-Marriage in Contemporary Egypt." *Domestic Tensions, National Anxieties: Global Perspectives on Marriage Crisis,* eds. Kristin Celello and Hanan Kholoussy, 231–54. Oxford: Oxford University Press.

Tucker, Judith. 1985. *Women in Nineteenth Century Egypt.* Cambridge, UK: Cambridge University Press.

Weitzer, Ronald. 2009. "Sociology of Sex Work." *Annual Review of Sociology* 35: 213–34.

Williams, Erica. 2013. *Sex Tourism in Bahia: Ambiguous Entanglements.* Urbana: University of Illinois Press.

Wynn, L. L. 2007. *Pyramids and Nightclubs.* Austin: University of Texas Press.

———. 2016. "'Like a Virgin': Hymenoplasty and Secret Marriage in Egypt." *Medical Anthropology* 35, no. 6: 547–59.

———. 2018. *Love, Sex, and Desire in Modern Egypt: Navigating the Margins of Respectability.* Austin: University of Texas Press.

———. 2022 "Masculinity under Siege: The Use of Narcotic Pain Relievers to Restore Virility." In *Arab Masculinities: Anthropological Reconceptions in Precarious Times,* edited by Konstantina Isidoros and Marcia Inhorn, 190–210. Bloomington: Indiana University Press.

Zelizer, Viviana. 2005. *The Purchase of Intimacy.* Princeton, NJ: Princeton University Press.

CHAPTER 11

Legal and Illegal Sex Work in Tunisia

Before and After the 2010–2011 Revolution

LAURENCE MICHALAK

Changing Patterns of Legal and Illegal Sex Work in Tunisia

Tunisia has legal female sex workers (FSWs) and legal brothels, which is rare in the Middle East and North Africa (MENA) region because Islam strictly forbids sex outside marriage. Under the French Protectorate, brothels in Tunisia were made legal and regulated by the government, and at independence in 1956 Tunisia retained this policy. An unmarried Tunisian woman between the ages of twenty and fifty can apply to the Ministry of Interior to become a legal sex worker and receive an identity card, which allows her to work in a legal brothel, with regular medical inspections for sexually transmitted infections (STIs). Only Tunisian women—that is, no foreign women and no men of any nationality—are eligible to become legal sex workers. Prostitution—defined as sex work outside the framework of legal sex workers and brothels—is against the law and punishable by up to two years in prison and/or a fine of up to 200 dinars (US$68).

On the eve of the Tunisian Revolution in 2010, there were fourteen Tunisian cities and towns with legal brothels (Dahmani 2014). In the parliamentary election of October 2011, Ennahda, an Islamist party, won 42 percent of the seats in the Constituent Assembly, formed a ruling alliance with two smaller parties, and remained in power for three years, during which the Assembly wrote a new constitution. Some observers expected that Ennahda would use its position of power to enact laws in keeping with Islam—such as abolishing legal sex work—but this did not happen.

During the months following the Revolution, Islamist rioters attacked legal brothels throughout the country—in Sousse, Medenine, Kef, Beja, Kairouan, Kebili, and elsewhere—looting and burning and driving out the FSWs. In some cases women were "hunted down and beaten" (Smoltczyk 2012). In Kairouan, the rioters not only attacked the brothel quarter but built a wall around it, sealing it off and isolating it. In some cities the legal brothels were closed administratively by order of the governor.

The legal brothels in Tunis and Sfax, Tunisia's two largest cities, were attacked, but the rioters were met by men who blocked them. A compromise was reached whereby these two brothel quarters were allowed to remain open, with the condition that they must close on Fridays and during the month of Ramadan and install gates that can be locked. These are now the only two official brothel quarters left in Tunisia.

However, despite the fact that the law allows legal sex work, since 2011 the authorities have been unofficially suppressing legal FSWs by refusing to renew their permits. As a result, between 2011 and 2019 the number of FSWs in Tunis and Sfax has decreased by over 90 percent. As of 2015, there were about sixty FSWs in Tunis and ninety in Sfax (Ministry of Health 2015, 24). By mid-2019 there were only thirty in Sfax and fewer in Tunis, while once there had been over two hundred FSWs at each site (Abdelmajid Zahaf, Personal communication, April 27, 2019).

In contrast to this sharp decline in legal sex work, illegal sex work has flourished. Many of the legal FSWs who lost their jobs when their brothels were closed have become "prostitutes." In Tunis and Sfax, even many legal FSWs no longer felt safe after the riots, so they left the legal brothels and became illegal FSWs. A study sponsored by the Ministry of Health in 2015 estimated that there are between fifteen thousand and twenty-five thousand illegal FSWs in Tunisia (Ministry of Health 2015, 106). This means that for every legal FSW there are between two hundred and three hundred illegal FSWs. Since illegal FSWs are not regularly inspected for STIs, this potentially presents a public health danger for the women, their clients, and the spouses of their clients for the potential spread of STIs, including HIV/AIDS.

Methods

The methodology for this study of sex workers begins with illustrative case studies that the author collected through interviews in Tunisian Arabic with three FSWs. The first case study is Sameh, formerly an illegal FSW and currently a legal FSW in Tunis. The author interviewed her briefly in April 2015 but most of her story comes from the published research of Mohamed Sadok Lejri (Lejri 2012, 2014). The second case study is Warda, an illegal FSW whom Lejri and the author interviewed for two hours in Tunis in May 2016, using a questionnaire and a tape recorder. The third case study is Semia, a former FSW and brothel proprietor; the author met her through a public health doctor and interviewed her in November 2016 while she took him on a walking visit to the ruined brothel quarter of Sousse. The author also interviewed public health doctors, an STI researcher, social scientists who have done research on sex work, and an Islamist member of the Tunisian parliament, informing all of them of the nature and purpose of the research project.

The author conducted the research for this article as a postdoctoral research affiliate of the Centre d'Études Maghrébines à Tunis (CEMAT), an overseas center of the American Institute of Maghrib Studies (AIMS), under a cooperative agreement between CEMAT and the Ministry of Higher Education of Tunisia, in conformity with Tunisian human subject protocols and informed consent. The author informed all those interviewed of the nature and purpose of the research. The author recruited the three Tunisian sex worker participants for case studies with assurances of confidentiality and has accordingly worded their case studies and changed their names to pseudonyms to protect their anonymity.

Case Studies

─────────── From Illegal to Legal Sex Work: Sameh's Story ───────────

Now in her mid-forties, Sameh has been a legal FSW in Abdallah Gueche, the legal brothel quarter of Tunis, for about fifteen years. Her situation is different from most FSWs because she does not work for a *batrona* (Engl., madam, Fr., *matrone*) but independently rents a single small cell-like room directly from a landlord, where she lives and works alone. She buys her meals from a family that caters food to sex workers because, like the other FSWs, she cannot leave the Abdallah Gueche quarter without a written furlough from the police.

Born and raised in the Sahel of Tunisia, Sameh was the youngest of four children in a modest working class family. She quit school at thirteen to work as a rug weaver to help support her family. In her mid-teens she fell in love with a neighbor boy who said he loved her too. When she became pregnant, he refused to marry her, claiming that he had paid her for sex. The boy's family was influential and the police threatened to arrest Sameh for prostitution, so she and her family had to drop the case.

Having a baby was a devastating experience for Sameh. She was barely past puberty and already her life was ruined. As an unwed mother, she had dishonored herself and her family. Her mother was angry, her father was stupefied, and Sameh felt completely lost. Sameh had no idea of how to take care of her baby boy, so she turned him over to her mother when he was only five days old. As the boy grew, he called his grandmother "mother" and called Sameh by her first name, as if she were his older sister.

Sameh moved away from home, shared apartments with fellow working women, and tried to support herself. However, even with occasional financial help from her father she found it hard to live on the wages she received in the low-skilled jobs she was able to find. She began to engage in sex in exchange for money that she described as "gifts"—only occasionally at first and then more often—although she did not consider herself a sex worker. This improved her finances and she was able to give money to her family to help them care for her child.

Sameh stopped working at low-paying jobs and for about ten years worked as a hostess in bars and cabarets accompanying customers. Her role was to encourage the customers to drink more. "The bar didn't pay me," she says, "but I got money from the clients of the bar when we would have sex at their places or in a nearby hotel."

At twenty-five Sameh became pregnant a second time. The father of the baby denied paternity and refused support. This time Sameh made no claim on him because she knew it would be useless. Twelve weeks had passed before she realized that she was pregnant. Although she could have had a legal abortion, she decided to have the baby— another boy.

Sameh had felt guilty about giving up her first child to her mother, but she was nine years older when her second child was born and she was determined to be a true mother to him. For five years, with the help of an elderly nursemaid, she participated actively in raising her second son. However, a second child meant increased expenses. When Sameh's nursemaid was no longer available, Sameh turned her second child over to her mother.

It was hard for Sameh's elderly mother to take care of two children. "I completely exhausted my mother with my problems," she says. "May God forgive me!" Sometimes they would quarrel but Sameh's mother was always there for her. She thought Sameh eccentric, but stood by her and would never acknowledge that her daughter was a sex worker.

Sameh's father died in 1995 and the family was reduced to near poverty. At the same time, her mother's health began to decline and the police began to crack down on illegal FSWs. Some of Sameh's fellow bar hostesses were arrested for prostitution and sent to prison, and many cabarets were driven out of business.

The danger of arrest and her deep fear of prison finally led Sameh to become a legal sex worker. One day she encountered a former bar girl friend who now wore nice clothes and jewelry and owned a car thanks to having become a legal FSW in Abdallah Gueche. So Sameh applied to the Ministry, got a sex worker card, moved to Tunis, and has worked in Abdallah Gueche ever since.

Like her fellow FSWs, Sameh now lives and works out of a small room in the brothel quarter. She leads a rather solitary life and after paying her rent and food bills she is able to contribute to the support of her two children. Her situation as a legal FSW in Abdallah Gueche and her interaction with her clientele mean that her clients pay her directly and, instead of working for a female brothel keeper, Sameh rents her room directly from a landlord and makes slightly more profit.

————————*An Illegal Sex Worker: Warda's Story*————————

Warda is a well-dressed woman in her mid-fifties, who works out of a Tunis bar. She and her fellow FSWs usually sit together at a table and the waiters are protective of them. She does not have a sex work permit from the Ministry of Interior, so she is legally a prostitute, subject to prison and a fine, but enforcing antiprostitution laws is a low priority for the Tunisian police.

Warda was born in the Tunis medina (the old Arab city with narrow, twisting streets). She was the middle child in a large family. Her parents were rural emigrants to the capital who met for the first time on their wedding night. Warda explains that this was not unusual in those days, when men often arranged marriages through male friends or exchanged sisters.

Warda's mother supported the family, working as a maid for an Italian family. Her father worked, but spent his money on alcohol. He beat his wife and, if the children were not in bed asleep when he came home in the evening, he also beat them. When Warda's mother was away, he would bring women home and through the keyhole of her bedroom Warda would watch them having sex.

Once when her mother was ironing clothes, Warda's father came home drunk. He was angry that dinner wasn't ready, grabbed Warda's mother by the hair, threw her to the floor and began kicking her. Warda seized the iron that was heating on a metal base filled with hot coals and hit her father on the head. She is very protective of her mother, with whom she still lives. "My mother is the world to me," she says.

When Warda was in the fourth grade, her father took her out of school because her breasts had started to grow and he thought it was time for her to marry. She married at fifteen or sixteen (she's not sure which) to a man about twenty years her senior. Her father brought the man to the house one night and told her, "He wants to marry you." She was three months pregnant by him when they married. Her new husband prostituted her by taking her to bars, bringing men to the table and then going home. At first she refused, but she needed the money and so she relented.

Warda had two children by the time she was twenty, then two

more. She became depressed and decided to commit suicide. She took her four children into the small kitchen, closed the door and the small window, and opened the valve on a bottle of butagas (liquid propane cooking fuel), but her sister arrived home and saved them.

Warda says that she is terrified of sexually transmitted infections, especially AIDS, and that she always insists that the man must use a condom. Once a month, she sees a doctor who examines her for STIs for free.

Warda's husband died in an accident a few years ago and she receives a monthly widow's pension of 420 dinars (US$140), but this is not enough to support a family of seven (herself, her mother, her four children, and her younger brother). She pays 10 to 20 dinars a day for food. She also pays for tutoring for her second daughter to help her prepare for the baccalaureate examination. Toward the end of the month she works part time out of the bar "to make ends meet."

Warda says she would never work in Abdallah Gueche because the FSWs there "are not 'free,'" unlike Warda, who can accept or reject men as she pleases. She acknowledges that men give her "gifts" and "help her out" but she does not think of herself as a sex worker. She will only go with a man if she "feels something for him in [her] heart." He has to be gentle and polite, woo her, buy her drinks, take her out to dinner, and take her to his house or to a nice hotel on the sea. She says that she does not go with Libyans, some of whom came to Tunis for sex and are looked down upon as nouveaux riches.

Her main concern is to take good care of her children and ensure their futures. Asked about her own future, she replies that she would like to remarry, but "a good man is hard to find."

──────*A Former Proprietor of a Legal Brothel: Semia's Story*──────

Semia had been sequentially an illegal FSW, a legal FSW, and the proprietor of a legal brothel in Bab El Finga, the sex work quarter of Sousse, when rioters attacked in 2011, chasing away the FSWs and looting and burning the buildings.

Interviewed in late 2016, Semia pointed out the vandalized and abandoned building where she and her five FSWs once lived and worked. There were twenty-one brothels in Bab El Finga, averaging four or five FSWs each, so Semia's brothel was typical in size. A few were tiny one-room cells with independent sex workers, but most were multiroom houses. The largest had eighteen FSWs. In 2016, five years after the riot, Semia's brothel and the other houses in Bab El Finga remained blackened shells strewn with burnt furniture and clothing; some had their doors and windows bricked shut or were barred with iron gates.

Semia was born in 1957 in the poor rural Northwest, a main source of sex workers. Her father divorced her mother, her mother remarried, and Semia's new stepfather threw her out of the house when she was a young teenager. To survive she became an illegal sex worker—first in Sfax, then in Tunis, where she was arrested at eighteen for prostitution. The police released her and told her, "Come back when you are twenty, apply to the Ministry of Interior and you can become a legal sex worker."

Semia continued doing illegal sex work from bars and cabarets until at twenty-two she followed the advice of the police and got a sex work permit. She refers to it as her *batinta* (business license). She worked in the brothels in Sfax and Tunis before eventually settling in Sousse.

After more than twenty years as a FSW Semia started her own brothel. Perhaps she was planning for when she would be over fifty and no longer be eligible for a sex work permit or perhaps she figured that she would make more money as a batrona. The legal brothels are run by women, usually former FSWs like Semia. For a thousand dinars (US$330) per month, she rented an apartment in Bab El Finga, launched her own brothel, and lived and worked there for nearly a decade until the rioters closed her down.

The procedure in the brothel was that a customer would buy a token from the *batrona* for 10 dinars (a little over US$3) and give it to the FSW for sex. At the end of the day the FSW would cash in her tokens with the batrona, dividing the fees. For example, if a FSW serviced twenty clients, she and Semia would split 200 dinars—100 dinars (US$33) each.

The basic charge covered only a brief physical encounter of perhaps five minutes or less. The FSW charged for "extras" such as kissing or touching, keeping these fees for herself. Semia says that in practice some of the sex workers had different rates, from 5 dinars for an older and less attractive FSW to as much as 100 dinars for a particularly desirable FSW.

Semia is still in touch with her former FSW workers and colleagues. She says that a few of them found legal sex work in Sfax, but most are now illegal FSWs or are unemployed. Some sell their blood to a blood bank, but that is allowed only once a week.

Of the looting and burning Semia says simply, "they made us flee." She is bitter toward the police, mayor, and governor, who did nothing to prevent the violence and who she says lack the courage to authorize the reopening of the legal brothels. She points out that she was operating a legal business. It was not she but the rioters who broke the law, stole money and property, destroyed buildings, and took away the livelihoods of about a hundred working women. Yet not one of the rioters has been punished.

Semia is proud that she ran a clean brothel with regular condom use and no STIs, paid rent, supported local businesses, treated her workers well, paid 6,250 dinars (US$2,080) a year in taxes, and provided livelihoods to women who would otherwise have been destitute. Semia is a vocal supporter of legal sex work and advocates for the reopening of Bab El Finga, pointing out the benefits of legal brothels. "Look at what has happened now," she laments, gesturing toward the Bab El Finga gate. "We used to have clean brothels with health inspections, but now people have sex by the city wall next to the drunks."

Sex Work in Sfax

Sfax is an important site for studying sex work because it is the country's second largest city and currently the only other city besides Tunis with a legal brothel quarter. The brothel quarter of Sfax consists of a long street that leads into the medina from El Djem Gate, where FSWs sit in the doorways waiting for customers. As in Tunis and as was formerly the case in Sousse, each brothel is run by a *batrona* who employs one or more FSWs, plus a few independent sex workers who rent directly, and the regular rate for sex is 10 dinars (US$3.33). The buildings in the Sfax medina are run down and have cheap rents of around 150 dinars (US$50) / month, which used to be much higher but have been dropping with the declining numbers of legal FSWs.

The most knowledgeable person about sex work in Sfax, and perhaps in all of Tunisia, is Dr. Abdelmajid Zahaf, a public health doctor, a defender of legal brothels, and an advocate for FSWs. He has been the health inspector for the sex workers in Sfax for over thirty years. He recounts that in late 2011, nine months after the start of the Revolution, a mob with clubs gathered to attack the Sfax brothel quarter. However, they were confronted by male defenders who threatened, "If you close our brothels, we will close your mosques." As in Tunis, it ended in a compromise that the brothel quarter would close on Fridays and during Ramadan and there would be the addition of a main gate with a lock to isolate the quarter. The FSWs in Sfax already had locks on their apartment doors following an incident in which a man released from prison had tried to "take revenge" on one of the FSWs by slashing her face with a razor.

In Sfax, as in Tunis, the authorities have made legal sex work increasingly difficult by not renewing existing permits. If a sex worker returns late from a furlough they refuse to reauthorize her permit. Even if she returns on time they may take her permit away for no apparent reason. It is rare for a new permit to be issued. There were formerly over two hundred legal sex workers in Sfax but by April 2019 there were only about thirty. Dr. Zahaf has made phone calls and written letters to the authorities to complain, but has received no response. Dr. Zahaf is active in the struggle against HIV/AIDS. He is a founding member and past president of ATL MST (the Tunisian Association for the Struggle against Sexually Transmitted Diseases and HIV/AIDS), a Tunisian NGO with branches in thirteen cities.

Most advocates of legal sex work support their position with a lesser-of-two-evils argument—that legal FSWs are medically monitored while illegal FSWs are not, so that illegal sex work increases the potential for the spread of STIs, especially HIV/AIDS. However, Dr. Zahaf believes that the main argument for legal sex work is that it provides a sexual outlet for men, thereby lowering the incidence of rape and other violence against women. He further argues that legal sex work provides an outlet for people in sexually unsatisfying marriages, protects the virtue of honest women, and is socially preferable to men seducing women for sex and then abandoning them (as, arguably, in the case of Sameh).

Dr. Zahaf is a controversial figure. After he appeared on Tunisian television in support of legal FSWs he received death threats. He has received grants to support his work with FSWs and other stigmatized groups such as drug users and people with leprosy, but the authorities have sometimes been slow to issue him permits to open centers. He has been physically attacked, access to his office has been blocked, and he has been the target of misinformation campaigns, but he perseveres in his public health advocacy activities.

Studies of Sex Work in Tunisia

Two general works about sexuality in the MENA region contain short sections about Tunisia (Bradley 2010; El Feki 2013), but there has been little research specific to Tunisia. For the pre-independence period, there are studies of legal sex work (Larguèche and Larguèche 1992; Kerrou and M'halla 1993). For the contemporary period, Sadoq Lejri has done a master's thesis and written an article about legal FSWs in Abdallah Gueche in Tunis (Lejri 2012, 2014), but there is almost no research about illegal FSWs, who are more than a hundred times more numerous.

A useful portrait of legal sex work before the Revolution can be found in an epidemiological study led by Dr. Abir Znazen, a public health doctor who in 2010 coauthored an article about STIs among sex workers in three legal brothel quarters—Tunis, Sousse, and Gabes (Sousse and Gabes no longer have legal brothels). In addition to their medical findings about STIs, Znazen and her colleagues provide a quick statistical portrait of legal sex work in Tunisia in 2007. At that time, there were legal brothels in fourteen Tunisia cities, four years before Islamist attacks closed down all but those in Tunis and Sfax.

Of the 188 sex workers in Znazen's sample, the average age was thirty-four, with 6.6 years in the profession. The FSWs reported an average of 25.5 clients per day. The study took place in the summer, a busy season for the brothels. If we lower the year-round estimate to twenty clients per day, six days per week, three weeks per month, and twelve months per year (before the Ramadan ban), at 10 dinars per client, this works out to 43,200 dinars gross income. Subtracting half of this for the batrona, who provides room and board, yields an annual net income of 21,600 dinars (US$7,200), not including tips and "extras." This is a very good income, over five times the Tunisian minimum wage.

Interviewed in 2016, Dr. Znazen recalled that many of the FSWs she examined were friendly and talkative and the stories they told her were disturbing. She was shocked to find that some had been essentially sold to the brothels by their fathers, including two young women from Kef. Dr. Znazen added that after the STI study, she was depressed for a long time (Personal communication, June 2, 2016).

To date the only substantial research on illegal sex work in contemporary Tunisia is a qualitative study on HIV and sex workers, sponsored by the Ministry of Health (2015), which estimated that Tunisia has 15,000–25,000 FSWs. The study was conducted through nine focus groups with a total of sixty-nine participants, led by a sociologist (Dr. Adel Ayari) and a public health doctor (Dr. Amel Ben Said). The study included interviews with twenty-one policy informants, including officials from three NGOs and five Tunisian ministries. The Ministry of Interior, which regulates legal sex work, refused to be interviewed (Adel Ayari, Personal communication, April 27, 2016).

Because a main concern of the study was HIV/AIDS, the focus groups included not only male and female sex workers but non–sex worker men who have sex with men (MSM) and injection drug users. The overall rate of HIV/AIDS in Tunisia is low—less than 0.1 percent (the percentage of adults aged fifteen to forty-nine infected with the virus). In 2014, there were 331 cases of HIV in Tunisia, of whom 189 (57 percent) were foreigners—mainly Libyans who came to Tunisia for treatment. Of those groups most at risk of HIV/AIDS, MSM are infected at a rate of 9 percent, people who inject drugs at a rate of 3.9 percent, and FSWs are a distant third at 0.94 percent. However, HIV/AIDS requires constant monitoring, and illegal sex workers do not receive regular medical checks, which creates a greater risk of an outbreak.

The Ministry of Health study offers important findings to which this short summary cannot do justice. However, a limitation is that it is based largely on focus groups and, as the authors acknowledge, a group setting might make it difficult for some participants to speak freely about intimate, illegal, and stigmatized activities. Sampling and estimating the sizes of FSW and MSW populations are also problematic.

Legal FSWs share the institutional framework of the regulated brothel and work under *batronas*, such as Semia, who are former FSWs. However, illegal FSWs are more diverse, working out of various venues that include bars, hotels, public parks, movie theaters, vehicles, abandoned buildings, and apartments rented for use as brothels. Some illegal FSWs are independent and some work through male intermediaries who rent apartments for sex work and communicate by cell phone to schedule sex appointments. Two of the nine focus groups consisted of minors (under eighteen). Of the twelve underage FSWs in the groups, three were pregnant from "close family members."

The Ministry of Health study included not only female but also male sex workers (MSWs). The authors estimated that there are three thousand to five thousand MSWs in Tunisia (Ministry of Health, 106). MSWs were among the fifteen male adults and ten male minors in the focus groups. All male sex work is illegal, and the penalty for sexual relations between consenting adults of the same sex is up to three years in prison—a year more than the maximum penalty for illegal female sex work (Ministry of Health 2015; interviews in 2016 and 2019).

Remunerated Sex: A Grey Zone

Especially as Tunisian society has become more urban, there has been a widening range of sexual behaviors that fall into an ambiguous "grey zone." Consider the following situations:

- A businessman has sex with his secretary who consents to some degree because she fears that he might dismiss her if she refuses
- A university professor has sex with a student to whom he gives high grades
- A man employs a woman who both cleans his house and has sex with him (sometimes called *une bonne à tout faire*)
- A university student from rural Tunisia lives in Tunis in a private *foyer* (student boarding house) and has sex with her landlord in lieu of paying rent
- A young woman accompanies a wealthy older man to dinner to a nice restaurant, receives expensive presents from him, travels abroad with him, and has sex with him
- A married man has a mistress whom he provides with a rented apartment and living expenses
- A FSW who is an addict provides sex to her dealer in exchange for drugs

In these situations, the man is in a position of greater power than the woman, raising issues of sexual harassment, sexual exploitation, and sex work. These scenarios also illustrate that sex can sometimes involve methods of compensation other than money and may involve ambiguity in terms of the degree to which the sexual reciprocity is explicit, and whether the woman or the man initiates the relationship can also contribute to the ambiguity. In some cases, an observer might need additional information to determine how to characterize a situation.

In an article on "student prostitution," Yasmine Chaouch describes three cases of women university students who work as escorts in Tunis. "Hana" lives in a student dormitory, works through a male intermediary, and escorts older men to dinners and social functions, receiving financial remuneration but not having sex with them. "Yossr," thanks to her escort income, has been able to move from the student dormitory into her own apartment, and has "developed a taste" for the escort lifestyle. She is thinking about leaving the university and "dedicating herself to this life." It is unclear whether Yossr has sex with her clients. "Marwa" had sex with her university professor to pass his course but was caught and expelled. She now cohabits with a man who arranges her escort services, which include sex, and has contracted HIV/AIDS. These three cases, two of which are not necessarily sex work, illustrate the ambiguity of "grey zone" sexual behaviors (Chaouch 2015).

For reasons of self-esteem, a woman might engage in remunerated sex but not consider herself a sex worker. Instead, she might view her situation in terms of romance, courtship, and/or love. The remuneration—even if it is monetary—becomes a "gift." Note that Sameh rationalized the remuneration for her early sex work as "gifts." Warda, even though she works from a bar and has sex with strangers for money, does not consider herself a sex worker in the same sense as the FSWs in Abdallah Gueche. The point is the ambiguity—that different observers and especially different participants might have different characterizations of the same situation.

Changing Sexual Attitudes

Tunisian sexual attitudes and practices have changed greatly in recent decades. At independence in 1956, Tunisians married at an early age; the average age at marriage was 25.96 for men and 19.35 for women. However, by 2014 the average age at marriage had increased to 32.96 for men and 28.30 for women (Ouadah-Bedidi, Vallin, and Bouchoucha 2017). Thus, over the course of several generations, men were waiting seven years longer and women nearly nine years longer before marrying.

An increasing percentage of Tunisians are unable to marry at all. Many men who would like to marry are unemployed or have low-paying jobs and cannot afford the appropriate housing and customary gifts required for marriage. Many women are unable to find partners. This is especially the case for professional women, because a woman doctor or lawyer cannot marry just anyone; a plumber or a taxi driver, for example, would be considered too low in social status for an educated, professional woman, given cultural norms against hypogamy. Even when people marry, Tunisia has a high divorce rate. One marriage in six, about 17 percent, ends in divorce, which according to Bendermel (2016) is the highest rate in the Arab world.

Lilia Labidi, an anthropologist and professor of psychology, writes that Tunisia is experiencing a "celibacy crisis"—that the inability to marry is preventing young people from becoming full members of the community and putting them in a social situation of "intense despair." The Revolution's "urgent demand for *karama*" (personal dignity) reflects aspirations of youth for fulfillment within a larger moral framework of sexuality, and Dr. Labidi sees this as a factor in the Arab Spring. She believes that involuntary celibacy in Tunisia has contributed to a widespread desire on the part of youth to emigrate and has motivated some young men to join jihadi movements in Libya, Iraq, and Syria. Dr. Labidi emphasizes a particular category of celibacy among women—educated women who take their religion seriously, are from educated, middle–class families, and come from cities other than the capital city of Tunis. However, when involuntary celibacy is prolonged, not only these women but also other women and men suffer from diminished value in society, and this affects their self-esteem and their morality (Labidi 2017; Personal communication, 2019).

With most Tunisians in their late teens and twenties remaining unmarried, it would be unrealistic to believe that this large population of young (and many not-so-young) men and women remains celibate. Psychologist Nedra Ben Smail cites a Ministry of Public Health statistic that by 2005, the average age of sexual initiation in Tunisia was 17.4 for boys and 16.4 for girls. Of this "new sexuality of Tunisian women," she writes that there has been "a blurring of lines of conduct which once were without nuance." (Ben Smail 2012, 10). Many Tunisians now engage in both nonpenetrative and penetrative sex before marriage. She argues that in Tunisia "a new sexual order" has been made possible by science and medicine, including hymen "repair" (a.k.a., hymenoplasty). Based on interviews with doctors, she estimates that only 20 percent of Tunisian women are "true virgins" at marriage (Ben Smail 2012, 86).

Dr. Zahaf notes that young women in Tunisia today begin to menstruate as young as twelve or thirteen, while men mature a little later, around fourteen or fifteen. He notes that the age at first sexual experience is now slightly younger for women than for men. Due to the increasing age at marriage, he asserts that both men and women are engaging more in premarital sex. He adds that Tunisian women today are more liberated and more accepting of sex before marriage. However, many men maintain a double standard and refuse to marry women who are known to have had premarital sexual relations.

An important factor that enables pre- and extramarital sex in Tunisia is that women have had easy access to effective contraceptive methods, including oral contraceptive pills, and safe and legal abortion services since the 1960s and 1970s, respectively. Since 2001, women have had access to emergency contraceptive pills through pharmacies and without prescription (Foster and Wynn 2012).

Tunisian anthropologist Kacem Ben Hamza suggests that legal sex work once served the function of sexual initiation for young men before marriage. The wedding night is highly stressful for both the bride and groom. The bride is expected to give evidence of her virginity by bleeding, but the groom must perform sexually, which can be difficult. The groom fears that he might be unable to perform on the wedding night, especially if he has never had sex before. Thus, the FSW served the function of initiating the future groom, providing him with practice and diminishing his performance anxiety. In contemporary Tunisia, however, media and the Internet have largely taken over the function of sex education. Young men nowadays are more likely to have had premarital experience with women other than sex workers. Dr. Ben Hamza argues that in this way, FSWs have lost their traditional function in society (Kacem Ben Hamza, Personal communication, April 15, 2015).

Opinions about sex work are complex. Some secular feminists find themselves in agreement with Islamists who believe that sex work should be illegal. The leadership of Ennahda apparently favors de facto abolition through not renewing permits. However, a contrasting Islamist position is that of Mehrezia Labidi, a member of Ennahda who in 2011 was elected to the national parliament and served as vice president of that body until

2014. During this time she was arguably the most prominent woman in politics in the Arab World. On March 11, 2014, eighteen months after rioters had destroyed the brothel quarter in Sousse, Ms. Labidi received a delegation of sex workers from Sousse who came to Tunis to protest their unemployment and present a petition with 120 signatures. Ms. Labidi was the only member of the parliament who would receive them. At her office in Bardo she received two young and three older FSWs, serving them tea and listening to their problems. Later she was criticized by some of her male colleagues who asserted that Islam teaches that prostitutes should be stoned or whipped, not received in parliament. Labidi replied that these women were Tunisian citizens who have the right to be heard, that her job was to uphold civil and not religious law, and that if it were not for the men who frequent brothels there would be no brothel problems. She believes that the situation of FSWs should be understood in the broader context of the oppression of women.

Labidi recalls that one of the older FSWs in the delegation wept throughout the meeting. Finally, Labidi asked, "Why are you weeping? Have I not received you with respect? The woman replied, "Women scorn me and men treat me like a thing to be bought; I weep *because* you are treating me with respect." Labidi points out that Tunisia also has MSWs. However, she reports that people do not bother them, but instead ignore them, as if they did not exist. On the street in her home town of Grombalia, she had recently seen an MSW that she had gone to school with and she greeted him. Her coworkers later told her that she should have ignored him, but she replied that all Tunisian citizens have the right to be recognized by their representatives. Her position illustrates the diversity of opinion about sex work, even among Islamists (Mehrezia Labidi, Personal communication, August 12, 2014).

Conclusion: The Likely Disappearance of Legal Sex Work and Its Consequences

Although a small minority of FSWs in Tunisia may make a comfortable living (Chaouch 2015), the great majority of them, both legal and illegal, are forced into sex work by poverty and engage in an activity that many argue is inherently dangerous and demeaning. An illegal FSW who gets into a car or goes to an unfamiliar apartment may be gang-raped. In a few notorious cases, illegal FSWs have been thrown from the balconies of buildings and killed (at least twice in Tunis and once in Sousse). An illegal FSW is often unsure that she will be paid. Some illegal FSWs sleep in parks or abandoned buildings. Dr. Zahaf met one illegal FSW who slept in a tree.

Policy pragmatists argue that, relative to illegal sex work, legal sex work is a lesser evil. From a public health perspective, legal brothels offer advantages for the control of STIs, especially HIV/AIDS. Legal brothels were once a framework that offered FSWs a degree of security, which could be restored if the Ministry of Interior were willing. The situation of legal FSWs could be improved through administrative changes, such as expanding their health care beyond STI testing and providing them with social security. The working conditions of legal FSWs could be improved by allowing them to leave the brothel quarters where they are now confined. Labor union representation would allow legal FSWs to articulate their views and promote their interests.

However, such an outcome seems unlikely. The maximum age for a legal FSW in Tunisia is fifty, and because new permits are not being issued, the category of legal FSWs is disappearing through attrition. The logical result is that soon there will be no more legal FSWs. Legal sex work will still exist in theory, but not in practice. This will happen without changing the law, and a parliamentary debate about a taboo topic will have been avoided. The old brothel quarters of Tunis, Sfax, and Sousse (and perhaps even the walled brothel quarter of Kairouan) might become ordinary run-down medina neighborhoods with a residual stigma. There will still be plenty of FSWs, but all of them will belong to the informal sector of illegal sex work.

ACKNOWLEDGMENTS

The author acknowledges the contribution of Sadoq Lejri. The case study of Sameh is based on Lejri's research (Lejri 2012, 2014) and the interview of Warda was conducted together by Lejri and the author.

REFERENCES

Bendermel, Rafika. 2016. "Why Do the Tunisian Women Divorce More and More Often?" Babelmed, November 18, 2016. http://eng.babelmed.net/article/7717-why-do-the-tunisian-women-divorce-more-and-more-often.

Ben Smail, Nédra. 2012. *Vierges?: La nouvelle sexualité des Tunisiennes.* Tunis: Cérès Éditions, 2012.

Bradley, John R. 2010. *Behind the Veil of Vice: The Business and Culture of Sex in the Middle East.* New York: Palgrave Macmillan.

Chaouch, Yasmine. 2015. "Prostitution des étudiantes: Voyage au coeur d'un tabou." Inkyfada, March 7, 2015. //inkyfada.com/2015/03/prostitution-etudiante-voyage-coeur-tabou-tunisie.

Dahmani, Frida. 2014. "Prostitution: Islamistes et maisons closes, le blues des filles de joie tunisiennes." *Jeune Afrique,* April 25, 2014. https://www.jeuneafrique.com/133742/societe/prostitution-islam.

El Feki, Shereen. 2013. *Sex and the Citadel: Intimate Life in a Changing Arab World.* New York: Pantheon Books.

Foster, Angel, and L. L. Wynn, eds. 2012. *Emergency Contraception: The Story of a Global Reproductive Health Technology.* New York: Palgrave Macmillan.

Kerrou, Mohamed, and Moncef M'Halla. 1993. "La prostitution dans la médina de Tunis au XIXe et XXe siècles." *L'Annuaire de l'Afrique du Nord,* no. 32. Paris: Centre national de la recherche scientifique, Iremam.

Labidi, Lilia. 2017. "Celibate Women, the Construction of Identity, Karam (Dignity), and the 'Arab Spring.'" *Gender,* 9, no. 1: 11–29. https://doi.org/10.3224/gender.v9i1.02.

Larguèche, Dalenda, and Abdelhamid Larguèche, 1992. *Marginales en Terre d'Islam.* Tunis, Cérès Productions.

Lejri, Mohamed Sadok. 2012. "Regards sur la prostitution, regards de prostitués: Enquête ethnographique dans le milieu de la prostitution à Tunis." Master's thesis, Université de Tunis El Manar, Institut Supérieur des Sciences Humaines de Tunis.

———. 2014. "Sameh, une prostituée au passé tumultueux: Des vagues qui conduisent au terraux de 'l'exile'." In *Ecrire sur les femmes: Retour réflexif sur une expérience de recherche,* edited by Sihem Najar and Lilia Othmane Challougui, 99–116. Paris: Harmattan, 2014.

Ministry of Health / Ministère de la Santé. 2015. *Direction des soins de santé de base, étude qualitative sur les facteurs de vulnérabilité au VIH des travailleurs et travailleuses du sexe en Tunisie.* Tunis: Ministère de la Santé.

Ouadeh-Bedidi, Zahia, Jacques Vallin, and Ibtihel Bouchoucha. 2017. *A Complete History of Male and Female Age at Marriage in Tujnisia since 1950.* Chicago: PAA. https://paa.confex.com/paa/2017/mediafile/ExtendedAbstract/Paper10972/PAA-Ouadah-Marriage-in-Tunisia-long_V2.pdf.

Smoltczyk, Alexander. 2012. "Islamist Intimidation: The Battle for the Future of Tunisia." *Der Spiegel,* December 3, 2012. http://www.spiegel.de/international/world/salafist-intimidation-campaign-threatens-young-democracy-in-tunisia-a-870680.html.

Znazen, Abir. 2010. "Sexually Transmitted Infections among Female Sex Workers in Tunisia: High Prevalence of Chlamydia Trachomatis. *Sexually Transmitted Infections* 86, no. 7: 500–505.

CHAPTER 12

Love, Sex, and Sexuality in Morocco

Navigating Barriers, Expanding Boundaries

GINGER FEATHER

Moroccans often view extramarital sexual relations as a taboo subject due to cultural sensitivities, moral propriety, and strict legal prohibitions. In Morocco, sexual relationships are only socially and legally sanctioned within a marital framework, while extramarital relationships are criminal offenses, punishable by up to one year imprisonment plus fines, with stiffer penalties if either partner is married (Penal Code 2003, Articles 490–491).[1] Similarly, sexual and reproductive health (SRH) education and services are circumscribed and exclusionary, targeting married couples through household-based contraception counseling and provision while systematically excluding adolescents and single women. Despite prohibitions against premarital sexual relations, 67 percent of Moroccan men and 33 percent of women admit to having premarital sexual relations (Bordat and Kouzzi 2010, 8). Consequently, Morocco's current laws and public policies lead to high rates of unwanted pregnancies, unsafe abortion (due to restrictive abortion laws, Penal Code 2003, Article 453), single motherhood, and "illegitimate" children, all gendered issues (Feather 2020). This chapter examines the gendered consequences of these laws and public policies in the lives of women and members of the lesbian, gay, bisexual, transgender, queer/questioning (LGBTQ) community who find love and intimacy outside the marital normative. Further, the chapter identifies the contestation in Morocco over the laws and public policies governing love, sex, and sexuality from within a feminist/religious dichotomy.

Zakia Salime (2011) richly contextualizes the polarization in the Moroccan women's rights movement prior to the 2004 Family Law reforms, characterizing it as an ostensibly secular/religious divide. Problematizing this polarization offers an opportunity for increased understanding and potential convergence, as demonstrated by recent scholarship that rejects the idea that feminist objectives and Islamic values are mutually exclusive. Instead, these scholars explore the compatibility of feminism with Islamic principles under names such as Muslim feminism, Islamic feminism, and third-wave feminism (Badran 2005, 2008, 2013; Mir-Hosseini 2006, 2011; Wadud 1999), some focusing on these debates in the Moroccan context (Gray 2015; Lamrabet 2014, 2016, 2018; Mernissi 1975; Rhouni 2010; Zvan-Elliott 2015). These scholars propose a potential melding or middle ground between "feminist" and "religious" cleavages that is simultaneously progressive, emancipatory, and sensitive to religious and cultural diversity.

The Moroccan feminists who emerged alongside second-wave feminism are "often in direct confrontation with fundamentalism, political Islam, and religio-nationalist trends" (Moghadam 2013, 66). These feminists did not reference religious texts to articulate their legal demands. Instead, they focused on "liberalizing" society and loosening its strictures, often taking a rights-based approach (Ennaji and Sadiqi 2011). Although most Moroccan feminists—men and women—still rely heavily on the United Nations (UN) human rights framework to challenge discriminatory laws, public policies, and cultural norms, some feminists also reference Islamic texts in their arguments. These feminists agree that formal and informal institutions place women in a subordinate and often vulnerable position while reinforcing a heteronormative, hegemonic, even toxic masculinity. They challenge gender discrimination as not evolving from Islamic principles and values, but in fact as incompatible with Islam as they practice their Islamic faith.

In contrast, conservative Islamic activists evoke primarily religious referents, including the Qur'an, sunna (words and deeds of the Prophet Muhammed), and hadith (sayings of the Prophet Muhammed), to affirm the relative rights and duties of men and women. While these activists often champion Moroccan women's socioeconomic rights, including equal opportunity to an education and public sector jobs, they often espouse complementary gender roles within the family. Consequently, the Islamic activists view the marital framework as sacrosanct, providing a protective economic safety net for compliant women, while sanctioning punitive measures for females and homosexual males who transgress accepted norms.

THEORY AND METHODOLOGY

The Advocacy Coalition Framework (ACF) provides the ideal theoretical approach for analyzing the competing coalitional cleavages within the Moroccan women's movement. Sabatier (1988), Sabatier and Jenkins-Smith (1993), and Sabatier and Weible (2007) developed and revised ACF to analyze polarization around contentious public policies. Scholars have since extended ACF to feminist issues such as domestic violence (Abrar, Lovenduski, and Margetts 2000), emergency contraception (Shorn 2005), and violence against women (Feather 2019). Nevertheless, scholars have yet to apply ACF to analyze polarization around the laws and public policies governing love, sex, and sexuality in a Muslim-majority country such as Morocco.

Using ACF, I examine the belief systems underlying the feminist/conservative Islamic contestation on these issues. I focus on each coalition's *core beliefs*, which are ontological, normative, and resistant to change, and *policy core beliefs*, which are prescriptive and more pragmatic (Sabatier and Weible: 2007, 194–95). As feminists and conservative Islamic activists compete to influence public policies, I analyze the differences in their policy prescriptions, stemming from their core beliefs, which divide along three criteria: the legal referent (human rights law or Islamic references), the unit of analysis (the individual or the family), and assumptions of familial gender relations (gender equality or gender complementarity) (Feather 2014). These beliefs drive the policy debates and the wedge between feminists and their conservative counterparts.

I base the analysis on in-depth interviews that I conducted with more than two hundred activists across the political spectrum in the Moroccan women's rights movement as well as activists focused on LGBTQ populations, single mothers, professional sex workers (PSWs), and men who have sex with men (MSM). In addition, I conducted a focus group discussion with twelve former or current sex workers, all single mothers and beneficiaries of the Association in the Fight against AIDS (ALCS) in Marrakech. I recruited participants through word-of-mouth and snowball sampling. I asked open-ended questions in Arabic, French, or English based on the respondent's preferences. I recorded, transcribed, and translated each response for later analysis. Each respondent gave permission to be identified by name and organizational affiliation in text. During my fieldwork in Morocco, I was affiliated with the Tangier American Legation Institute for Moroccan Studies in Tangier.

Relationships of Love in Morocco

The notion that love is an intrinsic part of a marital relationship is a relatively recent phenomenon in Morocco, according to several respondents, because arranged marriages between families, with the aim of forging political and financial alliances, were once the norm. Inevitably, newfound expectations of love and intimacy challenge traditional understandings in a country that is both European-influenced and socially conservative. Feminist activist Aicha Sakmassi, president of the Association of the Voices of Moroccan Women (AVFM) in Agadir, explained the ramifications of this "overnight" transition: "TV introduced the illusion of love into conservative rural regions with high illiteracy rates, rapidly altering young people's values, so a twelve-year-old girl who becomes pregnant claims, 'I was not harassed or raped. I love him. I was in a relationship with him.' Then she must leave her family, as her idea of love clashes with their conservative religious values." The juxtaposition of infatuations like in this example with statistics on the fallout from such relationships is striking. The National Human Rights Council of Morocco (CNDH) reported that of the 210,343 young Moroccan women who had children out of wedlock between 2003 and 2009, 90 percent were rejected by their families (2015, 11).

Nevertheless, "young and in love" couples are defying familial and societal expectations to push the boundaries of respectability and redefine love relationships and intimacy. Mahjouba Edbouche, president of Oum El Banine (OEB), an association that provides daycare for the children of single mothers in Agadir, paused during my interview with her to counsel

Salim and Aisha (pseudonyms), a young couple who had a child out of wedlock. Edbouche explained to me that the couple loved each other, but their love had broken their families, so she needed to "do a little sewing" to mend familial relationships. She told Salim that his girlfriend's parents are not bad people, just conservative, so it is normal for them to be mad, hurt, and offended that Aisha had had premarital sex. Edbouche advised the couple to reconcile with Aisha's parents and advised Aisha not to sleep with Salim again before getting married to avoid another pregnancy, which would only complicate their predicament. Edbouche counseled Aisha to instead "respect herself and others"; they were young and should not sabotage their relationships with their parents.

Despite the expectations of many families, young couples such as Salim and Aisha date, fall in love, and navigate intimacy. To comply with social expectations, some university students enter either temporary (*'urfi*) or traditional religious (*fatiha*) marriages in order to have sexual relations (Mdidech 2007). *Fatiha* marriages are especially common in the rural and remote regions of Morocco, where access to state institutions for the necessary documents is less convenient. However, these informal arrangements provide women scant legal recourse in the event of an unwanted pregnancy or abandonment, as the Moroccan state only recognizes government-documented marriages (Family Law 2004, Article 4).

A Premarital Sexual Double Standard

A clear double standard exists between Moroccan women and men with regard to premarital sexual relations. Secular feminists assert that Moroccan women face moral and legal double standards, living in a social context that values female chastity and male virility, with gendered recriminations and impunity. Prior to marriage, Moroccan society expects women to remain virgins—chaste and pure—with their families' honor contingent upon their daughters' intact hymens. Thus, the dominant sociocultural norms in Morocco exclusively hold women responsible for sexual outcomes—whether consensual or nonconsensual. Nora Fitzgerald is the founder of the Amal Association in Marrakech, which helps single mothers, "orphans" (girls who have lost their fathers), and other at-risk women to learn a trade such as cooking or baking to support themselves. She asserted that Moroccan society considers "sexual relationships which fall outside the legal marital framework and any progeny *persona non grata*, to be ignored and even ostracized."

Although Moroccan women who engage in premarital sex and become pregnant have few rights, after Morocco ratified the Convention on the Rights of the Child (CRC) their situation has improved due to their children. However, Edbouche stated that "single mothers have no rights and their children have very few rights." In compliance with the CRC, Morocco revised its Civil Status Act in 2002, allowing and obliging single mothers to register their child in the Civil Status Registry and to choose a name for the child (Articles 16, 20–21). However, Moroccan society can still identify "illegitimate" children by their identity papers, which stigmatize them as "bastards." Additionally, to comply with the CRC, Morocco revised its Nationality Code in 2007 to grant out-of-wedlock children the right to a nationality through their mothers (Article 6), thereby further exempting single fathers from parental accountability.

In contrast to single mothers and their children, men enjoy impunity for any sexual transgressions. If men are single and their partner becomes pregnant, they may (and according to my respondents often do) deny knowing the girl or discredit her as a "prostitute" to avoid paternal responsibility and criminal liability. If a couple is in an adulterous relationship and the man is married, he does not face criminal charges unless his wife files a complaint (Penal Code 2003, Article 492). Furthermore, in spite of Morocco's CRC commitments, illegitimate paternal filiation does not have any of the responsibilities of legitimate filiation (*nasab*), so illegitimate children are not entitled to their father's name, child support, or inheritance rights (Family Law 2004, Articles 54, 144, 148).

Feminist activists highlight several structural incentives Moroccan men may have to deny paternity. Nouzha Guessous, who served on the Royal Consultative Commission overseeing the 2004 Family Law reforms, indicated that, in the Moroccan context, the same Arabic word (shari'a) denotes both legitimacy and legality, blurring the lines between *legitimate/legal* and *illegitimate/illegal*, which discourages single fathers from recognizing their "illegitimate/illegal" children. Additionally, Hafida el-Baz, the director of Association Solidarity Feminine (ASF) in Casablanca, the most prominent Moroccan association working with single mothers and their children, said that Moroccan men who do not take responsibility for their out-of-wedlock children often justify this decision by referencing a legal ruling of fourteenth century Shaykh Khalil ibn Ishaq al-Jundi, the most revered legal scholar in Maliki Islamic jurisprudence. Shaykh Khalil stated, "A child of fornication is a bastard and remains a bastard. He does not take the name of his father, he does not inherit anything at all" (Mukhtasar Khalil, Article 446). El-Baz added that a 1983 court ruling upheld Shaykh Khalil's ruling. More recently, in 2017, the Tangier Court of First Instance, citing Article 7 of the CRC and Article 32 of the 2011 Constitution, ruled in favor of a child's right to filiation to her biological father, but the Tangier Court of Appeal later overturned the decision (El Masaiti 2017).

Marital Sexual Relations

As for marital sexual relations, marriage creates a husband-wife union with clearly defined gender roles, codified in law. Husbands are legally financially responsible for providing for (*qiwama*) their wives from "the moment the marriage is consummated . . . until a court orders the wife to return to the conjugal home and she refuses" (Family Law 2004, Articles 194–195). Husbands' designation as head of household and wives' obligation to show absolute obedience (*ta'a*) to him reinforced these monetized, sexualized, and gendered rights and responsibilities (Personal Status Code [PSC] 1993, Articles 1, 36), until the 2004 Family Law removed these designations in favor of shared spousal responsibilities (Articles 4, 51). Regardless, husbands' unfettered sexual access to their wives remains codified in Moroccan law, creating a sexualized power hierarchy between spouses, which effectually sanctions conjugal rape. Despite their efforts, Moroccan feminists have been unsuccessful in their attempts to pressure the government to explicitly define conjugal rape as a criminal offense (Penal Code 2003, Article 487).

FEMINISTS' VIEWS REGARDING SEXUAL RELATIONS

Many Moroccan feminists reference the UN human rights framework to cast sexual relations between consenting adults as a matter of personal freedom and control over one's body, under the protection of privacy (International Covenant on Civil and Political Rights, Article 17).[2] Further, feminists contend that conservative interpretations of Islamic texts undergird Morocco's family law and penal code, such that the codes relegate basic human rights, such as the freedom to decide one's own consensual adult relationships, to criminal offenses with gendered consequences.

El-Baz observed that the 2003 Penal Code Article 490 is not explicitly discriminatory, except regarding individual liberty; its consequences, however, are gendered. More importantly, the laws and norms in Morocco
both malign and persecute women—but not men—who have extramarital sexual relationships. Thus, el-Baz insisted, "when women have extramarital sexual relations, the state does not protect them enough and society does not protect them at all."

CONSERVATIVE ISLAMIC ACTIVISTS' VIEW OF EXTRAMARITAL SEXUAL RELATIONSHIPS

In contrast to the feminist rights-based approach, conservative Islamic
activists in Morocco take a moralistic stance. They cite passages from the
Qur'an that forbid sexual relations outside of marriage as *zina* (illicit sexual relations), whether fornication (Qur'an, 24:33) or adultery (Qur'an,
17:32), to prescribe abstinence from extramarital sexual relationships.
Hence, many conservatives equate extramarital sexual relations with
prostitution, emphasizing their illegality and immorality. Conservative
activists, such as Aziza Elbakali Kassimi, president of Forum Azzharae
for Moroccan Women (FAFM), which is affiliated with the moderate
Islamic Justice and Development Party (PJD), and Asmae Belghiti, at
Association al-Hidn, which formed to bring an Islamic legal reference
to the UN human rights discourse, oppose decriminalizing extramarital
sexual relations, despite the law's gendered effects. They feel the criminalization of extramarital sexual relations upholds the integrity of the
marital institution and protects the family and society. When I asked for
her views on extramarital relationships, Belghiti stated, "We are not for
extramarital sexual relations, . . . a mistress is just a sexual distraction
and one day he will throw her out. . . . If a man really loves a woman
he will marry her and give her rights." Belghiti viewed even underage
marriage as legal protection for women: "I prefer that a girl of seventeen
gets married and has legal papers with a legal husband and legal children,
than that she goes into hiding and has a boyfriend who leaves her with
his child." Similarly, Kassimi said, "Being a Muslim, I prefer that a girl
gets married at the age of seventeen, rather than having an affair without
marriage and risking becoming a single mother." Belghiti and Kassimi, however, dichotomize women's options as an early marriage, with legal rights
and economic protections, or debauchery, unwanted pregnancies, and
prostitution. They emphasize the marital framework—monogamous or

polygamous—as providing legal and economic security, but discount the rights of unmarried women.

Additionally, conservative Islamic activists are suspicious of the UN agenda, especially the Convention on the Elimination of All Forms of Discrimination against Women (CEDAW), which is the feminists' primary legal reference for promoting gender equality. Ilyass Bouzghaia at the Center for Women's Studies in Islam (CERFI) in Rabat stated that "the conservative Islamists' main concerns with CEDAW are its opposition to complementary gender roles and its promotion of sexual freedom." Bouzghaia conceded that "Islamic activists have a misconception of their secular counterparts as promiscuous," suggesting that Western movies fuel this notion. For example, he cited the 2011 American film *Friends with Benefits*, a romantic comedy in which two young professionals decide to be friends who have sex with "no strings attached." Bouzghaia remarked with concern that this "hook up" culture is increasing in Moroccan society, where young people use apps such as Tinder, Happn, and Spotted "to find someone, meet somewhere, and do whatever they like . . . benefits without responsibility." Nevertheless, Bouzghaia warned, "at the end of the day, what a person really needs is a companion and friend, not these purely sexual encounters."

THE GENDERED CONSEQUENCES OF THE CRIMINALIZATION OF EXTRAMARITAL SEXUAL RELATIONS

The criminalization of extramarital relations creates an odd incentive structure for single women with an unwanted pregnancy. If partners refuse to acknowledge the pregnancy, women may claim they were raped to deflect the blame and avoid prosecution. According to El-Baz, admitting a pregnancy came from a consensual sexual relationship is far less acceptable than claiming rape. Similarly, Sakmassi remarked that several AVFM beneficiaries were in personal relationships that developed into sexual relationships, but when the women became pregnant and their partner did not want to get married, the law and society compelled the women to portray themselves as the victims and the men as the aggressors. Sakmassi warned women in such circumstances that if they admit that they were in an extramarital relationship, the judge could sentence them to six months in prison. Likewise, Amina Byouz, the president of the Association Anaouat for Women and Children (AAFE) in Chichaoua, asserted that, in contrast, the man in such circumstances might insist that he does not know the woman or that he thought she was a prostitute in order to avoid potential prosecution for extramarital sexual relations and paternal responsibilities. During the focus group discussion that I led with ALCS beneficiaries, all of whom were single mothers and current or former sex workers, participants claimed that state officials are complicit in gendering the consequences of an out-of-wedlock pregnancy. One participant declared that if a single mother attempts to hold the child's father responsible by lodging a complaint, the man can simply pay the police to make the file disappear or he can pay off court officials to prevent the suit from progressing, while threatening to charge the woman with prostitution if she attempts to continue legal proceedings. Other participants agreed.

Underage Marriage and Polygamy

Moroccan sociologist Fatima Mernissi famously asserted that "Islam curbed and civilized women's sexuality, while making men's sexuality more promiscuous due to polygamy" (1975, 46). Although Morocco placed restrictions on polygamy and raised the minimum marriage age to eighteen for women to equal that of men (Family Law 2004, Articles 19, 40), feminist activists contend that the law also gave judges, most of whom are male, discretionary power to approve both underage and polygamous marriages that meet certain conditions (Family Law 2004, Article 20, 41). As Byouz at AAFE pointed out, although the marriage-age law is not discriminatory, its application is gendered because 99 percent of the petitions for underage marriage are for girls, not boys. Additionally, according to feminist activists, a legal loophole allows couples to register underage and polygamous marriages ex post facto (Family Law 2004, Article 16), sidestepping the restrictions on such marriages and placing child brides and co-wives in potentially precarious positions. Feminist Souad Benmassaoud, the president of the Federation of the Democratic League of Women's Rights (FLDDF) in Ouarzazate, viewed polygamy as the ultimate in male privilege and criticized the rising numbers of underage and polygamous marriages. Benmassaoud indicated that FLDDF advocates for the elimination of articles 16 and 20 to close the legal loophole facilitating ex post facto registrations and to curb judges' discretionary power to approve underage and polygamous marriages in advance.

In contrast, several of the conservative Islamic activists I interviewed regarded the increased age of marriage and current restrictions on underage marriage and polygamy negatively. Belghiti and Kassimi described marriage—monogamous or polygamous—as a social safety net for women and their children. Belghiti clarified, "When young people are attracted to one another, have sexual relations and a child, afterward the girl has neither studies, nor family, nor a social framework." Similarly, Kassimi argued that an underage marriage was preferable to an extramarital affair and becoming a single mother, since mistresses have no rights. Kassimi and Belghiti blamed the rise in single mothers, illegitimate children, and prostitution on the increased marriage age and recommended lowering the marriage age as a solution to debauchery, especially for poor rural girls. Kassimi asserted, "If a man really loves a woman, he marries her and gives her rights, his name, and legal children with paternal filiation." Nevertheless, some Islamic activists, such as Khadija Mouneen at the Initiative for Women's Development (IWD) in Marrakech, disagreed with Kassimi and Belghiti. In fact, Mouneen equated the marriage of underage girls to adult men with statutory rape.

As for polygamy, Moroccan men can legally marry up to four wives with judicial approval. Kassimi justified polygamy as permitted in the Qur'an and, thus, a man's right.[3] Belghiti described the Islamic allowance of up to four wives as an economic plan to protect women, by providing wives and children with certain financial security, which mistresses and illegitimate children do not enjoy. Feminist Fatima Mafdali, president of Association Wafae in Inezgane, disagreed, asserting that conservative activists only read the first part of the Qur'anic verse, but if they read the rest of the verse, then it is clear that the Qur'an actually limits men to one wife.[4] Consequently, Mafdali expressed skepticism about the Islamic precepts used to justify polygamous marriage, highlighting the abusive nature of some polygamous marriages, especially among ultra-conservative Salafis. She remarked that "Salafis forget God and interpret the Qur'an as they wish, marrying minors and divorcing them on a whim; whereas teenage girls, especially from poor families, fear not getting married, so they are hesitant to reject potential suitors."

RAPE AS AN AVENUE TO UNDERAGE MARRIAGE

Until the 2014 reform of Penal Code Article 475, the rape of a minor was a legally sanctioned pathway to marriage in Morocco. Due to the conflation of the loss of a girl's virginity—whether through consensual sexual relations or rape—with promiscuity and the loss of the family's collective honor, an accused rapist could escape prosecution by agreeing to marry his underage victim. Morocco closed this legal loophole following the high-profile 2012 case of Amina Filali in Larache. Filali was allegedly raped at fifteen and forced by her parents and the judge to marry her alleged rapist, who continued to rape and beat her during their marriage. Filali eventually committed suicide by drinking rat poison and died in the streets, sparking mass protests by both feminist and conservative Islamic activists against this law. Nevertheless, AAFE president Byouz asserted that despite the legal reform, the practice persists because families and even prosecutors claim the marriage of minors to their alleged rapist is a solution. However, Byouz added that since the reform, in the event of a rape, many families have stopped going to the police. Instead, they settle the matter among themselves to sidestep the revised code. In a personal interview with former PJD parliamentarian and current minister of Solidarity, Social Development, Equality and Family, Jamila Moussali, she explained that the law was designed as a way to allow couples who have engaged in consensual sexual relations to marry, not as legal protection for rapists.

CONJUGAL RAPE: AN OXYMORON

Feminists raised the issue of conjugal rape as a violation of a woman's right to bodily integrity and a human rights violation. In contrast to European countries, in Morocco, as in most other Muslim-majority countries, with the possible exceptions of Tunisia and Turkey, the government has yet to criminalize rape within a marriage. Instead, feminists and conservatives agree, several Islamic legal references have made conjugal rape an oxymoron in Morocco, as marriage implies a husband's sexual access to his wife. They enumerate the references that reinforce this understanding: a wife's obligation to obey her husband (*ta'a*), which was removed from the 2004 Family Law, Qur'an 2:223, and the 2004 Family Law provision conditioning a wife's right to maintenance on consummation of the marriage and remaining in the conjugal home (Family Law 2004, Articles 194–195).[5] Due to these references, even feminist activists consider conjugal rape an oxymoron.

A 2018 Tangier Court of Appeal case demonstrated an exception to the relative leniency shown conjugal rape. In this case, the court sentenced a Larache man to two years imprisonment for aggravated assault (Penal Code

2003, Articles 401–404), but not for marital rape, for sodomy (Morocco World News, February 14, 2019). Although conjugal rape is not a criminal offense, feminists and conservatives agree that the one exception is sodomy which is prohibited (haram) in Islam. FLDDF President Benmassaoud asserted, "The wife must be obedient to her husband in their sexual relations . . . never refusing his desire for sex, unless he forces her to do something outside the religious framework, specifically sodomy." Sakmassi agreed, "If a husband wants to make love, his wife must give way. It is not her right to refuse." However, Byouz disagreed with other feminists, saying, "The Islamists claim the husband can do whatever he wants in married life . . . even if it's violent, but this is wrong. In our religion, Islam, it is wrong. People do not understand the true content of our religion, which is the problem." Consequently, some feminists reject conjugal rape and domestic violence from within their Islamic faith, representing another area of convergence between the feminists and their conservative counterparts.

Despite such convictions, several feminists emphasized that the judiciary reinforces the impunity of husbands by reminding wives of their financial dependence on their husbands and encouraging them to drop complaints of rape or domestic violence. Mounir at AFS explained, "Even if wives go to the doctor and get a medical certificate, verifying a rape, prosecutors or judges say, 'he is your husband, you have children, do you want to put him in prison?'" As a result, husbands are only prosecuted if their wife sustains severe injuries and there are witnesses; in that case, they may be tried under assault charges for sodomy, as in the Tangier case.

Instead of viewing conjugal rape as a systemic gendered issue, like the feminists, the conservatives recommended additional analysis of the root causes for the violence. Kassimi suggested social factors, such as alcoholism and drug abuse, are often behind (sexual) violence in the marriage. Furthermore, she suggested studying the impact of potential solutions on the family as a whole, rather than on its constituent parts. Ultimately, however, Kassimi rejected violence as unacceptable in Islam, citing a hadith that forbids oppressing others.[6] Thus, although activists across the political spectrum often agree that husbands have unlimited sexual access to their wives, all the Moroccan activists whom I interviewed concurred that violence within the marriage, even conjugal rape, is against Islam, which suggests another potential avenue for cooperation across ideological divides.

The Criminalization of Homosexual Relations

As for LGBTQ rights, although the UN Human Rights Council adopted resolutions in 2011, 2014, 2016, and 2019 calling for protection against violence and discrimination based on sexual orientation and gender identity, the UN has yet to adopt a specific convention to define and protect the LGBTQ community.[7] Nidal Azhary, the executive director of the Union Feminine Liberale (UFL) in Rabat, which advocates for women's and LGBTQ rights, pointed out that the 2011 Moroccan Constitution asserts the security of the person, physical and moral integrity, and the protection of private life (Articles 21–22, 24). Nevertheless, neither the 2003 Penal Code nor the 2011 Constitution includes sexual orientation or gender identity in its list of protected categories (Penal Code 2003, Article 431–1; Constitution 2011, Preamble). Instead, Morocco criminalized "lewd or unnatural acts with an individual of the same sex," which are punishable by up to three years imprisonment plus fines (Penal Code 2003, Article 489). In 2016, two Moroccan teenage girls were arrested and stood trial for "kissing and hugging on the roof of a house" in Marrakech, but the judge eventually acquitted them.[8] Furthermore, according to Azhary, the police may arrest members of the LGBTQ community for lesser offenses such as nudity or obscenity under Section VI of the 2003 Penal Code, which regulates public modesty (*pudeur*) (Articles 483–496). Azhary stated that UFL advocates for the decriminalization of homosexual relations, the inclusion of sexual orientation and gender identity in the earlier-mentioned nondiscrimination clauses, and the establishment of public policies to protect LGBTQ people.

As with extramarital heterosexual relations, conservative Islamic activists reference religious restrictions on sodomy taken from the Qur'an, specifically the story of Sodom and Gomorrah.[9] However, more progressive readings of these verses suggest that they refer to gang rape, not consensual homosexual relationships. With the PJD's successive wins in 2011 and 2016 parliamentary elections, Azhary noted rising concern among activists over the potential for greater intolerance of sexual minorities. For example, in September 2017, when questioned by a reporter about homosexuality in Morocco, the PJD minister of human rights, Mustapha Ramid, called homosexuals "trash," which prompted UFL to launch a media campaign to highlight the contradictions in Morocco's promotion of equality among citizens. However, in the 2021 parliamentary elections the PJD suffered a major electoral defeat as the more liberal National Rally of Independents (RNI) and Authenticity and Modernity (PAM) parties took over half the parliamentary seats, marking a potential opening for more progressive policy shifts.

Although many feminist activists are more supportive of LGBTQ rights than their conservative Islamic counterparts, their activism for LGBTQ rights is limited. Hassan Naji at Association Ennakhil in Marrakech admitted that even the feminist associations are hesitant to advocate for "homosexual" rights, for fear they might jeopardize their dialogue with the state, partnerships with other associations, and the trust they have built in the community. Furthermore, Naji indicated that civil society lacks the training and support for how to work with the homosexual community, which the UN previously provided, especially how to work with the LGBTQ community to minimize the transmission of HIV/AIDS.

Despite the taboos in Moroccan society against homosexuality, Naji emphasized, there are a lot of homosexuals, but if they show "this part of femininity . . . in the streets, they may be assaulted, abused, or even beaten into a coma, not by the Ministry of Justice, but by the citizens." Additionally, Naji asserted, homosexuals immigrate to Morocco from sub-Saharan African countries where homosexuality is "normal," but in Morocco they find they are discriminated against. They may be beaten or even expelled. Due to these constraints, Naji said, rights-based associations only work with the LGBTQ community informally, under the umbrella of HIV/AIDS prevention. Despite the reticence, Naji admitted rights-based organizations cannot close their eyes indefinitely to the problems of the LGBTQ community.

Prostitution

Although Morocco criminalizes extramarital sexual relations as a type of prostitution, professional sex work is tacitly accepted in certain cities known for their sex tourism, such as Marrakech and Agadir. In fact, since the onset of HIV/AIDS, Morocco allows associations to work with female PSWs and MSM under the aegis of combatting HIV/AIDS. ALCS in Marrakech and the Association of the South in the Fight against AIDS (ASCS) in Agadir are two organizations that work with these at-risk populations.

ALCS's formal position is that they welcome people and accept bene-ficiaries as they are, with or without the virus. They aim to teach benefi-ciaries how to protect themselves through condom use and HIV testing. Through my ALCS focus group discussion with current or former sex workers, all of whom had children, it was clear that the recriminations and social policing experienced by single mothers for their "deviant" sex-ual behaviors are magnified among PSWs (Feather 2021). The lack of SRH education and services for single women leaves them uninformed, unpro-tected, and vulnerable. One ALCS beneficiary confided that her boyfriend told her that he was on "birth control," which led to her out-of-wedlock pregnancy and resorting to sex work to support herself and her child. Another focus-group-discussion participant explained that the adminis-trative offices and police can identify them as single mothers based on their child's documents and they treat the women like prostitutes. The ALCS beneficiary clarified that although single mothers can give their child a fictitious father's name beginning with the prefix *'abd* when they register the child in the civil status registry, the mother cannot add a grandfather's name to the child's legal documents which identifies the child as born out-of-wedlock (CSA 2002, Article 16). Subsequently, the officials either tell them directly that they are prostitutes or make them feel like they have no rights.

The feminists viewed sex workers as disadvantaged women who often resorted to remunerative sex to support themselves and their children. Sakmassi initiated a micro-credit program to help PSWs find an alterna-tive source of income, known as the Amélie Project, in cooperation with the Social and Development Agency (ADS) and ALCS. The project ran for three years with several success stories, but the former PJD minister of Solidarity, Women, Family, and Social Development Bassima Hakkaoui cut funding to the program because it targeted sex workers.

Fatima Elallaoui, a sociologist at ASCS, said the organization provides social and medical assistance to PSWs, MSM, and people living with HIV/AIDS. She explained that the PSWs ASCS assisted included single women, single mothers, divorcees, and widows, while their MSM beneficiaries included gay, bisexual, and cross-dressing men, "gigolos," dominants, and submissives. Doctors conduct biweekly HIV/AIDS testing on-site and if they detect HIV, social workers accompany the beneficiary to the Center for Contagious Diseases for confirmatory testing. Social workers also help with administrative and legal issues. Elallaoui indicated that ASCS provides hotlines and uses the educator-peer-leader (EPL) model to distribute condoms and lubricants to the PSWs and MSM in the bars, discotheques, and beaches of Agadir. Each EPL receives almost MDH 500 (US$52) to distribute lubricants and condoms to five more PSWs or MSM, with the process repeating.

Elallaoui emphasized, however, that ASCS is not an association of homosexuals and is not encouraging the homosexual population or advocating for increased LGBTQ rights, since homosexuality is haram. Instead, ASCS's mission is to fight AIDS, so neither the King's royal gendarmerie nor the police interfere with its work. As MSM and PSWs are among the populations most affected by HIV/AIDS, they go to ASCS for assistance. Elallaoui reiterated that, "as social workers, they do not discriminate or differentiate between categories of people . . . as social work exists apart from sex, convictions, beliefs, or sexual orientations." She acknowledged, however, that there are men in Morocco who are homosexuals and who need legal protections and rights, as their situation is precarious. Elallaoui said that when she works with homosexuals, they tell her that "ASCS is the only organization that helps the homosexual community and gives us guidance." Hence, Elallaoui asserted, "ASCS has become a home to them, where they found violence and aggression elsewhere."

Analysis and Conclusions

Moroccans are navigating love and intimacy in a society steeped in both European influences and Islamic values. Instead of arranged marriages, couples are pursuing love and intimacy as they cross and expand the boundaries of acceptability in a conservative society. However, this new terrain poses challenges, especially for single women, who may enter sexual relationships in search of love, marriage, and security but find just the opposite: social ostracism, family rejection, and punitive legal and administrative hurdles.

Due to the concerted efforts of associations such as Association Solidarity Feminine and Oum El Banine, Moroccans have had to acknowledge the existence of single mothers. Consequently, the Moroccan state has gradually taken steps toward their reintegration into Moroccan society, primarily through ensuring their children's rights. The former PJD-led government made a concerted effort to ensure that out-of-wedlock children enjoy their rights in compliance with the CRC. Feminist Khadija Mounir, the president of the Association Women of the South (AFS) in Ait Milloul, explained that the state and civil society have conducted numerous campaigns in remote and rural regions to register children in the civil status registry in order to give them a legal identity. This initiative illustrates a possible area of convergence between feminists and conservatives in which discrimination against single mothers is addressed by securing the rights of their children.

Similarly, within marriage, Moroccan women can find themselves disadvantaged and often vulnerable as patriarchal laws and norms perpetuate hegemonic, even toxic, masculinities. Underage and polygamous marriages establish gendered power hierarchies between husbands and wives. Many wives' economic dependence on their husbands and widespread understandings that marriage implies husbands' sexual access to their wives blur the lines between power, sexuality, and violence, which permissive laws reinforce.

Against this background, polarization along core and policy core beliefs between feminist and conservative Islamic activists provides an opportunity to examine the gendered outcomes of certain laws, such as the criminalization of extramarital sexual relations and the increased minimum marriage age. Though the laws are indiscriminate, feminists demonstrate how legal loopholes produce gendered outcomes, in effect vilifying women and exonerating men for their extramarital sexual transgressions. Additionally, Morocco's laws and public policies, such as household-based contraceptive counseling and provision and the criminalization of same-sex relations, privilege married couples and heterosexual men, while marginalizing single women and sexual minorities who breach societal norms.

As Morocco continues to harmonize national laws with its human rights commitments and 2011 Constitution, feminists highlight the gendered nature of crime and punishment in Morocco, while Islamic conservatives identify potential social factors contributing to these phenomena. Through feminists' efforts, greater gender equality, more inclusive communities, and less punitive normative frameworks are emerging, especially vis-à-vis the treatment of out-of-wedlock children. Likewise, conservative Islamic activists are conducting their own studies and analyses of these problems. They suggest that solutions must consider men's as well as women's perspectives, causing some feminist organizations, such as Ennakhil, to incorporate men's perspectives into potential and more holistic solutions.

Whether citing UN human rights law or the Qur'an, both poles agree that all sexual relations should be consensual and violence has no place in a marriage. Perhaps by dispelling the notion that feminists are amoral and necessarily nonreligious and that Islamic activists cannot also promote women's rights, an enhanced understanding between feminists and their conservative counterparts can lead to a shared path forward.

ACKNOWLEDGMENTS

I would like to thank the many Moroccan activists and academics who gave freely of their time and expertise to answer my many questions, and Mounir Yahyani for his valuable assistance transcribing many of the interviews.

NOTES

1. Information about the laws cited in this chapter is available at Mobilising for Rights Associates, https://mrawomen.ma/our-resources/english-translations-of-laws.
2. The International Covenant on Civil and Political Rights can be found on the website of the United Nations Office of the High Commissioner for Human Rights, https://www.ohchr.org/en/instruments-mechanisms/instruments/international-covenant-civil-and-political-rights.
3. The verse from the Qur'an that Kassimi cited was "You may marry other women who seem good to you: two, three or four of them. But if you fear that you will not be just, then [marry only] one or those your right hand possesses. That is more suitable that you may not incline [to injustice]" (Qur'an 4:3).
4. The verse from the Qur'an that Mafdali cited was "try as you may, you cannot treat all your wives impartially" (Qur'an 4:129).
5. "Your wives are as a tilth unto you, so approach your tilth when or how ye will, but do some good act for your souls beforehand; and fear Allah and know that you are to meet him" (Qur'an 2:223).
6. According to the hadith, the Prophet Muhammad said, "Oh my servants, I have forbidden oppression for myself, and made it forbidden amongst you, so do not oppress one another." See Sunnah.com, https://sunnah.com/muslim:2577a.
7. General Assembly resolution 60/251, Human Rights Council, A/RES/60/251 (15 March 2006), available from undocs.org/en/A/RES/60/251; Human Rights Council, 17/19, A/HRC/RES/17/19 (17 June 2011), available from undocs.org/en/A/HRC/17/19; Human Rights Council, A/HRC/RES/27/32 (26 September 2014), available from undocs.org/en/A/HRC/27/32; Human Rights Council, A/HRC/RES/32/2 (30 June 2016), available from undocs.org/en/A/HRC/32/2; Human Rights Council, A/HRC/RES/40/5 (21 March 2019), available from undocs.org/en/A/HRC/40/5; and Human Rights Council, A/HRC/RES/41/18 (12 July 2019), available from undocs.org/en/A/HRC/41/18.

8. Sharman, Jon. "Teenage Girls Acquitted after Being Put on Trial for Kissing." *Independent*, December 9, 2016, https://www.independent.co.uk/news/world/africa/teenage-girls-acquitted-kissing-marrakech-morocco-a7466396.html.

9. The story of Sodom and Gomorrah contains the majority of the verses against "men approaching men" instead of women, which is used in Morocco to condemn both homosexual and heterosexual anal sex. Qur'an 29:28–31; Qur'an 26:165–68; and Qur'an 27:54–55.

REFERENCES

Abrar, Stefania, Joni Lovenduski, and Helen Margetts. 2000. "Feminist Ideas and Domestic Violence Policy Change." *Political Studies* 48, no. 2: 239–62.

Badran, Margot. 2005. "Between Secular and Islamic Feminism/s: Reflections on the Middle East and Beyond." *Journal of Middle East Women's Studies* 1, no. 1: 6–28.

———. 2008. "Engaging Islamic Feminism." *Islamic Feminism: Current Perspectives* 96: 25–36.

———. 2013. *Feminism in Islam: Secular and Religious Convergences*. London: Oneworld Publications, 2013.

Bordat, Stephanie W., and Saida Kouzzi. 2010. "Legal Empowerment of Unwed Mothers: Experiences of Moroccan NGOs." In *Legal Empowerment: Practitioners Perspectives*, edited by Stephen Golub, 179–202. Legal and Governance Reform: Lessons Learned. No. 2/2010. Rome: International Development Law Organization.

El-Masaiti, Amira. 2017. "Minister of Family Wants DNA Test, Still Needs Courses in Family Law." *Morocco World News*, December 21, 2017. https://www.moroccoworldnews.com/2017/12/236851/paternity-dna-test-family-law-bassima-hakkaoui.

Ennaji, Moha, and Fatima Sadiqi. 2011. "Contextualizing Gender and Violence in the Middle East." In *Gender and Violence in the Middle East*, edited by Moha Ennaji and Fatima Sadiqi. New York: Routledge Taylor and Francis.

Feather, Ginger. 2014. "Competing Frameworks: Feminists Differ over Best Path to Moroccan Women's Rights." *Journal of Women and Human Rights in the Middle East*, no. 2: 19–41.

———. 2019. "Legal Discrimination and Violence against Women Analyzed through a Feminist Lens Using the Advocacy Coalition Framework." *Journal of Applied Language and Culture Studies*, no. 2: 103–28.

———. 2020. "Proactive versus Reactive Sexual and Reproductive Health Rights: A Comparative Case Study of Morocco and Tunisia." *Femina Politica*, no. 2: 76–89.

———. 2021. "The Conflation of Single Mothers and Prostitutes in Morocco: Qiwama, Legal Exclusion, and Paternal Impunity." *Journal of Middle East Women's Studies* 17, no. 2: 294–303.

Gray, Doris H. 2015. *Beyond Feminism and Islamism: Gender and Equality in North Africa*. New York: Palgrave MacMillan.

Lamrabet, Asma. 2016. *Women in the Qur'an: An Emancipatory Reading*. Markfield, UK: Kube Publishing.

———. 2014. "An Egalitarian Reading of the Concepts of Khilafah, Wilayah and Qiwamah."

In *Men in Charge?: Rethinking Authority in Muslim Legal Tradition*, edited by Ziba Mir-Hosseini, Mulki Al-Sharmani, and Jane Rumminger, 65–87. London: One World Publication.

———. 2018. *Women and Men in the Qur'ān*. New York: Palgrave MacMillan.

Mdidech, Jaouad. 2007. "Relations sexuelles avant le marriage, les jeunes en parlent." *La Vie Eco*, May 6, 2007.

Mernissi, Fatima. 1975. *Beyond the Veil: Male-Female Dynamics in a Modern Muslim Society*. Cambridge, MA: Schenkman.

Mir-Hosseini, Ziba. 2006. "Muslim Women's Quest for Equality: Between Islamic Law and Feminism." *Critical Inquiry* 32, no. 4: 629–45.

———. "Beyond 'Islam' vs. 'Feminism.'" *IDS Bulletin* 42, no. 1 (2011): 67–77.

Moghadam, Valentine M. 2013. "What Is Democracy?: Promises and Perils of the Arab Spring." *Current Sociology* 61, no. 4: 393–408.

Morocco World News. 2019. "Tangiers Court Denies Charging Man with Marital Rape." February 14, 2019. https://www.moroccoworldnews.com/2019/02/265779/tangiers-court-marital-rape.

National Human Rights Council of Morocco (CNDH). 2015. *Gender Equality and Parity in Morocco: Preserving and Implementing the Aims and Objectives of the Constitution*. Rabat: National Human Rights Council of Morocco. https://www.cndh.org.ma/an/thematic-reports/gender-equality-and-parity-morocco-preserving-and-implementing-aims-and-objectives.

Rhouni, Raja. 2010. *Secular and Islamic Feminist Critiques in the Work of Fatima Mernissi*. The Netherlands: Koninklijke Brill NV.

Sabatier, Paul A. "An Advocacy Coalition Framework of Policy Change and the Role of Policy-Oriented Learning Therein." *Policy Sciences* 21, no. 2–3 (1988): 129–68.

Sabatier, Paul A., and Hank C. Jenkins-Smith. 1993. *Policy Change and Learning: An Advocacy Coalition Approach*. Boulder, CO: Westview Press, 1993.

Sabatier, Paul A., and Christopher M. Weible. 2007. "The Advocacy Coalition Framework." In *Theories of the Policy Process*, edited by Paul Sabatier, 189–220. New York: Routledge Taylor and Francis.

Salime, Zakia. 2011. *Between Feminism and Islam: Human Rights and Sharia Law in Morocco*. Minneapolis: University of Minnesota Press.

Shorn, Mavis. 2005. "Emergency Contraception for Sexual Assault Victims: An Advocacy Framework." *Policy, Politics, and Nursing Practice* 6, no. 4: 343–53.

Wadud, Amina. 1999. *Qur'an and Woman: Rereading the Sacred Text from a Woman's Perspective*. New York: Oxford University Press.

Zvan-Elliott, Katja. *Modernizing Patriarchy: The Politics of Women's Rights in Morocco*. Austin: University of Texas Press, 2015.

CHAPTER 13

(Un)hiding the Samaritan's Sexuality in Egypt

Insights from a Coptic Woman's Journal

MINA IBRAHIM

"She Knocks on the Door": A Second Chance for the Foolish?

I first encountered her journal in the summer of 2018, while I was doing my doctoral studies fieldwork in Cairo, Egypt. I am grateful to her for allowing me to borrow her private journal, which contains her daily memoirs. She writes her meditations in Arabic, and I asked her if I could translate them for my research tracing the difficulties of repentance and salvation among Coptic Christians in Egypt. She usually writes late in the night, a few minutes before dawn. Copts know this in biblical terms as the "fourth watch of the night," when Jesus is believed to come for the second time declaring the end of the world. Sometimes She writes these mediations when She is sober, but usually when She is drunk and/or high on different types of drugs. She writes using the third person. She never mentions her name and prefers to write using the pronouns "she" and "her." She told me that this allows her to write more and to reflect all her feelings and thoughts. Hence, I will also follow her by not mentioning her name or even using a pseudonym.

The first entry I read in her journal was a fresh reading, at least for me, of the story of the ten virgins in the Bible. Well-known to Christians around the world, this is one of the few fictive parables that Jesus told to his disciples and followers to give them a more empirical and familiar understanding of the relationship between God in heaven and people on earth. According to the parable, ten virgins were waiting for the bridegroom (God) with their lamps (faith). Five of them were "wise" and brought enough oil to lighten their lamps; the other five virgins were "foolish" and did not keep a sufficient amount of oil. When the groom came, he took with him the wise virgins to celebrate the wedding (heaven). The foolish ones, who had left to get more oil, returned after the doors were closed (Matthew 25:1–13).

And I thought that the story was over, as She and I have learned at Sunday School at our Cairene neighborhood parishes, which have been centralized by the clerical hierarchy of the Coptic Orthodox since the mid of the twentieth century. With respect to this parable, young Copts generally learn that there is no hope for the foolish virgins, who will be tortured eternally in darkness (i.e., hell), forever weeping, suffering, and gnashing their teeth. But for her, the story wasn't over then. "But she waits up until late at night for you, my Lord; she is the foolish virgin, who did not buy enough oil for her lamp," She writes in her journal. After everyone thought that the story was over and the door was closed, "she comes back and knocks on the closed door. She knows the groom would tell her with anger: 'Who are you? What do you want? Did not I tell you to leave and never to come back?'" In her journal, She responded, "Cannot the foolish virgin still get another chance?"

The owner of the journal is a Coptic Christian woman in her late twenties. The journal is made of leather, composed of thick paper. A friend brought her the journal from Granada, Spain. During the previous few years, She had many sexual partners, a few of whom She loved and others who remunerated her with money, a job, or a classy outing. Although She considers herself to be one of the foolish virgins, She insisted on knocking on the closed door and not giving up on another chance to join the wise ones. In this chapter, I reflect on how She and her multiple sexual relationships are not only transgressions of hegemonic interpretations of the contemporary Coptic Orthodox tradition but also new ethnographic readings of and knockings on the closed doors of Christian theology in Egypt.

She allowed me to scan a copy of her journal after I published a short piece with Egypt Migrations (formerly the Coptic Canadian History Project [CCHP]) in May 2018 (Ibrahim 2018). In that short piece, I suggested that the study of Coptic Christians in Egypt together with other minorities in the Middle East should be expanded to include theologically and socially negated places such as brothels, coffeehouses, bars, weed gatherings, summer vacations, casinos, and nightclubs. I did not originally intend to conduct ethnographic research in those places myself, but as my fieldwork evolved so did the locations of my research. She was not the only of my Coptic interlocutors from whom I have learned the importance of getting closer to the social and political insights embedded in ordinary writings (Makatou 2007, 173). Several others, who did not think that their stories and memoirs were worth telling in a book about a religious community that often negates their practices, nevertheless shared their stories with me.

Before hearing or reading each person's story, I strongly emphasized that I am not in the position of judging people because I am not studying how to be a "wise man" in such an evil world. "I am not a priest to whom you would confess or a spiritual father from whom you would ask for advice," I told her during one of our many meetings over a one-year period before I returned to Germany to write my dissertation.[1] "I am here to learn from and about your life," I added. Against this backdrop, in this chapter I reflect on a few snapshots of her journal in which She makes sense of invisible meanings of living as a Coptic Christian in contemporary Egypt. In doing so, I emphasize how a Coptic woman's sexuality, which is condemned and negated on communal and national levels, has the agency to produce critical theological knowledge that takes into consideration misrepresented desires and anxieties.

"She Loved Him": At the Courtyard of the Neighborhood Parish

"Why does the Church always focus on the *zina* [adultery or illicit sexual relations] of the biblical women but never men?" She writes. "Why are men who commit *zina* like Prophet David, Solomon, or Lot never condemned like the females who did the same?"

During one of our conversations, I suggested this answer. As a result of the so-called Revival Movement (Hasan 2003, 71), the religious education and theological knowledge of the Copts have become more institutionalized and dominated by clergymen.[2] As part of what historian Lucie Ryzova (2014; see also Jacob 2011) called the Age of the Effendiyya, this male-dominated movement carried out a theological, social, political, economic, and moral project that reflected the broader nationalist movement of Gamal Abdel Nasser and the then powerful Islamist movement of the Muslim Brotherhood. While women have played various roles in writing the history of modern Copts (van Doorn-Harder 1995; Beshara 2019), I use her journal to explore the social and political effects and paradoxes of the construction and negotiation of the sinful figure among Copts. I show how her sexual experiences have the potential to dismantle the masculine, moral, social, and political project(s) of the *effendiyya* (middle class elites; sing. *effendi*).

She hides the journal in a locked small wooden drawer next to her bed. She tells her parents that this drawer has her private menstrual pads. "Bleed, for those who bleed will see God," She once wrote in her journal using her menstrual blood; She didn't tell me why She did so.[3] She also repeatedly writes, "Ask, knock, and seek," before starting to narrate each of her sexual adventures. Her previously mentioned comment on the parable of the ten virgins is connected to another biblical verse where Jesus said, "Ask, and you will receive. Search, and you will find. Knock, and the door will be opened to you" (Matthew 7:7, Common English Bible [CEB]). For her, this verse is the most revolutionary (*thawriyya*) quote in the Bible. By asking, knocking, and seeking, She struggles to immerse herself in topics that seem to be finished and locked. By "asking, knocking, and seeking," She insists on opening up new meanings and ways of negotiating her sexual life and those of her partners.

In many cases, Coptic Christians in Egypt have their first romantic relationships, and sometimes their first sexual encounters, through their friends and acquaintances in their neighborhood parishes. The latter are central to the religious cultivation of Coptic Christians from childhood, not only through formal Sunday School services but also as a result of the tight social connections that Copts build through entertaining and spiritual summer activities (Hasan 2003, 138–39). Within this context, "she loved him," as She puts it, writing with bold red ink in her journal. She knew him through a choir group of university students in which She used to sing and where he used to be the drummer. Moreover, they had also both joined the parish scout group when they were young.

In addition to its prestigious role in providing security to the church during the celebrations of mass on Christmas, Easter, or New Year's Eve (Roux 2018), the scout group is one of the very few activities in the parish where boys and girls frequently interact.[4] Boys and girls are segregated in most of the church's activities. When they are eight or nine years old, they learn about Jesus, Mary, the Bible, and the Coptic Orthodox tradition in isolation from each other, before they assemble again when they start attending university. "We did not learn much about sex at Sunday School or during summer activities," She once told me when I asked her about her first sexual encounter. "We just learned the scientific stuff we already learn at our schools. We discovered ourselves by ourselves," She added. "Discovering oneself" sometimes happened through pornographic movies or friends. In her case, it was her first lover who allowed her "to touch her body with her hands, before he touched it with his hands, lips, and penis," She describes in her journal.

In his teachings, Bishop Mousa, of the Coptic Orthodox Church Bishopric of Youth, argues that sex is a spiritual act (Haddon 2012, 35). He also mentions that bringing boys and girls together might result in sin. Moreover, at Sunday School, we have been taught that sex is one of the skills (*wazna*) that God gave to people in the world to share with Him in the act of creation. In this regard, the agency of the sexual partners has a secondary value after God's will and plan. While the contemporary hegemonic interpretation of Coptic Church tradition minimizes sex and confines its importance to the making of faithful sons and daughters of God, it is interesting to see how the activities sponsored by the Church allow for sexual talk and encounters.

While the clerical authority of the Church together with Sunday School teachers provided social spaces to control the spiritual and sexual activities of their congregants (Oram 2004, chapter 4), I have become more interested in how my interlocutors differently produce and consume the very same spaces. They are the courtyards of the neighborhood parishes where boys and girls meet following their gender-segregated activities. Even before they are allowed to officially assemble when they finish high school, they also meet at the kiosks and mini-markets next to the parishes where the first sight, touch, and maybe kiss usually happen.

Her encounter with her first love was around 2009, a time when Facebook began to be popular among Egyptians. Men and women born during the 1980s and 1990s were finally able to follow each other's updates without the need to know each other's mailing addresses, and to chat on Yahoo without exchanging phone numbers. Moreover, one needed only to know the name of her or his crush and search for it on Facebook. Even better, one might find a picture of the person she or he liked and use that to confirm identity. "I liked his muscles that were made visible when he was playing drums; he was sexy, and I fell in love with him even before he came and told me about his feelings and even before we added each other on Facebook," She told me.

The lover's family went to Alexandria to spend some time during the summer holidays. She was nineteen and he was twenty-one. He took her to his house one evening after She had finished the rehearsal of a play She was acting in as part of the parish's theatrical group and after they drank her favorite Schweppes beverage at the kiosk of the courtyard. They had previously kissed in a park and while watching a film in the cinema a few months before they met in his house. He opened the door to her and they immediately started to kiss. "He was a bit tipsy," She wrote in her journal, "and she quickly got drunk because she was not used to drink . . . she got undressed and offered herself to him without any hesitation."

A few years later, after they had had sex many times and traveled together on vacations to Alexandria, Dahab, and Sharm El-Sheikh, he left her without giving any reason. It was then that She started to write her meditations in her journal. "He dropped all the promises that he would marry her and that they would live forever happy together," She wrote. He stopped answering her messages on WhatsApp and Facebook Messenger. She learned that he was telling their mutual friends in the neighborhood parish about their sexual adventures. Hence, She decided to leave him as well, to start a new chapter of her life. In this chapter, She questioned not only what real love was but also her relationship with her neighborhood parish and its Sunday School, summer activities, choir, theatrical group, and scout group.

She found herself adding a lot of boys to her list of Facebook friends and exchanging numbers with them. She became emotionally and physically drained and lost control over her body and feelings. "She was literally falling in love with everyone who just smiled at her," She wrote. She also mentioned in her journal that, following her first love, She had become like the Samaritan woman, who hides from everyone due to her bad reputation but who would still have sexual relations to fulfill her desires and pain. In the New Testament, Jesus met the Samaritan woman by Jacob's Well around noon, and asked her to give him some water to drink (John 4:7 CEB). Asking her for water was strange because Jesus was a Jew, and Jews were not friendly with the Samaritans during this time. He offered to give her a kind of water "that bubbles up into eternal life" (John 4:14 CEB).

During their encounter, Jesus implicitly depicted the Samaritan woman as a prostitute, when he told her that she had "five husbands, and the man you are with now isn't your husband" (John 4:18 CEB). Intentionally, according to her journal, Jesus went to meet the Samaritan woman at a time when it was too hot for anyone else to bring water. Knowing that the Samaritan woman might be too embarrassed to meet her neighbors and acquaintances due to her reputation, Jesus made sure to take care of her emotional wounds and her fear of other people's judgment.

"But the Samaritan woman was lucky," She writes in her journal. For her, Jesus offered the Samarian woman the water of eternal life when she was already a sinner, and *before* her repentance. However, our protagonist in this chapter had already been tasting this water for years, before She was traumatized by her first sexual partner and at the parish that witnessed their first look, touch, and smile. The figure of the sinful person is indeed central to any Christian theology, and that figure reflects the essence of the message of redemption by Jesus Christ. But what would the situation be if Jesus was not able to fulfill her thirst for redemption and acceptance through the institutions of the Coptic Orthodox Church, which had promised since childhood to represent, protect, and take care of her spiritual, social, and political needs?

She has learned since childhood that the neighborhood parishes of the Coptic Church should be more like hospitals that take care of their prodigal sons and daughters than like hotels that selectively host people according to their social and economic capital. While the story of the Samaritan woman and the other well-known biblical story of the woman taken in adultery (John 8:1–11) tell us that all sins are forgiven and forgotten, a woman with a bad reputation in the contemporary Coptic Church is always condemned, negated, and abandoned. We will see in the coming sections how her multiple sexual relationships have allowed her to provide alternative theological understandings of being a sinful person. Similarly, I have paid attention to gaps in the academic literature that have argued about (and against) the political and social victimhood narratives of the largest Christian minority in the Middle East.

"She Was Naked and They Kept Staring at Her":
Inappropriate for Policy-Makers

After one of our meetings, I went home and continued reading through my copy of her journal. "She was easily dragged by the simplest word," She writes. She once told me that She knows that they (her sexual partners) just want to ejaculate through their sex calls or sexting. She becomes important for them only at night, when they are horny (*haygānīn*). For them, She has become like a sex toy that replaces pornography. When She wakes up the next morning, "they forget about her, and it would be rare if they would text her," She writes.

Gender is performed, as Judith Butler reminds us, and so are gender roles (Butler [1990] 2006, 187). The dominant and the dominated in a sexual interaction are not essentialist static categories; they are exchangeable and depend on the movements and the acts of one's body. In her case, moreover, this contingency is connected to the changes in her tone of voice and the words She says before and after her sexual partners' ejaculations. In this regard, She decided that sexual pleasure should not be a free gift, as anthropologists like myself learn from the classic work of Marcel Mauss (2002, 61), at least for those whom She does not like. She started asking for money, classy outings, or a job from those who want to ejaculate while hearing her voice or reading her texts, in addition to those who want to touch her body and let her touch their penises. Notably, She would make sure to ask for her favors before their ejaculations, that is, when She imagines She is in control of the sexual encounter.

"She was naked, and they kept staring at her," She writes, while referring to her abandonment by the childhood friends of her neighborhood parish due to her "bad reputation." This specific entry was an interpretation of one of the biblical verses that She likes in the Gospel of Matthew: "I was naked and you gave me clothes to wear. I was sick and you took care of me. I was in prison and you visited me" (Matthew 25:36 CEB). She thinks that Jesus also referred not only to naked bodies but also to the naked souls of those who would need protection. For years the Egyptian state has promised to protect Copts from being victims of the violence committed by extremist groups. Sometimes, Copts can be also victims of state violence, as happened with the 2011 Maspero massacre (Shenoda 2011). In this case, Copts might present their victimhood to and seek protection from international human rights organizations. Going beyond describing

Copts in terms of victimization, scholars have also argued about Copts' agency, as they have struggled to find a place for their faith and identity in Egypt (Sedra 2009, 1050). Whether they are victims or agents, her story highlights some aspects in the lives of Egyptian Copts that remain largely unrepresented in these dominant narratives.

"Because I Am a Sharmūṭa*": Rumors and Gossip*

"So, are not you afraid that one of your friends might see us?" She asked me during one of our gatherings at a bar located in one of Cairo's elite neighborhoods.

"Why would I?"

"Because I am a *sharmūṭa* [whore], or so they describe me."[5]

"I do not care," I responded. And I was lying. Of course, I do care. Being seen with someone known to have her bad reputation in different Cairene bars and nightclubs might disrupt my relationships with other interlocutors, if they were to see me with her.

Why did I want to become invisible while meeting her? A Coptic Christian myself, I have always been thinking about the positioning of the sinful in academic studies of the Copts. I also left my neighborhood parish a few years before I started my doctoral studies in 2016. Like her, I have had nonmarital sexual relationships; that definitely labels me as a sinful person. Like her, I have stopped confessing, receiving the communion, and attending spiritual meetings. Yet, unlike her, I have succeeded in hiding from and lying about these facts to my community. When someone would ask me, "Are you still a believer?" I usually responded with, "I do not like these kinds of questions."

She has been asked similar questions as well and responds with the same answer. For both of us, it is not a yes or no question; it is more about our ability to implement what Michel de Certeau called tactics (1984, 38) that allow us to be invisible to friends and acquaintances in our neighborhood parishes and hide from that most repressive entity, *kalām innās*—the rumors people fabricate about each other. It is this panic-inducing specter of gossip that we Egyptians always have to take into consideration as we navigate through our everyday lives. As Unni Wikan (1996, 121) puts it, *kalām innās* "arises without anyone quite knowing where or how." Given its randomness and contingency, one would never be able to predict when one might be perceived as unrespectable (Wynn 2018, 35; Al-Tal 2017, 205).

Of course, the intensity of the work we must perform to evade *kalām innās* is significantly connected to our prescribed gender roles and how we perform them. It is usually women who occupy more space within the entity of *kalām innās*. During his long papal period (1971–2012), Pope Shenouda III of the Coptic Orthodox Church devoted many of his books and sermons to argue how the modern Coptic woman should be a virtuous (*faḍīla*) one, who takes care of her husband and brings up her children according to the orthodox teachings of the Church (Armanios 2002, 110–11). He also warned that her body, her tight (or any) clothes, her eyes, her laughter, her hair, and even her makeup are the cause of any violation of communal and national moral codes. In theological terms, the hegemonic interpretation of the Coptic Orthodox Church always puts the blame on women, describing them as *'athara* (a stumbling block) that causes others to commit sins. In these theological interpretations, Pope Shenouda III made use of the Gospel of Luke's argument, "how terrible it is for the person through whom they happen. It would be better for them to be thrown into a lake with a large stone hung around their neck than to cause one of these little ones to trip and fall into sin" (Luke 17:2–3 CEB).

It is true that some of the sermons I attended during my fieldwork at various Coptic Orthodox parishes inside and outside Cairo argued that men might also be sources of *'athara*. Nonetheless, the number of these sermons cannot compare to the dominance of those gendered discourses that criticize the actions and words of women, and that reduce their contemporary roles within the Coptic Church to nuns, deaconesses, or wives (Beshara 2019). When I lied to her that I do not care about being seen with her as a *sharmūṭa*, I was referring to my masculinity, or perhaps I should say my fragile masculinity, which might be threatened by us sharing food or some drinks. During my fieldwork, for example, many of my friends (or those who used to be my friends) were quite sure that I was sleeping with her. They were not convinced that someone would do his doctoral studies about the story of a *sharmūṭa*. Others doubted that She would be a "good" representative of the Coptic community when I presented my work to non-Coptic audiences in Egypt or in the West.

In the coming lines, I would like to share my thoughts about the "West," which is another entity that similarly doubts whether the sexual adventures of a Coptic Christian are worth telling. Indeed, the problem was not that She will cause people to commit sins due to the more secularized moral imaginaries in the West. Moreover, it is true that there are related narratives of *kalām innās* that might similarly label some people as "unrespectable," "perverts," or "sluts" in Western countries. However, a girl who is labeled a *sharmūṭa* in Egypt and other countries in the Middle East might be killed or sent to prison for violation of public morality, thus drawing our attention to the real physical dangers of *kalām innās* for women.

In September 2019, I attended a workshop organized by one of the most prestigious policy-making organizations in Washington, DC. I presented the topic of my doctoral dissertation as part of a panel concerned with Christian and other minority rights in the Middle East. I received no questions or feedback, and the chair of the panel immediately moved to the next talk. I was disappointed. During the welcome dinner, I was approached by one of the presenters, who told me that my work was important, but that it was not appropriate to use terms such as *sharmūṭa* or *mitnākah* (slut) at a roundtable that included ambassadors and diplomats. In this sense, I was again faced with the importance of the performance of embodying certain rules at certain spaces and times.

Studying or presenting the lives of Coptic Christians in Egypt has always been connected to a process of making and becoming that totally dismisses the rubble (Gordillo 2014, 54) of Coptic stories and experiences. By *rubble* I refer to those whose grievances are unrepresented because they might annul and haunt other "more urgent" and necessary ones. Sociologists, anthropologists, political scientists, and historians have recently tried to depict Copts as agents who play roles in Egyptian society and not (only) as victims of violence or discrimination (Guirguis 2016, 82; Lukasik 2016, 109; Heo 2018, 40). They have reflected on the heterogeneity of the Coptic identity, faith, and activism (Shenoda 2010, 9; Tadros 2013, chapter 1; van Doorn-Harder 2017, 4). Nevertheless, there is a clear lack of investigation into the lived experiences of those who cannot visibly and loudly assert their Copticness (Ibrahim 2019, 374).

Put differently, I have not read about the exhausted bodies and souls who, like her, cannot claim a place either at a roundtable of diplomats or in historical or ethnographic research about what scholars call the "Coptic Question" (Elsässer 2014, 213). In this regard, I have been thinking about how the integration of her sexual agency or victimhood, before and after her partners' ejaculations, might act as a stumbling block that disrupts the credibility of the narratives of people who are predominantly described through their religious identity. Considering how this identity is differently performed and contested in academic and nonacademic circles, I wonder about why Coptic Christians' sexual activities in general and those of women in particular have been silenced and made invisible. Although we "see her naked," we keep "staring at her" without inviting her to any of our academic and policy-making discussions. This passive staring is true not only on the level on the international human rights discourses but also with respect to the Muslim majority in Egypt.

"They See Mary on Porn Sites": Writing about Competing Penises

The figure of the sinful is central to the theological arguments made by the Coptic Orthodox tradition. As previously discussed, this centrality is paradoxically met with its complete absence on political, social, and academic scenes that argue about the lives of the Copts. "Why do you want to put our dirty laundry [i.e., scandals] on display?" I was once asked by a prominent *khādim* (lay servant) at the Sunday School service in the neighborhood parish of my childhood. He made this comment when I told him about my research topic. Although the *khādim* was one among many others who taught me how Jesus loves sinners, he preferred to confine this love to the walls of the Church, not only in light of the repressive dynamics of *kalām innās* but also in parallel with the performative politics of diplomacy.

What the *khādim* accused me of is a famous Egyptian proverb that one would say to another person who would expose the wrongdoings of their shared family/community/group to outsiders. This saying has been used in one way or another against political activists since the 2013 coup in Egypt, whenever someone posts a picture on her or his social media account reflecting government corruption, the poverty of the populace, or the brutality of the Egyptian security forces. It has also been used within activist circles when a woman writes about an incident of sexual harassment committed against her by a self-proclaimed "revolutionary" or "activist" man. In both cases, there is the fear of visibility. In my case, it has been specifically about the audience of Muslim others who might think that all Coptic women are *sharāmīt* (plural of *sharmūṭa*) and who might further spread the rumors that Copts have sex inside their neighborhood parishes.[6]

Back to her, whose (in)visible sexual adventures and writings have been unpacking my masculine fragility together with the social and political negation of the paradoxically dominant and masculinized theology of sins and the sinful. Together with Dina Georgis's (2013, 58) insistence that even the "ghosts" of the dead can speak, I follow Spivak's (1994, 194) reading of her interlocutor, who left her dead body and menstruation blood as "dissenting possibilities" that fight against hegemonic discourses. "She started sending nude pictures and videos to one of her sexual partners, who promised to secure a job for her in one of the most famous real estate companies in Egypt," She writes. One of the videos was leaked on the internet. She does not know whether he did it himself or if someone stole it from his phone. In recent years, porn sites have been flooded with short clips of girls who had sent nudes to their sexual partners. Indeed, Egypt does not have a professional pornography industry. Yet, the most famous porn sites have "Egypt" as one of their categories (Charbel 2016). In most cases, men hide their phones in secret corners of the rooms where they have sex with their partners. The videos are then posted to porn sites either when the men's phones are stolen or when the videos are intentionally leaked by the male partners for blackmail or revenge.

In the video in question, "she was wearing a cross, . . . the famous Coptic cross tattoo was clearly seen on the wrist of her right hand, . . . [and] the icon of Mary appears in the movie. She was the reason why they see Mary on porn sites," She notes. The visibility of Mary or other Coptic Saints via divine apparitions or miracles has been the subject of much academic attention over the previous two decades resulting from its much longer embeddedness within popular and traditional narratives among the Copts. When a Saint is made visible, Copts proudly take the opportunity to prove the truthfulness of their faith vis-à-vis Muslims. Moreover, sometimes the visibility of saints, crosses, and bibles in public spaces might reflect the nationalist harmony between Muslims and Copts (Shenoda 2010, 114; Heo 2018, 20). On the other hand, the visibility of Christian signs might sometimes put Copts in physical danger and cause public disorder (*balbala*). Hence, on many occasions, the Coptic Church has allied with the Egyptian state to contain the publicness of the Copts and their symbols (Heo 2013, 154).

But her visibility on porn sites cannot be easily contained or controlled given that sexuality is a public secret (Altink 2019, 1) in Egyptian society that all people talk about in scattered and privatized public spaces, that is, without collective consent about the importance of debating and learning about such a topic. Her appearance might not (only) contribute to the killing or the torturing of the Copts. More importantly, due to *kalām innās*, the Coptic Orthodox Church Revival Movement and its masculinized imagination of the Coptic faith, identity, and history might fall into pieces, as the *khādim* warned me. While the blood of the martyrs, who died for the sake of their faith, is an essential component of the modern Coptic tradition, physical and verbal violence that might result from sexual "scandals" can belittle the cause of the Copts as religious minority. Seeing Mary on porn sites can also diminish the power of Coptic activists, who sometimes deploy the apparition of Mary and other Christian symbols in the streets to contest not only the Islamized Egyptian state and society but also the hegemonic power of the Coptic Orthodox Church (Sedra 2012; El Gendi and Pinfari 2020).

Following the "scandal," She kept following the clip here and there. She sent dozens of emails to the porn site administrators asking them to delete it. Although She has achieved some success in doing so, through the efforts of her friends, She believes that many people would have downloaded the clip on their cell phones and computers and might re-upload it on the internet. Her ghost came into a brutal fight with the ghosts of *kalām innās*. "She started to see her nude clip in the eyes of everyone in the streets," She writes. She changed her hair color, put in contact lenses, and wore large sunglasses that covered her facial features to appear as a different person. For months, She entered into a state of severe depression that She was not able to reflect in her journal. She was afraid that her parents might find out and kill her. She had suicidal thoughts and started to visit a psychiatrist. Last but not least, as I was writing the lines of this chapter, She reported to me that She was afraid of being arrested. This fear has emerged with the recent raids by Egyptian police(men) against female social media influencers, whom they accuse of "spreading debauchery" and "violating public morals" (Ahmed 2020).

While chasing the clip on different porn sites, She was reading comments about the "beauty of the Christian girls' flesh, boobs, and asses." The comments section of the movies placed under the category of "Egypt" on porn sites has turned into a sectarian space where male Coptic and Muslim consumers of porn debate who owns the honorable women and who has the stronger and longer penises to fuck each other's women. Beyond this masculine battlefield, She felt that everyone was sleeping with her, Copts and Muslims alike. On different occasions, She was advised to emigrate or to hide for a long time until people forget. Others suggested She repent like the Samaritan woman, "but is this even possible?" She despaired in her journal.

The story of the Samaritan woman did not end with her meeting with Jesus, as hinted above. The Gospel of John tells us that "Many Samaritans in that city believed in Jesus because of the woman's word when she testified" (John 4:39 CEB). This radical shift from a sinful person who was hiding from her neighbors to a visible preacher has been a research interest of mine during my fieldwork in general. I asked my male Coptic interlocutors about the story of the Samaritan and whether they would accept hearing about Jesus from someone who is labelled a *sharmūṭa*. "The problem is that whatever she does, people would still remember what she did," one of them said. He was right; they will never marry or even give credibility to Samaritan women due to the historically embedded patriarchal society they live in and reproduce with their and her bodies (Ghannam 2013, 134).

Recalling my fear of sitting with her at a shared table, She cannot be a preacher like the Samaritan woman because of her inability to hide her sexual relationships, which disrupts Coptic attempts to become visible and loud about their faith, history, and identity. She cannot join a demonstration of Copts calling for their rights. She cannot teach kids about the word of God at the Sunday School service. She can only be visible through her journal. This chapter is devoted to and built around this peculiar and unrepresented kind of visibility and to its impressive and inspiring theological, political, and social insights.

ACKNOWLEDGMENTS

I would like to thank *her* for allowing me to write about her journal. I am also grateful for Professors Lisa L. Wynn and Angel M. Foster for the kind invitation to contribute to their volume. I am grateful to Egypt Migrations (formerly the Coptic Canadian History Project [CCHP]) and its editors Miray Philipps and Michael Akladios for publishing my piece about the Coptic coffeehouses in May 2018. It is this piece that led to my encounter with the ethnographic material that produced this chapter. Last but not least, the fieldwork that gave birth to this chapter was funded by the Excellence Initiative of the German Research Foundation and the Orient Institute Beirut (OIB)- Max Weber Foundation. The field research was conducted in accordance with the ethical guidelines of the University of Gießen (JLU).

NOTES

1. Within the Coptic Orthodox Church there is a difference between fathers of confession and spiritual fathers. While the former should be clergymen, the latter may be laymen (but never laywomen, as far as I know) who can help Copts build a good spiritual life. In some cases, Copts can ask their fathers of confession to be their spiritual fathers.
2. Also known at the Sunday School Movement.
3. She derived this meditation from the Sermon on the Mount, when Jesus uttered His blessings and curses.
4. Over the previous two decades or more, and specifically with the recent church bombings in Egypt, the scout teams of the neighborhood and village parishes have been responsible for checking the congregants' bags and belongings before they enter the parishes, leaving the police forces to stand with their weapons a few meters away from the gates of the parishes.
5. See Wynn 2018, 127, for a detailed description of the distinction between *sharmūṭa* and prostitute/sex worker.
6. Because the parishes are surrounded by high fences that prevent outsiders from seeing what happen inside them, sexual rumors emerge regarding what Copts do inside those walls. The funniest and strangest one I have heard is that Copts kiss each other when the lights are turned off during the celebration of the New Year's Eve. Here, I should emphasize that Copts do not kiss or have sex *inside* their neighborhood parishes. I have never seen something like this before or during my official period of fieldwork. However, as I earlier mentioned in the chapter, Copts might hold hands and kiss when they *leave* their parishes and *after* they finish their spiritual and entertainment activities.

REFERENCES

Ahmed, Ghadeer. 2020. "Up in Arms over a TikTok Star: Public Morality and the State." *Mada Masr*, April 29, 2020. https://madamasr.com/en/2020/04/29/opinion/u/up-in-arms-over-a-tiktok-star-public-morality-and-the-state.

Al-Tal, Suhair. 2017. "Being a Revolutionary and Writerly Rebel." In *Bad Girls of the Arab World*, edited by Nadia Yaqub and Rula Quawas, 199–211. Austin: University of Texas Press.

Altnik, Henrice. 2019. *Public Secrets: Race and Colour in Colonial and Independent Jamaica*. Liverpool: Liverpool University Press.

Armanios, Febe. 2012. "The 'Virtuous Woman': Images of Gender in Modern Coptic Society." *Middle Eastern Studies* 38, no. 1: 110–30.

Beshara, Aida. 2019. *Egyptian Women in the Coptic Orthodox Church of Egypt*. Meadville, PA: Christian Faith Publishing.

Butler, Judith. 2006 [1990]. *Gender Trouble: Feminism and the Subversion of Identity*. New York: Routledge.

Charbel, Jano. 2016. "Egypt's Shady World of Sex Videos." *Mada Masr*, March 11, 2016. https://www.madamasr.com/en/2016/03/11/feature/society/egypts-shady-world-of-sex-videos.

de Certeau, Michel. 1984. *The Practice of Everyday Life*. Translated by Steven Rendall. Berkeley: University of California Press.

El Gendi Yosra, and Marco Pinfari. 2020. "Icons of Contention: The Iconography of Martyrdom and the Construction of Coptic Identity in Post-Revolutionary Egypt." *Media, War and Conflict* 13, no. 1: 50–69.

Elsässer, Sebastian. 2014. *The Coptic Question in the Mubarak Era*. Oxford: Oxford University Press.

Georgis, Dina. 2013. *The Better Story: Queer Affects from the Middle East*. New York: State University of New York Press.

Ghannam, Farha. 2013. *Live and Die Like a Man: Gender Dynamics in Urban Egypt*. Stanford, CA: Stanford University Press.

Gordillo, Gaston R. 2014. *Rubble: The Afterlife of Destruction*. Durham, NC: Duke University Press, 2014.

Guirguis, Laure. 2016. *Copts and the State Security: Violence, Coercion, Sectarianism in Contemporary Egypt*. Stanford, CA: Stanford University Press.

Haddon, Hazel. 2012. *Gender and Identity in Contemporary Coptic Society*. Master's thesis, American University of Cairo.

Hasan, Sana S. 2003. *Christians Versus Muslims in Modern Egypt: The Century-Long Struggle for Coptic Equality*. New York: Oxford University Press.

Heo, Angie. 2013 "The Bodily Threat of Miracles: Security, Sacramentality, and the Egyptian Politics of Public Order." *American Ethnologist* 40, no. 1: 149–64.

———. 2018. *The Political Lives of Saints: Christian-Muslim Mediation in Egypt*. Berkeley: University of California Press.

Ibrahim, Mina. 2018. "Gathering for Shisha during St. Mary's Time: Another Story of (Un)Employed & (Un)Faithful Copts." *Egypt Migrations*, May 27, 2018. https://egyptmigrations.com/2018/05/27/gathering-for-shisha-during-st-marys-time.

———. 2019. "A Minority at the Bar: Revisiting the Coptic Christian (In-)visiblity." *Social Compass* 66, no. 3: 366–82

Jacob, Wilson. 2011. *Working Out Egypt: Effendi Masculinity and Subject Formation in Colonial Modernity, 1870–1940*. Durham, NC: Duke University Press.

Lukasik, Candace. 2016. "Conquest of Paradise: Secular Binds and Coptic Political Mobilization." *Middle East Critique* 25, no. 2: 107–25.

Makatou, Krystallia. 2007. "Ordinary Writing in Greece: Young People's Diaries." In *Ordinary Writings, Personal Narratives: Writing Practices in 19th and early 20th-Century Europe*, edited by Martyn Lyons, 173–90. New York: Peter Lang.

Mauss, Marcel. 2002. *Essay on the Gift: Forms and Functions of Exchange in Archaic Societies*. Translated by Ian Cunnison. New York: Routledge.

Oram, Elizabeth. 2004. *Constructing Modern Copts. The Production of Coptic Christian Identity in Contemporary Egypt*. PhD diss., Princeton University.

Roux, Martin. 2018 "Securing Coptic Churches: The Necessary Role of the Scouts." *Mada Masr*, April 8, 2018. https://madamasr.com/en/2018/04/08/feature/society/securing-coptic-churches-the-necessary-role-of-the-scouts.

Ryzova, Lucie. 2014. *The Age of the Effendiyya: Passages to Modernity in National-Colonial*

Egypt. Oxford: Oxford University Press.

Sedra, Paul. 2009. "Writing the History of the Modern Copts: From Victims and Symbols to Actors." *History Compass* 7, no. 3: 1049–63.

Sedra, Paul. 2012. "Reconstituting the Coptic Community amidst Revolution." *Middle East Report*, no. 265: 34–38.

Shenoda, Anthony. 2010. *Cultivating Mystery: Miracles and a Coptic Moral Imaginary.* PhD diss., Center for Middle Eastern Studies, Harvard University.

———. 2011. "Reflections on the (In)visibility of Copts in Egypt." *Jadaliyya*, May 18, 2011. https://www.jadaliyya.com/Details/24007.

Spivak, Gayatri C. 1994. "Can the Subaltern Speak?" In *Colonial Discourse and Post- Colonial Theory: A Reader*, edited by Patrick Williams and Laura Chrisman, 66–111. Hemel Hempstead, UK: Harvester-Wheatsheaf, 1994.

Tadros, Mariz. 2013. *Copts at the Crossroads: The Challenges of Building Inclusive Democracy in Egypt.* Cairo: American University in Cairo Press.

van Doorn-Harder, Pieternella [as Nelly], ed. 2017. *Copts in Context: Negotiating Identity, Tradition, and Modernity.* Columbia: University of South Carolina Press.

———. 1995. *Contemporary Coptic Nuns.* Columbia: University of South Carolina Press.

Wikan, Unni. 1996. *Tomorrow, God Willing: Self-Made Destinies in Cairo.* Chicago, IL: University of Chicago Press.

Wynn, L. L. 2018. *Love, Sex, and Desire in Modern Egypt: Navigating the Margins of Respectability.* Austin: University of Texas Press.

Sexual Emergence in the Middle East and North Africa

Ten Insights from the Ethnography

MARCIA C. INHORN

More than forty years have passed since the Egyptian physician and feminist activist Nawal El Saadawi published her critical memoir, *The Hidden Face of Eve: Women in the Arab World*. First published in Arabic in 1977, and then in English in 1980, this book documented El Saadawi's own experience of female circumcision (*tahara*) as a girl in Upper Egypt, a practice that she would later come to condemn as one of the "hidden faces" of Middle Eastern women's oppression. Since then, multiple books, academic articles, documentary films, and activist campaigns have been devoted to this topic, with major initiatives to eliminate "female genital mutilation" (FGM) supported by the World Health Organization, the United Nations Population Fund (UNFPA), and UNICEF. Although "female genital cutting" (FGC)—a less sensationalist term promoted by some Indigenous advocacy organizations such as Tostan International—has never been practiced in most parts of the Middle East and North Africa (MENA), it has become synonymous with Middle Eastern women's sexual oppression.

It took nearly forty years for the next book on sex in the MENA region to be written by another Egyptian-born journalist and public health activist, Shereen El Feki. Called *Sex and the Citadel: Intimate Life in a Changing Arab World* (2013), the book describes the Arab world as a citadel, with a fortress mentality surrounding sex that leads to lack of sex education and, hence, knowledge of both sexual pleasure and safety. More recently, the award-winning French novelist Leila Slimani has published a journalistic account called *Sex and Lies: True Stories of Women's Intimate Lives in the Arab World* (2020). Through return to her home country of Morocco and interviews with women there, she has produced a story of Arab women's sex lives advertised as "harrowing" to Western readers.

On the one hand, it is extremely important that Middle Eastern–born women themselves have opened up a conversation about sex, including attitudes and practices that they deem harmful to women across the region. On the other hand, such accounts may fuel Western Orientalist stereotypes of Muslim women as painfully oppressed, including in the sexual realm. In her critically acclaimed book *Do Muslim Women Need Saving?* (2013), Columbia University anthropologist Lila Abu-Lughod questions this constant negative reinforcement of Muslim women's oppression. In particular, she takes issue with the genre of writing that she calls "pulp nonfiction," in which "pornographies of pain" highlight women's abuse in an imagined place that Abu-Lughod calls "IslamLand." A prime example of this genre of pulp nonfiction would be Somali émigré Ayaan Hirsi Ali's book, *The Caged Virgin: An Emancipation Proclamation for Women and Islam* (2004). In it, Ali decries the treatment of women in Islam, arguing that the religion's demands of premarital chastity turn Muslim women into "caged virgins." This image, and the book itself, have played well with Western audiences who are prone to Islamophobia.

Arguing for a much-needed corrective, Abu-Lughod turns to her own discipline, anthropology, as a scholarly path to redemption. In her book *Do Muslim Women Need Saving?*, Abu-Lughod gives precedence to the voices and stories of women who she has come to know through more than three decades of anthropological immersion in communities in both rural and urban Egypt (see, for instance, Abu-Lughod 1986, 1993), as well as among her own Palestinian female family members.

Abu-Lughod advocates for anthropology as the most humanistic form of social inquiry. Through anthropology's unique method of ethnography, scholars learn local languages, live with communities for extended periods of time, engage in both participant observation and in-depth interviewing, and attempt to represent the life worlds of interlocutors through writing that is "thick" with ethnographic description. The ultimate object of this research is to produce "ethnographies"—usually book-length accounts that render nuanced portrayals of lives as lived, giving voice to those whose stories would otherwise remain unaccounted for or otherwise muted.

Since the mid-twentieth century, nearly six hundred book-length Middle East ethnographies have been published in English, constituting a remarkable anthropological corpus (Inhorn and Isidoros 2021). Yet, remarkably, only ten of these ethnographies are devoted to sex. Sexual studies are what I have described as a "road less traveled" in Middle East anthropology:

> We know very little about what we might call "lived sexuality," including between men and women as married and unmarried couples. Fortunately, some younger-generation scholars are beginning to open the path of lesbian, gay, bisexual, and transgender studies in the Middle East. . . . [But] Middle East anthropologists are far behind in scholarship on sexuality. This is especially egregious in the era of HIV/AIDS. . . . There is not a single ethnography on HIV/AIDS or its impact in the Middle East. It is time for Middle East anthropologists to be bold and bring sexuality into focus. (Inhorn 2014, 72–73)

One of the first bold scholars to do so was the Iranian-American anthropologist Pardis Mahdavi (2008), who published a path-breaking ethnography on young people's sex lives in Tehran. Her next book (2011) was an ethnographic study of labor migrants and sex workers in the United Arab Emirates, in which she argued that some Middle Eastern women actually *choose* to engage in sex work, thereby challenging human rights discourses of "sex trafficking," with all women sex workers in need of "saving."

Since then, a new focus on queer sexuality in the Middle East has emerged, perhaps inspired by Princeton University anthropologist John Bornemann's 2007 autoethnography of his own gay desires and encounters in the Syrian city of Aleppo (prior to the 2011 civil war). Over the past decade, mostly younger scholars have begun to study queer life and sex, particularly among men in some of the Middle East's major cities, including Beirut, Lebanon (Merabet 2015; Moussawi 2020), Istanbul, Turkey (Özbay 2017), and Tehran, Iran (Kjaran 2019; Najmabadi 2013). These books chart the ways Middle Eastern gay men are navigating urban, and sometimes transnational spaces and activist circles (Atshan 2020), in order to express same-sex desires and enjoy relationships with other men. Yet, all of these ethnographies also focus on gay men's struggles in their own societies against inequalities and discrimination, homophobia, religious condemnation, threats of violence and detention, and human rights violations. Although the threat of HIV/AIDS is a reality for men who have sex with men across the MENA region, few of these ethnographies pay attention to this topic. As of 2020, there is still not a single ethnography devoted to people living with HIV/AIDS (PLWHA) in the region.

This Volume and Its Ethnographic Insights

Given these scholarly openings and omissions, it is important to bring together the work of anthropologists who have made sex in the MENA region a topic of their ethnographic inquiries. The present volume is groundbreaking in this regard—the first to focus explicitly on sex in multiple settings across the region. The editors, Lisa L. Wynn and Angel M. Foster, are among the first anthropologists to devote their own research to MENA sexuality studies. Together, they have documented the rise of emergency contraception in the region (Foster and Wynn 2012), as well as the introduction of a number of other sexual and reproductive health technologies (Wynn and Foster 2017). Wynn, who is a past president of the Australian Anthropological Association, is a long-term ethnographer of Egypt. She has published two ethnographies documenting the lives and loves of her interlocutors, including their sexual relationships and challenges (Wynn 2007, 2018).

In this volume organized by Wynn and Foster, most of the contributors are younger-generation anthropologists, both men and women, whose research covers a wide swath of the Middle East, ranging from Morocco in the west to Iran in the east. Through their work, we meet multiple categories of sexual subjects, including married and unmarried people, gay men and women, pregnant women, sex workers, prisoners, virgins, pornography users, and masturbators.

Through this multi-sited, richly peopled anthropological approach, we learn much about *sexual emergence* in the MENA region. Based on the definition of "emergence" forwarded by Marxist scholar Raymond

Williams—namely, "new meanings and values, new practices, new relationships and kinds of relationship [that] are continually being created" (Williams 1978, 123)—we might think of sexual emergence as the new knowledge, attitudes, beliefs, practices, and social mores around sex that are in constant creation in the MENA region.

This volume is replete with examples of sexual emergence. In what follows, I summarize ten facets of sexual emergence that are clear in this volume's ethnographic accounts.

1. THE ETHNOGRAPHY OF SEX

As noted above, the disciplinary hallmark of anthropology is ethnography, a process of research and writing that is unique as a form of social inquiry. Participant observation and interviewing are how most anthropologists come to know about the lives of their interlocutors. However, in the realm of sex, "observing" is generally impossible—although some ethnographers have pushed the ethical boundaries of the discipline by providing autoethnographic descriptions of their own sexual encounters in the field (e.g., Merabet 2015). Still, asking questions and hearing answers about sex can be done sensitively and with proper consent. In this book, we see the results of this kind of sexual inquiry. The book provides numerous sexual narratives and stories, particularly from Middle Eastern women. Through their willingness to "sexually self-report," we learn about sexual desires and gratifications, as well as sexual disappointments and struggles. Overall, the ethnographic message is clear. In the MENA region, people are attempting to pursue meaningful sex lives within the constraints of their local social worlds.

2. THE MORALITY OF SEX

Harvard anthropologist Arthur Kleinman (1992) was the first to forward the concept of "local moral worlds," which he defined as the "particular local patterns of recreating *what is most at stake* for us, what we most fear, what we most aspire to" (129, italics in original). In the realm of sex in the MENA region, local moral worlds do matter. From an orthodox Islamic religious standpoint, heterosexual conjugal sex is the only permitted form of sex, with all other forms—including premarital sex, extramarital sex, homosexual sex, and, according to most religious scholars, masturbation—strictly forbidden. Furthermore, acts of *zina* (illicit sexual relations) are punishable religiously and by law in most MENA countries (see Hayes, this volume). Thus, enacting sex that is *zina* can lead to moral approbation, as well as legal risk and criminal punishment. Having said that, as seen throughout this volume, *zina* is widespread, especially among the younger generation. In various chapters in this volume, we read about young men and women masturbating to porn, meeting up through dating apps, hooking up in furnished rental apartments and family homes, establishing sexual partnerships through "secret" marriages, and for gay men and women, finding each other through gay sex apps and clubs catering to a queer clientele. In short, in today's Middle East, young people are not only questioning the local social mores surrounding chastity and heterosexuality, they are doing so in ways that literally mitigate the power of *zina* as a local moral discourse.

3. THE DELAY OF SEX

Changing moral discourses are, in part, a reflection of changing political-economic realities across the region. As noted in several chapters, the age of marriage for both men and women is increasing across the MENA region as a result of changing marriage laws, women's increasing education, and the burdensome costs of marriage for both men and women. Middle East political scientist Diane Singerman (2007, 2013) coined the term "waithood" to describe this widespread pattern of marriage delay (see also Inhorn and Smith-Hefner 2020). In countries such as Egypt, Jordan, and Morocco, it may take years, even decades, for young men to accrue sufficient material resources to marry and establish a household. While still residing in their parents' homes, with little opportunity for sex, these young men—and the women they cannot yet marry—may feel frustrated and blocked in their passage to full adulthood. This "marriage crisis" or "celibacy crisis," as some in the MENA region have called it, redounds throughout the chapters of this volume. Yet, we also learn about the many ways young people are pursuing their sexual desires without "waiting" for marriage to happen—at least "official" marriage, performed before friends and family. 'Urfi, or customary, marriages are becoming frequent among young couples (see Salem, this volume), allowing those who are dating to have sex with their partners while hidden in a state of "secret" matrimony. In addition, women who are tired of "waiting" and have had sex before marriage are turning to hymenoplasty, or hymen repair, to "renew" their virginity if and when the time comes to marry. In short, young Middle Easterners are becoming increasingly savvy in finding ways to date, have sex, and have fun, even when economic realities make marriage and the transition to full adulthood beyond their individual control.

4. THE MEDIATIZATION OF SEX

Young people's ability to pursue relationships before marriage has been profoundly enhanced through the massive expansion of media technologies in the MENA region, including computers, cell phones, the Internet, and a wide variety of social media platforms and applications. The chapters in this volume provide numerous examples of what might best be described as the "mediatization of sex," from the use of "hookup apps" such as Tinder and Bumble (see El-Mowafi and Foster, this volume), or Grindr and Scruff for gay men (see Gagné, this volume), to the widespread dissemination and use of pornography, even among the most religiously observant (see Saramifar, this volume). These forms of new media have allowed young people to connect, to meet, and to find safe zones for sex. They have also become fruitful sites for cultivating new forms of sexual desire and pleasure. And, from a reproductive and sexual health standpoint, they have provided crucial forms of knowledge and information, for example, about sexually transmitted infections, contraception, and safe abortion.

5. THE REPRODUCTIVITY OF SEX

This volume also reminds readers that sex can lead to reproduction. As we see in some chapters, pregnancies are planned by Middle Eastern couples, leading to desired births, for fathers as well as mothers (see Chalmiers, this volume). But pregnancies can also happen by mistake, leading to desperate decision-making, safe and unsafe abortions, and in some cases, impoverished single motherhood (see Michalak, this volume). Overall, sexual and reproductive health services are unevenly distributed across the MENA region, with problems of access for unmarried young people, who are assumed, by default, to be sexually inactive. Acquiring access to contraception can thus be very difficult (see MacFarlane, this volume). And because abortion is legally restricted in most countries across the region

(Hessini 2007), abortions are performed in secrecy, often unsafely. But as shown in this volume, emergency contraception pills (so-called "morning after" pills) are making their way to the Middle East, even if the market is unregulated. Furthermore, in many Middle Eastern countries, the majority of reproductive-aged women can name at least one—and often many—forms of contraception (Inhorn 2018a). Sexual and reproductive technologies—from intrauterine devices (IUDs) to in vitro fertilization (IVF) (Inhorn 2003, 2012, 2015) to vibrators (Wynn and Foster 2017)—have made their way across the Middle East, serving to further disassociate sex from reproduction. This is perhaps especially true in the case of Palestinian couples, who find ways to make babies through "sperm smuggling," even when husbands are incarcerated for years in Israeli prisons (see Ferrero, this volume).

6. THE CONJUGALITY OF SEX

The case of these imprisoned Palestinians' "marriage by proxy" demonstrates how highly marriage is valued across the MENA region. Marriage for Muslims is said to be "half of the religion," and Middle Easterners are among the "most married" people in the world (Omran and Roudi 1993; Rashad, Osman, and Roudi-Fahimi 2005). This "marriage imperative" can be difficult, not only because of the aforementioned economic constraints, but also for individuals in the Middle East who do not identify as heterosexual (Atshan 2020; Najmabadi 2013). In short, marriage, though valorized, can be multiply problematic. Yet, as shown throughout this volume, young people who want to marry are finding creative ways to do so, particularly through 'urfi marriages among Sunni Muslim youth (see Salem, this volume), and temporary mut'a marriages among the Shi'a (Haeri 1989). Whether these marriages are customary, temporary, or "official," conjugal sex is being enjoyed, partly through the help of sex manuals, online sex therapists, and a booming marketplace of internet porn, which even the Islamic Republic of Iran is unable to completely censor (see Saramifar, this volume). Although we know far too little about how married couples in the Middle East experience their sex lives together, new forms of "marital ethnography" (Inhorn 2012, 2014) are beginning to emerge, revealing what marriage means to both men and women, as well as their hopes for romance and their desires for sexual fulfillment.

7. THE QUEERING OF SEX

Until about five years ago, we knew almost nothing about the lives of lesbian, gay, bisexual, transgender, and queer/questioning (LGBTQ) people in the MENA region. But through the work of young queer-identified anthropologists, the life worlds of gay men (see Gagné, this volume), lesbians (Le Rebard 2014, and transgender people (Najmabadi 2013) are beginning to be revealed. In several chapters in this volume, we see the ways LGBTQ identities and communities are beginning to take shape, partly through the gay sex apps that have become prevalent in countries like Lebanon (see Gagné, this volume) and social media and dance clubs in places like Dubai (see Hassanein and Wynn, this volume). An increasing openness to the LGBTQ community is apparent in places like Beirut, Casablanca, Dubai, Istanbul, and Tehran, where commercial venues such as bars and nightclubs cater exclusively to a gay clientele. In short, the queering of sex in the MENA region is coming out into the open, at least in some of the region's more cosmopolitan centers. Still, as shown in this volume, compulsory heterosexuality and masculinity norms continue to haunt queer spaces, leading to what University of Texas anthropologist Sofian Merabet (2015) has called "internalized homophobia." This is apparent in the chapter by Matthew Gagné, where more effeminate Lebanese men who do not conform to desired Arab "bear" masculinity (i.e., muscular and hairy) experience bodily objectification and discrimination. In other words, the queering of sex in the Middle East has opened new possibilities for some men but not for others, thereby suggesting that norms of masculinity require further unseating and transgression (Inhorn and Isidoros 2021).

8. THE TRANSACTION OF SEX

Sex, whether straight or gay, can also be transactional in nature. The final section of this volume includes contributions devoted to transactional sex, which can be difficult to define in the Middle East, where not all transactions fall within the realm of legal or illegal sex work (see Wynn, this volume). Prostitution has existed in the Middle East for centuries, with Islamic court records documenting the regulation of the sex trade during the Ottoman period (Baldwin 2012). In the contemporary period, some MENA countries such as Tunisia have allowed and regulated legal

278 SEX IN THE MIDDLE EAST AND NORTH AFRICA

sex work, although it has been challenged by Islamist political parties (see Michalak, this volume). Although knowledge may not yet be widespread, "transactional safe sex" has come to the Middle East, thereby reducing the risk of HIV/AIDS and other sexually transmitted infections (STIs).

9. The Risks of Sex

Remarkably, the rate of HIV/AIDS infections in the MENA region is among the lowest in the world, at a current prevalence rate of just 0.1 percent (Gökengin et al. 2016). Still, there has been a 31 percent increase in new infections since 2001, most of them sexually transmitted. Beyond the risk of HIV/AIDS and other STIs, the risk of sex in the MENA region takes on a much broader meaning, as shown throughout multiple chapters in this volume. Women who decide to have sex outside of "conjugal confines" (Gürtin 2016) face many risks, among them the loss of virginity, reputation, and honor, as well as partners' abandonment, and, in worst-case scenarios, death at the hands of family members (see El-Mowafi and Foster, this volume). Stories of sex are also replete with fear—fear of discovery, stigma, shame, dishonor, and moral punishment (see Ibrahim, this volume). Furthermore, for women, sex can bring the risky physical embodiment of unwanted pregnancy, unsafe abortion, maternal mortality, or single motherhood (see Hayes, this volume). Sex, especially for young Middle Eastern women, can be very costly (see Feather, this volume). Thus, despite the new sexual freedoms and mores that are shown to be emerging across the MENA region, this volume also reminds us that sex is often a high-stakes affair, especially for Middle Eastern women.

10. THE POLITICS OF SEX

Finally, this volume demonstrates that sex is political—from the most intimate realm of the sexual body and its desires, to the highly gendered negotiations surrounding sex and reproduction, to the nation-state and its efforts to criminalize sex, sex work, homosexuality, and abortion (see El-Mowafi and Foster, this volume). Furthermore, the politics of sex become apparent in the lacunae—for example, missing sex education, inadequate sexual and reproductive health services, and lack of sexual-harm reduction efforts. But perhaps the most striking example of sexual politics is found in the aforementioned chapter on Palestinian sperm smuggling. As shown in Laura Ferrero's poignant ethnography, thousands of Palestinian men spend decades of their lives in Israeli prisons, making impossible their chances for ordinary marriage and conjugal sex. Yet, in a most creative move—supported by Palestinian women, their families, local IVF clinics, and political parties—Palestinian prisoners are being "married by proxy" to women who are willing to become their wives and the mothers of their children. So-called sperm smuggling out of Israeli prisons, accompanied by conceptions in Palestinian IVF clinics, are enabling the birth of Palestinian children, including by women who are otherwise sexual virgins.

This story is a haunting one. But it also speaks to political agency among one group of people in the Middle East whose lives have been profoundly constrained by settler-colonialism and its violent effects. Such stories are vitally important, and need to be pursued by anthropologists in other parts of the MENA region. In the midst of the world's worst refugee crisis— with the majority of refugees coming from the Middle Eastern countries of Afghanistan, Iraq, and Syria, and with millions of internally displaced persons in Libya and Yemen (Inhorn 2018b; Inhorn and Volk 2021)—it is important to understand how sex and reproduction are being thwarted by conflict and forced displacement, experienced by refugees in bleak camps scattered across the MENA region, and questioned in Euro-American communities where refugees are ultimately resettled (see Chalmiers, this volume). In other words, anthropologists must begin to explore sex both *in* and *out* of the MENA region. This is another road barely traveled in Middle East anthropology, but one that is critical for a region with the world's highest rates of forced displacement.

In short, there is still much more to be done. But this volume is a critical beginning.

References

Abu-Lughod, Lila. 1986. *Veiled Sentiments: Honor and Poetry in a Bedouin Society.* Berkeley: University of California Press.

———1993. *Writing Women's Worlds: Bedouin Stories.* Berkeley: University of California Press.

———. 2013. *Do Muslim Women Need Saving?* Cambridge, MA: Harvard University Press.

Ali, Ayaan Hirsi. *The Caged Virgin: An Emancipation Proclamation for Women and Islam.* New York: Free Press.

Atshan, Sa'ed. 2020. *Queer Palestine and the Empire of Critique.* Stanford, CA: Stanford University Press.

Baldwin, James E. 2012. "Prostitution, Islamic Law and Ottoman Societies." *Journal of the Economic and Social History of the Orient* 55, no. 1: 117–52.

Borneman, John. 2007. *Syrian Episodes: Sons, Fathers, and an Anthropologist in Aleppo.* Princeton, NJ: Princeton University Press.

El Feki, Shereen. 2013. *Sex and the Citadel: Intimate Life in a Changing Arab World.* New York: Anchor.

El Saadawi, Nawal. 1980. *The Hidden Face of Eve: Women in the Arab World.* London: Zed.

Foster, Angel M., and L. L. Wynn, eds. 2012. *Emergency Contraception: The Story of a Global Reproductive Health Technology.* London: Palgrave Macmillan.

Gökengin, Deniz, Fardad Doroudi, Johny Tohme, Ben Collins, and Navid Madani. 2016. "HIV/AIDS: Trends in the Middle East and North Africa Region," *International Journal of Infectious Diseases* 44: 66–73.

Gürtin, Zeynep B. 2016. "Patriarchal Pronatalism: Islam, Secularism, and the Conjugal Confines of Turkey's IVF Boom." *Reproductive BioMedicine and Society Online,* no. 2: 39–46.

Haeri, Shahla. 1989. *Law of Desire: Temporary Marriage in Shi'i Iran.* Syracuse, NY: Syracuse University Press.

Hessini, Leila. 2007. "Abortion and Islam: Policies and Practice in the Middle East and North Africa." *Reproductive Health Matters* 15, no. 29: 75–84.

Inhorn, Marcia C. 2003. *Local Babies, Global Science: Gender, Religion, and In Vitro Fertilization in Egypt.* New York: Routledge.

———. 2012. *The New Arab Man: Emergent Masculinities, Technologies, and Islam in the Middle East.* Princeton, NJ: Princeton University Press.

———. 2014. "Roads Less Traveled in Middle East Anthropology—and New Paths in Gender Ethnography." *Journal of Middle East Women's Studies* 10, no. 3: 62–86.

———. 2015. *Cosmopolitan Conceptions: IVF Sojourns in Global Dubai.* Durham, NC: Duke University Press.

———. 2018a. "The Arab World's 'Quiet' Reproductive Revolution." *Brown Journal of World Affairs* 24, no. 2: 147–57.

———. 2018b. *America's Arab Refugees: Vulnerability and Health on the Margins.* Stanford, CA: Stanford University Press.

Inhorn, Marcia C., and Konstantina Isidoros. 2021. "Middle East Anthropology and the Gender Divide: Reconceiving Arab Masculinity in Precarious Times." In *Arab Masculinities: Anthropological Reconceptions in Precarious Times,* edited by Konstantina Isidoros and Marcia C. Inhorn, 1–33. Bloomington: Indiana University Press.

Inhorn, Marcia C., and Nancy J. Smith-Hefner, eds. 2020. *Waithood: Gender, Education, and Global Delays in Marriage and Childbearing.* New York: Berghahn.

Inhorn, Marcia C., and Lucia Volk, eds. 2021. *Un-settling Middle Eastern Refugees: Regimes of Exclusion and Inclusion in the Middle East, Europe, and North America*. New York: Berghahn.

Kjaran, Jón Ingvar. 2019. *Gay Life Stories: Same-Sex Desires in Post-Revolutionary Iran*. London: Palgrave Macmillan.

Kleinman, Arthur. 1992. "Local Worlds of Suffering: An Interpersonal Focus for Ethnographies of Illness Experience." *Qualitative Health Research* 2, no. 2: 127–34.

Le Renard, Amélie. 2014. *A Society of Young Women: Opportunities of Place, Power, and Reform in Saudi Arabia*. Stanford, CA: Stanford University Press.

Mahdavi, Pardis. 2008. *Passionate Uprisings: Iran's Sexual Revolution*. Stanford, CA: Stanford University Press.

———. 2011. *Gridlock: Labor, Migration, and Human Trafficking in Dubai*. Stanford, CA: Stanford University Press.

Merabet, Sofian. 2015. *Queer Beirut*. Austin: University of Texas Press.

Moussawi, Ghassan. 2020. *Disruptive Situations: Fractal Orientalism and Queer Strategies in Beirut*. Philadelphia, PA: Temple University Press.

Najmabadi, Afsaneh. 2013. *Professing Selves: Transsexuality and Same-Sex Desire in Contemporary Iran*. Durham, NC: Duke University Press.

Omran, A. R., and F. Roudi. 1993. "The Middle East Population Puzzle." *Population Bulletin* 48, no. 1: 1–40.

Özbay, Cenk. 2017. *Queering Sexualities in Turkey: Gay Men, Male Prostitutes and the City*. London: I. B. Tauris.

Rashad, Hoda, Magued Osman, and Farzaneh Roudi-Fahimi. 2005. *Marriage in the Arab World*. Washington, DC: Population Reference Bureau.

Singerman, Diane. 2007. *The Economic Imperatives of Marriage: Emerging Practices and Identities among Youth in the Middle East*. Middle East Youth Initiative Working Paper no. 6. Washington, DC: Brookings Institution, Wolfensohn Center for Development.

———. 2013. "Youth, Gender, and Dignity in the Egyptian Uprising." *Journal of Middle East Women's Studies* 9, no. 3: 1–27.

Slimani, Leila. 2020. *Sex and Lies: True Stories of Women's Intimate Lives in the Arab World*. New York: Penguin.

Williams, Raymond. 1978. *Marxism and Literature*. Oxford: Oxford University Press.

Wynn, L. L. 2007. *Pyramids and Nightclubs: A Travel Ethnography of Arab and Western Imaginations of Egypt, from King Tut and a Colony of Atlantis to Rumors of Sex Orgies, Urban Legends of a Marauding Prince, and Blonde Belly Dancers*. Austin: University of Texas Press.

———. 2018. *Love, Sex, and Desire in Modern Egypt: Navigating the Margins of Respectability*. Austin: University of Texas Press.

Wynn, L. L., and Angel M. Foster, eds. 2017. *Abortion Pills, Test Tube Babies, and Sex Toys: Emerging Sexual and Reproductive Technologies in the Middle East and North Africa*. Nashville, TN: Vanderbilt University Press.

Glossary

List of Acronyms and Abbreviations

ACF	Advocacy Coalition Framework
AÇSAP	Maternal-child health and family planning centers (Turkey)
AFS	Association of Women of the South (Morocco)
AIDS	Acquired immunodeficiency syndrome
AIMS	American Institute of Maghrib Studies
AKP	Adalet ve Kalkınma Partisi (Justice and Development Party, Turkey)
ALCS	Association in the Fight against AIDS (Morocco)
ART	Assisted reproductive technology
ASCS	Association of the South in the Fight against AIDS (Morocco)
ASF	Association Solidarity Feminine (Morocco)
ATL MST	Tunisian Association for the Struggle against STDs and HIV/AIDS
AVFM	Association of the Voices of Moroccan Women
BDSM	Bondage, discipline, sadism, and masochism
CCHP	Coptic Canadian History Project
CEDAW	Convention on the Elimination of All Forms of Discrimination against Women
CEMAT	Centre d'Études Maghrébines à Tunis
CERFI	Center for Women's Studies in Islam

CRC	Convention on the Rights of the Child
DHS	Demographic Health Survey
EC	Emergency contraception
EPL	Educator-peer-leader
FAFM	Forum Azzharae for Moroccan Women
FHC	Family health center (Turkey)
FGC	Female genital cutting
FGM	Female genital mutilation
FLDDF	Federation of the Democratic League of Women's Rights (Morocco)
FSW	Female sex worker
HIV	Human immunodeficiency virus
ICSI	Intracytoplasmic sperm injection
INSAF	National Institute of Solidarity with Women in Distress (Morocco)
IPS	Israel Prison Service
IRB	Institutional review board (United States)
IRC	Internet Relay Chat
ISF	Internal Security Forces
ISIS	Islamic State of Iraq and Syria
IUD	Intrauterine device
IVF	In vitro fertilization
IWD	Initiative for Women's Development (Morocco)
JCAP	Jordan Communication, Advocacy, and Policy
JPFHS	Jordan Population and Family Health Survey
LGBTQ	Lesbian, gay, bisexual, transgender, queer/questioning
MENA	Middle East and North Africa

MOH	Ministry of health
MSM	Men who have sex with men
MSW	Male sex worker
NGO	Nongovernmental organization
NSA	No strings attached
ob-gyn	Obstetrician/gynecologist
OCP	Oral contraceptive pill
OEB	Oum El Banine (Morocco)
PJD	Justice and Development Party (Morocco)
PLWHA	People living with HIV/AIDS
PRCS	Palestine Red Crescent Society
PSC	Personal Status Code (Morocco)
PSW	Professional sex worker
REB	Research ethics board (Canada)
SRH	Sexual and reproductive health
STI	Sexually transmitted infection
TFR	Total fertility rate
UFL	Union Feminine Liberale (Morocco)
UN	United Nations
UNRWA	United Nations Relief and Works Agency
UX	User experience
VPN	Virtual private network

Terms

'a'la	extended kinship networks
amr waqe'	fait accompli
'athara	stumbling block

azadi	freedom
'azl	withdrawal
balbala	public disorder
batinta	business license
batrona	madam, matrone
bint	girl
boya	tomboy
bukhoor	incense
butagas	liquid propane cooking fuel
chador	black outer women's coat worn in Iran
coitus interruptus	withdrawal, or more colloquially, pulling out; the practice of removing the penis from the vagina prior to ejaculation
Dār al-Ifta' al-filastiniyya	government body established as a center for Islamic legal research
dakhal 'al khas	entered my private messages
du'a al-istikhara	prayer to guide decision-making
effendiyya	middle class elites
'end	stubbornness
fadila	virtuous
fāqidat	woman who has been deprived of something/someone
fatiha	first Sura of the Qur'an (also traditional religious marriage, Morocco)
fatwa	religious opinion or ruling offered by a qualified Islamic jurist (pl. fatwas)
film e super / film e mõstahjan	pornography
foyer	student boarding house
fqih	Islamic scholar
ghalban	pitiable

ghalat	wrong
gharaez	impulses
hadith	sayings of the Prophet Muhammed
halal	permissible, licit
haram	prohibited, illicit
hashari	horny
hijab	modest women's head covering worn in public
hshouma	shame
imam	Muslim cleric, religious leader
intifada	uprising
ishhar	announcement (also public acknowledgment of a union)
istashhad	martyred, killed by the Israeli army
isteqlal	independence
jinn	spirits
jomhuri islami	Islamic Republic
kalām innās	rumors
karama	personal dignity
khādim	lay servant
khalas	enough, stop
koshary	traditional Egyptian dish of noodles, rice, lentils, and fried onions
kouboul	talisman which makes its wearer loved by all
mahr	bride wealth
mar'a ajnabia	foreign woman
ma'zoun	registrar
medina	traditional downtown area
mitnākah	slut
molokhiya	jute

munhalleen	deviant
muqawwama	resistance
nasab	legitimate filiation
nasle soukhte	the "burnt generation"
pudeur	public modesty
qanoonan	outside the Egyptian personal status code
qiwama	providing for a wife
rasmy	official, formal
resaleh	textual treatise compiling all ordinances of a learned jurist
rugu'	second marriage
rujula	manliness
safir al hurreya	ambassador of freedom
shar'an	evil
shari'a	Islamic law (also legitimacy, legality, Morocco)
sharmūta	whore
shawafat	female practitioners
shurut	conditions
siḥr	magic
shimagh	traditional male headdress
simsara	middlewoman
sunna	words and deeds of the Prophet Muhammed
taa'	absolute obedience
tahara	female circumcision
tahrīb al nuṭaf	sperm smuggling
temiz	clean
thaqāf	complete impotence
thawriyyah	revolutionary
thobe	white robe worn by Saudi men

tilth	place to sow seeds
toukal	magic that is ingested via food or drink
une bonne à tout faire	cleaning woman who has sex with her male employer
'urfi	customary
usra	nuclear family
velayate faqih	guardianship of a learned jurist
wali	consent of the bride's male guardian
warta	bind
waznah	skills
zina	illicit sexual relations, adultery

Contributors

MORGEN A. CHALMIERS is an MD/PhD candidate in psychological and medical anthropology at the University of California San Diego Medical Scientist Training Program.

I. M. EL-MOWAFI holds an MSc in interdisciplinary health sciences from the University of Ottawa.

GINGER FEATHER holds a PhD in political science with a minor in women, gender, and sexuality studies. She works for IMS Expert Services on domestic violence and child custody cases involving Moroccan and international laws.

LAURA FERRERO holds a PhD in anthropology and is an adjunct professor of anthropology of the Middle East at Turin University, Italy.

ANGEL M. FOSTER is a professor in the Faculty of Health Sciences and the 2011–2016 Endowed Chair in Women's Health Research at the University of Ottawa. She is also the co-founder of Cambridge Reproductive Health Consultants.

MATHEW GAGNÉ in assistant professor in the Department of Sociology and Social Anthropology at Dalhousie University. His research examines the impacts of digital media within the intimate lives of queer Beiruti men.

SAFFAA HASSANEIN is an artist, activist, and PhD candidate in visual arts at the University of Sydney.

SHANNON HAYES is a monitoring and evaluation officer at Education for Employment, an international nonprofit that provides employment training and job placement to youth in the Middle East and North Africa.

MINA IBRAHIM recently completed his PhD at the University of Gießen, Germany, and is currently an affiliate researcher at the Leibniz-Zentrum Moderner Orient (ZMO) in Berlin. He is also the founding director of SARD for History and Social Research (Shubra's Archive) and the project coordinator of the MENA Prison Forum.

MARCIA C. INHORN is the William K. Lanman Jr. Professor of Anthropology and International Affairs and chair of the Council on Middle East Studies in the MacMillan Center for International and Area Studies at Yale University.

KATRINA MACFARLANE holds an MSc in interdisciplinary health sciences from the University of Ottawa. She has previously served as a research fielding manager at the Guttmacher Institute and an assistant research scientist at NYU.

LAURENCE MICHALAK is a cultural anthropologist and retired vice chair of the Center for Middle Eastern Studies of the University of California at Berkeley.

RANIA SALEM is an associate professor in the Department of Sociology at the University of Toronto.

YOUNES SARAMIFAR is an assistant professor in the Faculty of Humanities, Department of Art, Culture, History, and Antiquity at the Vrije Universiteit Amsterdam.

L. L. WYNN is an anthropology professor in the School of Social Sciences at Macquarie University and previous president of the Australian Anthropological Society.

Index

www.ingramcontent.com/pod-product-compliance
Lightning Source LLC
Chambersburg PA
CBHW030642270326
41929CB00007B/173